Sustainable Development
and
Climate Change

Editors

Dr. Mamta Sharma   Dr. Hukam Singh

Dr. Upendra Singh

Pustak Bharati
Toronto Canada

Editors : Dr. Mamta Sharma
Dr. Hukam Singh
Dr. Upendra Singh

Book Title : Sustainable Development and Climate Change

Cover Picture : By Dr. Anil Kumar Chhangani, D. Sc.

Published by :
Pustak Bharati (Books India)
180 Torresdale Ave, Toronto Canada M2R3E4
email : pustak.bharati.canada@gmail.com
Web : www.pustak-bharati-canada.com

Published for
Raj Rishi Government Autonomous College,
Alwar, Rajasthan, India

Financial Assistance
Rashtriya Uchchatar Shiksha Abhiyan
(RUSA-2.0)

Preface

"Our planet is slowly dying, and if we don't do anything about it soon enough, it would eventually begin to deteriorate and everything would be used. The world would become a barren place without any resources. We need to cater to the needs of our planet, and we need to change our life styles so that it becomes beneficial to the planet. We need to become much more eco-friendly, so that no harm is dealt to the planet by our existence. Many people don't realize that they waste large amounts of energy and other resources in various unnecessary things that could otherwise be saved."

This series of books is an extension of the three days international conference on **Multidisciplinary Approach Towards Sustainable Development and Climate Change for A Viable Future (ICMSDC-2022)** held from 12th -14th August 2022 at Raj Rishi Government Autonomous College, Alwar, Rajasthan.

We are very happy and delighted to publish our series of books which are accumulation of research papers of knowledgeable experts in the field of sustainable development and climate change.

Climate change is the most significant challenge to achieving sustainable development, and it threatens to drag millions of people into grinding poverty. At the same time, we have never had better know-how and solutions available to avert the crisis and create opportunities for a better life for people all over the world. Climate change is not just a long-term issue. It is happening today, and it entails uncertainties for policy makers trying to shape the future.

There is a dual relationship between sustainable development and climate change. On the one hand, climate change influences key natural and human living conditions and thereby also the basis for social and economic development, while on the other hand, society's priorities on sustainable development influence both the greenhouse gas emissions that are causing climate change and the vulnerability.

Climate policies can be more effective when consistently embedded within broader strategies designed to make national and regional development paths more sustainable. This occurs because the impact of climate variability and change, climate policy responses, and associated socio-economic development will affect the ability of countries to achieve sustainable development goals. Conversely, the pursuit of those goals will in turn affect the opportunities for, and success of, climate policies.

With these books, we aim to reach to as many people as we can, and spread awareness about sustainable development and climate change and its in-depth analysis through our didactic research papers. We hope that the thought with which ICMSDC-2022 was executed is taken forward through this series of books and the inception of an idea of saving the environment is rooted in the minds of our readers.

The articles in these books have been contributed by eminent research scholars, scientists, academicians and industry experts whose contributions have enriched this book series. We thank our publisher, Pustak Bharati, Toronto, Canada for joining us in this initiative and helped in publishing this series of books.

Finally, we will always remain indebted to all our well-wishers for their blessings, without which ICMSDC-2022 and series of these book would have not come into existence.

Financial Assistance provided by Rashtriya Uchchatar Shiksha Abhiyan (RUSA-2.0) is gratefully acknowledged.

Dr. Mamta Sharma
Dr. Hukam Singh
Dr. Upendra Singh

Contents

1. High Time to Go Green in Living

Dr. Mamta Sharma*
Dr. Hukam Singh**
Dr. Upendra Singh***

Green living is a lifestyle that strives to create balance in preserving and protecting Earth's natural resources, habitats, human civilization and biodiversity.

In short, green living is a means of developing sustainable habits in one's daily life so that their daily routines work alongside the resources of nature instead of depleting them, or doing more long-term damage to the environment or ecological system.

The most common way the people become more cognigant of the vital aspects to green living are through the need to reduce pollution, to protect our wildlife from going sources, predominantly, people recognize that green living can alleviate the rapidly increasing rates of climate change and global warming.

Green Living and Healthy Life

Therefore, Green living also refers to the practice of living a lifestyle that is environmentally friendly. There are many benefits of green living, and it is becoming more popular in the world. Green living can be a good way to reduce carbon footprint, save money, and improve your health. It also helps you reduce stress and anxiety levels by providing more time for yourself. The most important thing about green living is that it is sustainable in the long term. It does not cause harm to the environment or any other life form in order to sustain itself. These days, many living all by pursuing modern lifestyle.

Some Simple Steps to create Green Living are Mentioned as given below :

1) Use Natural Light Instead of Artificial Light at Home :

Busting the myth that natural light is less effective than artificial light, the use of artificial light at home can lead to health and safety

1

issues. Artificial lighting has been linked to skin cancer, eye damage, and increased risk of depression. The most cost-effective way to shield your family from these risks is by simply turning-off the lights in your home when you are not using them.

2) Make Sure that you have an Eco-Friendly Cleaning Solution for your Home :

Eco-friendly cleaning products are a hot commodity in today's market. There are many eco-friendly cleansers available that clean home without harming the environment. Some of these products include green tea, vinegar,and coconut oil. There are so many natural ingredients that impart better results-than chemical ones. Lemon juice, for example, is the best replacement for acids, when it comes to washing utensils. Whenever possible, do consider the natural cleaning solutions which are quite reliable.

3) Save Energy :

Installing solar panels on your roof is a great way to start saving money while you save the environment. Solar panels are installed on rooftops , and they generate power of the grid when it is sunny-out. You will pay less for electricity than you would do by purchasing electricity from the grid and could potentially save a lot through renewable energy resources. The amount of energy that you could get for free using solar panels in enormous.

4) Keep your Heating and Cooling Systems Natural :

It is important to keep your heating and cooling system natural, as they may be one of the most significant changes to make in your home. Keeping your heating and cooling system to a minimum will help save money and reduce energy consumption, which is good for the environment. The way of construction changes the way your home keeps cool and warm.

5) Go for Cloth Napkins over the Paper Ones :

Placing cloth napkin on your dining table is an easy way and inexpensive way to keep the environment clean and healthy. A single cloth napkin can be used for multiple uses such as cleaning, wiping, or drying. Using a cloth napkin also saves trees from being cut down and saves money because of lower energy consumption.

6) Use Reusable Water Bottles instead of buying Disposable Ones :

Disposable water bottles are a huge waste of money and a menace to the environment. Reusable water bottles are much more convenient. Reusable bottles can be washed, refilled and reused. And most importantly, these bottles are the safest for our health and for nature's health as well.

7) Grow your own Organic Garden :

Organic gardening is a sustainable and environmentally friendly way to grow food. It could be easily done in small gardens that are surrounded by a fence or wall. Although it can be done in large gardens as well. There are many benefits of growing your own organic garden. It is fun to create the perfect garden; you will save money on grocery bills and enjoy fresh fruits and vegetables year-round.

8) Switch to CFLs or LEDs :

CFLs and LEDs are both lighting solutions that use less energy and re better for the environment CFLs or compact fluorescent lamps, have a lifespan of around 10,000 hours while LEDs have a lifespan of around 50,000 hours. CFLs produce less heat than incandescent bulbs do and they can last up to 10 years. They also produce a brighter light that is more natural to our eyes than the light produce by traditional bulbs.

9) Avoid Plastic and Paper as much as Possible :

Plastic bags could be replaced with paper ones. However, for greener living, think of an alternative that even replaces paper. Because paper bags won't protect you from rains and they can't even carry heavy items. Consider cloth bags, consider long-lasting materials. When it comes to containers, think of bamboo, stainless steel, and copper. When it comes to packaging, think of coconut shells, leaves, jute rope and so on.

The new decade is upon us, and many of us have the same goal in mind: to be more eco-friendly. Living a more sustainable lifestyle can be very rewarding but also a bit daunting. There are 3 R's of Green living which would be the stepping stone that we can apply to everyday life:

Reduce, Reuse and Recycle :

Reduce

The first step to this eco-friendly trio is to reduce, which seems self-explanatory-just use less. Each year, we use 1 billion plastic shopping bags, creating 300,000 tons of landfill waste. One can start reducing use of plastic by:

- Bringing reusable bags to the grocery store and buying in bulk whenever you can
- Using a washcloth instead of a paper towel when cleaning –up kitchen messes
- Taking shorter showers
- Hand washing dishes instead of using the dishwasher
- And avoiding single-use plastic (plates, bowls, cups, Styrofoam, straws, water bottles, etc.)

Whether you are reducing your waste, water usage-or buying habits a little effort goes a long way for the environment.

Reuse

Next up to but is reuse, which is as simple as it stands. When you reuse products, you are able to make use of them multiple times or in multiple ways. In less than 15 years, world-wide waste is expected to double. So, instead of throwing away, find a way to reuse items you would otherwise loss!

Some super simple ways to reuse what you already have and keep trash-out of landfills are:

- Purchase a reusable water bottle instead of using single use plastic bottles.
- Use your old toothbrush to scrub small, hard to reach areas when cleaning the house

- Turn a broken frame into an earring holder by attaching wire across frame and hanging earrings from wire.
- Cut the top off of an old soda bottle and hang it from a tree with birdseed for an easy bird feeder.

There are endless ways to reuse items that would typically be going to waste, but the best way will be successful with this step is to be creative!

Recycle

The third "R" on the list, recycling, is the process of turning waste into new materials or objects. In some cases, producing waste is inevitable. However, it is important to be aware of waste you are producing and how to recycle as much of that waste as possible. For example:

- If you have to use a plastic spoon, clean it thoroughly and make sure it is recycled.
- Find a local recycling centre to recycle old electronics bin.

The recycle materials in the US waste stream would generate over $7billion, if they were recycled. It is important to produce as little waste as possible, but when you produce waste, determine how much of it can actually be recycled, clean it off and throw it in the recycling bin.

Conclusion

These days, it is hard to turn back the clock to a time when people did not worry about environmentalism. The more we learn and understand, the harder it is to resist doing our part. All of us have duties and responsibilities in this respect.

With the world's population growing, the demand for resources is increasing. The fastest and most effective way to combat this is using less and recycling. This ensures that our energy usage can remain low and that we continue to enjoy our lifestyle while being environmentally conscious.

References :
- o *Green living lovetoknow.com*
- o *Green coast.org*
  https://www.byui.edu/university-operation/facilities-management-statistics
  https://www.recycleacrossamerica.org/recycling-facts
- o *Greenbiz.com*

*Associate Professor (Zoology)
**Professor
*** Associate Professor (Chemistry)
Raj Rishi Government (Autonomous) College
Alwar, Rajasthan 301001,India.
email : mamta810@gmail.com ;
drhukamsingh63@gmail.com
dr.usingh09@gmail.com

2. Green Chemistry for Sustainable Development

Dr. Sudha Sukhwal Shringi

Abstract

Green chemistry is a rapidly growing field that focuses on the design and development of chemical products and processes that reduce or eliminate the use and generation of hazardous substances. Its principles and practices can play a significant role in promoting sustainable development by reducing environmental impacts, conserving natural resources, and improving human health. Green chemistry is the use of chemicals which are environment friendly and cause no pollution.

The term green is synonymous to life, pure and fresh non-polluting things. This research is based on using the processes in which chemicals used do not cause pollution. This involves the design and optimization of processes and products such that there is no pollution and environment harm. Green chemistry is based on 12 Principles which are taken into account when designing any process or product based on green chemistry. In this paper, we provide an overview of the principles of green chemistry and their application in various industries. Our analysis suggests that while green chemistry has the potential to contribute significantly to sustainable development, more research is needed to fully understand and overcome the challenges faced in its implementation.

Keywords : Green Chemistry, Sustainable Development, Environment

Introduction

Sustainable development is a global challenge that requires the integration of economic, social, and environmental goals. One of the key strategies for achieving sustainable development is the use of green chemistry, which aims to design and develop chemical products and processes that reduce or eliminate the use and generation of hazardous substances. Green chemistry has been recognized as a powerful tool for improving the environmental and human health impacts of chemical products and processes, and has the potential to contribute significantly to sustainable development.

Principles of Green Chemistry

There are certain principles on which green chemistry is based.

1. **Prevention :** It is best to prevent waste than to clean up after same has been created.

2. **Atom Economy :** Synthesis of products should be designed in such a way so as to maximize the incorporation of all raw materials into final product. Atomic economy is the ratio of weight of final product and all raw reactants in percentage.

3. **Less Hazardous Chemical Synthesis :** Design processes for chemical substances in a way that toxicity is minimum to humans and the environment.

4. **Designing Safer Chemicals :** Chemical product should be designed in such a way so it can perform the desired function and toxicity is minimized.

5. **Safer Solvents and Auxiliaries :** The use of additives like solvents, agents should be safe and harmless.

6. **Energy Saving :** Energy requirements of chemical processes must be recognized for their environmental and economic impacts. If possible, a synthetic method should be performed at room temperature and pressure

7. **Use of Renewable Feedstocks :** Raw materials should be renewable rather than depleting.

8. **Reduce Derivative :** Unnecessary use of blocking groups, protection / deprotection, temporary modification of process / chemical physical factors should be reduced or avoided – if possible, because such measures require additional reagents and can produce waste.

9. **Catalysis :** Catalytic reagents are superior to stoichiometric reagents and should be used.

10. **Design for Degradation :** Chemical products should be designed in such a way that at the end of their function they break down into non harmful degradation products.

11. **Real-time analysis for Pollution Prevention :** The analytical methodology needs to be further developed to enable real-time, in-process monitoring and control before the formation of hazardous substances.

12. Inherently Safer Chemistry for Accident Prevention : Substances used in a chemical process should be chosen to minimize chemical accidents, including releases, explosions and fires.

Green Chemistry Technology

There has been a growing emphasis on using and developing new technology for chemical synthesis and reactions which are as per principles of green chemistry.

Ultrasound Activation

Ultrasound activation (sonochemistry) is modern method for speeding up chemical processes. It has big potential for use in green chemistry. Number of scientific researches on sonolysis have been published.

Sound is sonic waves that propagate through a medium and create vibrations in it. Substantially, all sonochemical reactions initiated in the aqueous solutions under the effect of acoustic oscillations are due to the cavitation process. Cavitation is the formation of cavities (cavity bubbles, cavity pockets) in a liquid filled either with gas, vapor, or their mixture. Reaching the threshold value during the sonolysis is the required condition for the onset of cavitation. The high threshold power density (over 3 MHz) can conversely hinder the cavitation, which makes some of the reactions impossible. Sound frequency used in sonochemistry can vary from 20 kHz to 2 MHz

Microwave Activation

With all modern technologies associated with the use of microwave radiation comes a long history of its gradual transition from defense industry through consumer electronics finally reaching the science and production sector. Today, microwave enhancement is commonly involved in various industrial processes (e.g., food dehydration, wood desiccation and bonding, manufacturing of porcelain, building and construction work,etc.).

Benefits of Microwave

• Integration of processes (e.g., dissolution of the reagents and direct energy transfer to the reaction mixture combined)
• Carrying out microwave heating under pressure can often homogenize slightly soluble starting compounds into a single

phase which is extremely difficult or even impossible with conventional heating;
• Ability to monitor and control the main parameters of the reaction (pressure, temperature, time, and power)
• Safety
• Ease in checkout and automatic monitoring.

Photochemical Activation

Photochemical activation of reactions has been well established and used for a long time. There are a number of photochemical processes that are of the utmost importance for both a biont and the biosphere as a whole. It is primarily regarded as a process of photosynthesis, as well as the synthesis of vitamins, such as vitamin D produced in the human skin, etc. The photochemical decomposition of the silver halides underlies the photo process. There are photochromic materials that are capable of changing color or opacity on exposure to light, which are particularly used either for photo- chemical recording or for sunglasses manufacturing. Photochemical reactions are also used in the chemical industry.

The mechanism of the photochemical processes boils down to the reaction initiated by the absorption of a photon of light by a reactant molecule which entails its excitation. Generally, molecules with an even number of electrons upon photoexcitation initially switch to the excited singlet state Photochemical reactions usually proceed from the lower excited singlet state or from the triplet state via intersystem crossing from an excited singlet.

Green Chemsitry and Sustainable Development

Definition of sustainable development as per UN report "development which meets the needs of the present without compromising the ability of future generations to meet their own needs."

There is no fixed definition it is multidimensional model which includes various definitions including "sustainable development—is the development based on a balanced consideration of the needs of people and the environment, which allows us to meet the needs and aspirations of both present and future generations. It limits economic growth and social development to within nature's resource limits and capacity for self -regeneration."

Thereby, three aims of sustainable development can be distinguished:

(1) Ecological (maintenance of environmental integrity, conservation of biodiversity and biosphere at large);
(2) Economic (economic growth and effectivization);
(3) Social (improvement of living conditions, constitutional evolution, realization of social equity).

Use of Green Chemstry for Sustainable Development
Green Chemistry in Education

Some of the benefits of incorporating green chemistry into education include:

Promoting Environmental Sustainability : By teaching students about the principles of green chemistry, they can learn about ways to reduce the negative impact of chemical processes on the environment.

Encouraging Innovation : Green chemistry principles can inspire students to develop new, more sustainable ways of synthesizing chemicals and designing processes.

Enhancing Safety : Green chemistry can help students learn about ways to design chemical processes that are less hazardous and therefore safer for workers and the environment.

Improving Economic Competitiveness : As industries increasingly prioritize sustainability, learning about green chemistry can help students develop skills that will be in demand in the workforce.

In terms of importance and application, Green chemistry education can help students in many different areas, such as chemical engineering, materials science, pharmaceuticals, biotechnology and environmental science, as well as in interdisciplinary fields, to develop the knowledge and skills necessary to design safer, more sustainable chemical products and processes.

Also it is important to note that not only in chemical field but also in many other areas like medicine, agriculture, energy, chemical manufacturing and research and development, the principles and practice of green chemistry is employed, thus providing an important and applicable subject for students to study.

Biomass and Phytomass for Fulfilling Energy Needs

Biomass and phytomass are plant-based materials that can be used as a source of renewable energy in green chemistry. One of the main applications of biomass and phytomass in green chemistry is in the production of biofuels. Biofuels are fuels that are produced from renewable, organic materials such as plants and algae. Examples of biofuels include ethanol and biodiesel. These biofuels can be used in place of fossil fuels, such as gasoline and diesel, to reduce greenhouse gas emissions and dependence on non-renewable resources.

Another application of biomass and phytomass in green chemistry is the production of bioplastics. Bioplastics are plastics that are made from renewable, biodegradable materials such as starch, cellulose, and lignin. These bioplastics can be used in place of traditional plastics, which are made from fossil fuels and are not biodegradable.

Additionally, biomass and phytomass can also be used as feedstock for producing chemicals and materials such as bio-based lubricants, adhesives and resins, thus replace fossil-based chemicals.

Furthermore, Biomass and Phytomass can also be used to generate electricity through methods such as direct combustion, gasification, and anaerobic digestion. They also can be used in combined heat and power (CHP) systems to increase energy efficiency.

Overall, the application of biomass and phytomass in green chemistry can help to reduce the use of fossil fuels and non-renewable resources, reduce greenhouse gas emissions and promote sustainable development, thus playing an important role in fulfilling energy needs.

Moral responsibility for future generation forces the industrial nations to aspire to sustainability. Sustainability, in the long term, cannot rely on finite resources and phytomass as renewable raw material could correspond to this concept.

Use of Nanoparticles

Nanoparticles are incredibly small particles with at least one dimension measuring less than 100 nanometers. These particles have unique properties that make them particularly useful in a variety of applications, including green chemistry.

In green chemistry, nanoparticles are used to catalyze chemical reactions, create new materials, and clean up pollutants. Some examples of specific uses include:

- Catalyzing reactions: Gold nanoparticles, for example, can be used as catalysts in organic synthesis reactions, making them more efficient and reducing the amount of waste produced.
- Creating new materials: Researchers are using nanoparticles to create new types of composite materials that are stronger and more durable than traditional materials.
- Cleaning up pollutants: nanoparticles have a high surface area to volume ratio, which makes them ideal for use in cleaning up pollutants like heavy metals, oil spills, and pesticides.
- Photocatalysis- use of nanoparticles as photocatalyst to bring about chemical reactions on exposure to light.
- Agriculture, as a tool in pest management, as pesticidal nanoparticles.

In all above use case, the use of nanoparticles helps to reduce the usage of chemical compounds and also reduces the waste production which is one of the principles of green chemistry.

Antimicrobial Bandages Bandage is a material which is used to cover up the wounds or injured body parts. It provides support to the wound and the surrounding tissues. Green synthesis of nanoparticles is done for making wound healing bandages. The nanoparticles are then impregnated on the bandages. For example, silver nanoparticles were synthesized by using the weed plant Tridax procumbens (impregnated on the bandage), which has shown antimicrobial activity against gram-positive and gram-negative bacteria.

Using Green Solvents Green solvents are based on the principal of green chemistry and are excellent choice for green chemistry. Water, ionic liquids and Glycerol have enormous potential for use as solvents in food and pharma industry.

Conclusion

In conclusion, this study has shown that green chemistry has the potential to contribute significantly to sustainable development through the reduction of environmental impacts, the conservation of natural resources, and the improvement of human health. However, the implementation of green chemistry principles is not without challenges, and more research is needed to fully understand and overcome these challenges. Future research should focus on developing a consistent and standardized definition of green chemistry, as well as identifying and addressing the economic, social, and cultural barriers to the implementation of green chemistry principles.

Chemists, researchers and pharmaceutical companies must use the principles of green chemistry while designing the reaction mechanism and selecting catalyst. By applying green chemistry procedures, we can minimize the waste materials, reduce the use of toxic chemicals, maintain the atom economy, and save the environment which is heritage of our next generation. To combine technological progress with the safeguard of the environment is one of the challenges of the new millennium. Chemists will play a key role in the realization of the conditions for a sustainable development and green chemistry may be their winning strategy. Research, technology transfer, and education in the field of green chemistry will be important in determining the future of raw materials in the context of sustainable development.

References

1. Monika B, Anupam B, et al. Green synthesis of gold and silver nanoparticles.2015;6(3):1710-1716.
2. Ivanković A, Dronjić A, et al. Review of 12 Principles of Green Chemistry in Practice. 2017; 6(3): 39-48 2)
3. Berkeley W and Zhang J. Green process chemistry in the pharmaceutical industry. 2009;2(10):193-211 3)

4. Nydia T, Cecile B. Green and sustainable chemistry. 2018;8(3):1-10
5. Gupta M, Paul S, et al. General aspects of 12 basic principles of green chemistry with application. 2010;99(10):1341-1360.
6. Peng, G., & Weijun, L. (2011). Green Chemistry and Sustainable Development
7. Clark, J. H., & Macquarrie, D. J. (Eds.). (2008). Handbook of green chemistry and technology. John Wiley & Sons.
8. Anastas, P. T., & Warner, J. C. (1998). Green chemistry: Theory and practice. Oxford, UK: Oxford University Press.

Associate Professor,
Department of Chemistry,
Rajrishi College Alwar,
Rajasthan

3. Management of Conservation and Wildlife in India

Dr. Rajesh Kumar Verma* and Pushpa Khatnal**

Keywords : Biodiversity, Wildlife, Coservation Management, Species. Biosphere etc.

Introduction

Wildlife includes all non-domesticate plants, animals and other organisms. Domesticating wild plant and animal species for human benefit has occurred many times all. This has effects are all over the planet, and has a major impact on the environment, both positive and negative. Wildlife can be found in all ecosystems. Deserts, rain forests, plains, and other areas including the most developed urban sites, all have distinct forms of wildlife. But today most of the wildlife around the world is affected by human activities. This has been a reason for debate throughout recorded history.

Wildlife of India

Wildlife of India is a mix of species of diverse origins.The regions rich and diverse wildlife is preserved in numerous national parks and wildlife sanctuaries across the country. Since India is home to a number of rare and threatened animal species, wildlife management in the country is essential to preserve these species. According to one study, India along with mega diverse countries and is home to about 60-70% of the world's biodiversity. India, lying within the Indomalaya ecozone, is home to about 7.6% of all mammalian, 12.6% of avian, 6.2% of reptilian, and 6.0% of flowering plant species.

Wildlife in North India

- Naturally blessed this part of India is home to the vast Himalayas and the great Gangetic Plains.
- Due to its favorable climatic conditions and topographical diversity North India supports a rich mix of flora and fauna.
- North India provides shelter to some of the finest and the rarest wildlife and wildlife sanctuaries.
- Some of the species unique to this part of the country are;

16

bluesheep, Himalayan marmots, snow partridges, snow leopards, goats like ibex, Himalayan wolfs, makhor, etc.

- The list of most frequented wildlife sanctuaries in North India include; Corbett National Park, Ranthambore National Park, Rajasthan and Bharatpur National Park.

Wildlife in East India

- Unique and diverse the wildlife of East India attracts millions of tourist from different parts of the globe.
- Home to some of the finest endangered species like Hispid Hare, Pigmy Hog, the One-horned Rhinoceros and the Wild Buffalos the wildlife in this part of the country is very different from the rest of India.
- The two most important wildlife sanctuaries in East India are the Sunderbans, West Bengal, and the Kaziranga Wildlife Sanctuary, Assam.

Wildlife in South India

- South India is popular all across the globe for its extraordinary, unusual and varied flora and fauna.
- Characterized with lush greeneries South India houses a fascinating wildlife that consists of about 500 specics of mammals, 1225 varieties of Birds and 1600 types of reptiles.
- Some of the famous wildlife sanctuaries in the southern part of India include; The Periyar Wildlife Sanctuary, Kerela, Bandipur Wildlife Sanctuary, Karnataka and the Dandeli Wildlife Sanctuary, Karnataka. The wildlife common to South India are; Bison, Malabar Trogon, Antelopes etc.

Wildlife in West India

- Ideal for the wildlife enthusiasts the western part of India supports a prominent part of India's wildlife. Supporting the growth of a distinct flora and fauna this part of India resides more than 40 mammals species and about 450 birds species.
- Blessed in terms of topography and climate West India is home to some of the most popular wildlife sanctuaries in India.
- There are about 300 Asiatic Lions in the Sasangir, Wildlife Sanctuary which is situated in Gujarat.

- The other important wildlife sancturies in West India include; Dhangadhra Sanctuary, Wild Ass, Gujarat the Velavadar National Park, Gujarat, Marine National Park, Gulf of Kutch and many more.

Need Conservation of for Wildlife in India

- The need for conservation of wildlife in India is often questioned because of the apparently incorrect priority in the face of direct poverty of the people.
- Many rare species of animals that are only found in India are getting extinct day by day.
- Examples are Bengal tigers, Asiatic lions found in India, many species of reptiles etc
- Wildlife Protection Act The Wildlife Protection Act of 1972 refers to as weeping package of legislation enacted in 1972 by the Government of India.
- The Act provides for the protection of wild animals, birds and plants; and for matters connected therewith or ancillary or incidental thereto.
- The act came in action in 1972, and thereafter increased the protection of wildlife to higher level.

Tiger Protection

- The framework was then setup to formulate a project for tiger conservation with an ecological approach. Launched on April 1, 1973, Project Tiger has become one of the most successful conservation ventures in modern history.
- The project aims at tiger conservation in specially constituted tiger reserves which are representative of various bio-geographical regions falling within India. It strives to maintain a viable tiger population in their natural environment.
- Today, there are 39 Project Tiger wildlife reserves in India covering an area more than of 37,761 km².
- Some Biosphere Reserves The Indian government has established 15 Biosphere Reserves of India.
- which protect larger areas of natural habitat and often include one or more National Parks and/or preserves
- along buffer zones that are open to some economic uses.

- Protection is granted not only to the flora and fauna of the protected région, but also to the human communities who inhabit these regions, and their ways of life.

Bio-Reserves in India

1. Sunderbans 2. Gulf of Mannar 3. The Nilgiris Nanda Devi 4. Nokrek Great Nicobar 5. Manas Simlipal 6. Dihang Dibang 7. Dibru Saikhowa 8. Agasthyamalai 9. Kanchenjunga 10. Pachmarhi 11. Achanakmar Amarkantak 12. Kachchh

Conservation Challenges

- The challenges to conservation of large mammals in a developing country like India are complex.
- The needs of a increasing human population and the consequent growth of the market where India has become part of the expanding global economy has been at the centre of conservation problems of our country.
- The protected wildlife areas constitute a mere 3% of the total land mass with ever-increasing pressure on this fragmented landscape.
- Any further exploitation of the last remaining bits of protected areas to meet human and development needs, which in any event need to be met by using 97% of the landscape, will surely lead to the decimation of large mammal assemblages.
- Conservation of large mammal's in India is beset with serious problems such as habitat loss, fragmentation of forests, illegal hunting, commercial exploitation of forest products, livestock grazing, forest fires, unscientific management practices and ignorance of the need for wildlife conservation.
- The Progressive loss of habitat include fragmentation>> Illegal hunting and wildlife trade>> Commercial exploitation of forests>> Removal of dead and fallen trees>> Collection of minor forest produce>> Livestock grazing
- Also fire in the forest causes Habitat destruction and fragmentation Deforestation
- increased road-building in the forests are a significant concern because of increased human encroachment upon wild areas, increased resource extraction and further threats to biodiversity.

How can one help Conserve the Environment and Wildlife?

- Public opinion and awareness are two critical factors that will finally make a difference.
- Here are outline of some activities that we can consider for awareness and to save forests and wildlife in India.
- Try to learn as much as possible about India's wildlife (from books, the internet, seminars and talks) and about the importance of the 'Web of Life'.
- Get people involved in your cause - in your colony, in your colleges and schools as well as your local MLAs.
- Organize trips to local wildlife areas, or botanical gardens and the zoo.
- Keep in touch with media people.
- Keep in touch with Forest Department - often they need volunteers for some of their field activities.
- Keep in touch with the Honorary Wildlife Warden and conservation NGOs in your area. Offer assistance wherever possible.
- In day to day life, remember the six Rs: Refuse Reduce Re-use Reinvent Recycle (paper, plastic etc) Replenish (water harvesting, planting trees etc)

Conclusion

➢ The natural world is a complex system. Only by understanding how species relate to each other and their environment can we hope to properly protect wildlife and preserve their habitat for the future.

➢ The best scenario would imply integrated community development and wildlife conservation promoted by national park managers and supported by local populations.

➢ Community-based conservation should give indigenous people the right to limited and sustainable use of natural resources while promoting tolerance towards wildlife, responsible interaction with their natural villagers, appreciate nature's intrinsic value and agree with the necessity to protect forests and their wildlife inhabitants for future generations.

➢ In order to enhance protected area effectiveness, conservation should be based on sound scientific knowledge, practical local indigenous knowledge and collaboration.

➤ Also there must be awareness in people for saving animals.

➤ Jawaharlal Nehru had truly said "A country is known by the way it treats its animals".

*Assistant Professor,
PG Department of Zoology,
Agrawal PG College, Jaipur, INDIA
email : rkzoology@gmail.com
**Assistant Professor,
Department of Zoology,
Saint Soldier PG College for Girls, Jaipur, INDIA
email : pkzoology2@gmail.com
Correspondig email : rkzoology@gmail.com

4. Seed to seedling Transmission of *Pseudomonas Virdiflava* causing Bacterial Spot Disease of Faba Bean

Manju Meena* and Ashwani Kumar Verma

Abstract

Legume plants such as dry and green beans, green peas and chickpeas are the key components of food for diet of human beings. *Vicia faba* L. is the third most important legume after *Glycine max* and *Pisum sativum*. Faba bean is a rich source of essential amino acid lysine and presenting high amount of protiens, fibers, vitamins, minerals, and compounds possessing antioxidant and anticarcinogenic properties. *Pseudomonas virdiflava* phytopathogenic bacteria with a broad host range which is responsible to causing bacterial spot disease in faba bean. *P. virdiflava* causes not only pathogenic infections such as bacterial spot but also reduce the growth of Faba bean crop and yield.

Keywords : Faba bean, *Pseudomonas virdiflava,* phyto-pathogen, transmission, bacteria.

Introduction

Legumes are the main source of protein and are well known for their nutritional value. They are relatively cheap source of protein. Leguminous crops such as lentils, peas, broad beans and soya beans are main components of a healthy diet (Nene, 1988). *Vicia faba* L, is important grain legume of family leguminosae. It has several common names such as Bakla, Kalamatar, Broad Bean, Horse Bean etc. The term 'Fava' bean is taken from the Italian word 'Fava' which means broad bean is extensively used in different countries. They are good source of protein, carbohydrate, dietry fiber, minerals and secondary metabolites such as phenolics, L-DOPA (Rabey et. al., 1992).The protein content of Faba bean is the range being approximately 20-40% depending upon the seed quality of different varities (Vidal-Valverde et.al., 1998).

Faba bean green pods and dry seeds used vegetable and dal respectively. They also help to increase vital nitrogen in the soil

(Etemadi et. al., 2018). Faba bean is infected by many pathogens. Some important fungal, bacterial and viral disease are Chocolate spot, Rust, Black root rot, Foot rots, Halo spot, Bacterial brown spot, Bean yellow mosaic virus etc. *Pseudomonas viridiflava* was first described by Burkholder in 1930 as a bean (*Phaseolus vulgaris*) pathogen. It is multi host pathogen. It can produce a variety of symptoms including necrosis, rots, blight and spots affecting different plant parts (Lipps et. al., 2022). It can cause bacterial blight in peas, rots in carrot, bacterial canker in stone fruits, bacterial leaf spot in pumpkin and soft rot in tomato and the model plant species *Arabidopsis thaliana*. Typical symptoms infection in tomato are a general wilting and yellowing of the plants and brown black spots developing at the pruning sites of stem (Sarris et. al., 2012) In poppy infected plants were obseverd to turn brown to black streaks woth translucent olive green edges at the base of stem and leaves. Whereas in pumpkin olive green, water soaked spots were observed which developed into pale brown leisons (Wilkie et. al., 1973). In peas pathogen affects the leaves, stipules and stems and showed water soaked, soft brown leisons.

In the present study affected seed to seedling transmission of *Pseudomonas viridiflava* causing bacterial spot disease of faba vean was observed.

Materials and Methods

The most common bacterial pathogen on faba beans are *Pseudomonas syringae*, *P. aeruginosa*, *Xanthomonas campestris* and *Pseudomonas viridiflava*. The infected plant debris or infected seeds of faba bean were the primary source of bacterial pathogen for new infection.

Faba bean growing fields were surveyed and infected plant samples were collected. Two types of seed samples of Faba bean carrying 80% and 89% natural infection of *Pseudomonas viridiflava* were selected to disease transmission studies. The experiment was done in triplicate forms. 30 seeds of per infected sample were placed on moist cotton blotters (10 Seed per plate) at equal distances.

To study phyto-pathological affect healthy faba bean seeds artificially treated with isolated bacterial broth culture were placed on moist cotton beds in petriplates and inculated for 7 days at above described optimum conditions. After that seedlings were again treated artificially with isolated bacterial broth culture by stabbing the cotyledons and performed blotter method and incubated 25 c for 7 days.

The percentage of seed germination, ungerminated seeds asssociated with pathogen, symptomatic seedling and mortality of seedlings were recorded timely.

In the pot experiment 30 infected seeds per category per sample were sown in plastic pots (5 seeds per pot). All the petriplate and pots were incubated at 25 C for 12-12 hour atternating cycles of light and dark photoperiod for 7 days. During the experimental studies percentage of seed germination, seedling symptoms and seedling mortality were recorded. There after bacterial colonies were isolated from infected seedling and seed to isolate pathogenic bacteria (Jain and Agarwal, 2011)

Result and Discussion

There are many seed borne bacteria, while a number of bacteria are serious pathogen on floweres and maturing seeds.These bacterial pathogen reduce the seed quality. The seed associated bacteria survive and proliferate by using nutrients and therefore, subsequently become pathogenic on seedlings and growing plants. Pathogenic bacteria proliferate in intercellular space after entering through stomata. These pathogens deliver some toxins into the plant cell to affect their fitness.

In the petriplate method 80% and 50% seed germination rate were recorded with 80% and 89% faba bean infected seeds in the present study respectively.

Some un-germinated seeds were shrivelld and rolled out of these one seed of 89% infected seed sample is comletely covered with white bacterial growth with rotting.Where as the radicles of germinated seeds were also dried within 7 days. Accordingly 20% and 50% mortality was observed with 80% and 89% infected seeds respectively.

In pot experiment 30% rate of seed germination was recorded with 80% faba bean infected seeds and 10% germination with 89%

infected seeds. According to results 70% and 90% mortality was observed with 80% and 89% infected faba bean seeds respectively. The non-germinated seeds showed shriveling and rotting. Due to heavy infection of the pathogen green and white bacterial growth on and around the bean seeds appeared. The infected radicle and plumule were used to isolate bacterial pathogen and identified using biochemical characteristics representative isolate of *Pseudomonas spp.* were identified as *Pseudomonas viridiflava* based on the determinative scheme as proposed by previous researchers (Lelliott et. al., 1987).

Phyto-pathological study of artificially treated seed with *P. viridiflava* showed 60% germination that were higher rate of germination in comparision to rate of control(40%). The length of shoot and root of control sample was 18.42cm and 4.75cm respectively. Where as radicle formation was not recorded in *P. viridiflava* infected seed sample. The present study revealed that *Pseudomons viridiflava* was found with heavy occurrence on faba beans. The bacterial pathogen was found transmitted with seed borne inoculum from seed to seedling to plant and causing bacterial spot in the crop. The results of this study concluded tha t bacterial infection of plants reduce the seed viability and growth of beans.

References
1. Etemadi, F., Hashemi, M., Autio, W., Mangan, F., Zandvakili, O. Accumulation and distribution trend of L-Dopa in different parts of eight varieties of faba bean plant through its growth period. J Crop Sci (2018): 6: 426–434.
2. Goumas, D.E., Malathrakis, N.E., Chatzaki, A.K. Characterization of *Pseudomonas viridiflava* associated with a new symptom on tomato fruit. European Journal of Plant Pathology. (1999): 105: 927–32.
3. Jain, R. and Agrawal, K. Incidence and seed transmission of *Xanthomonas axonopodis* pv. cyamopsidis in cluster bean. J. Agri. Tech., (2011): 7(1): 197-205.

4. Lelliott, R.A. and Stead, D.E., Methods for the diagnosis of bacterial diseases of plants. In Methods in Plant Pathology, Blackwell Scientific Publication, Oxford, London. (1987): 2: 216.
5. Lipps, S.M., Lenz, P., Samac, D.A. First report of bacterial stem blight of alfalfa caused by *Pseudomonas viridiflava* in California and Utah. Plant Disease, (2019): 103: 3274.
6. Rabey, J.M., Vered, Y., Shabtai, H., Graff, E., Korczyn, A.D. Improvement of parkinsonian features correlate with high plasma levodopa values after broad bean (*Vicia faba*) consumption. Journal of Neurology, Neurosurgery & Psychiatry, (1992): 55:725–727.
7. Sarris, P.F., Trantas, E.A., Mpalantinaki, E., Ververidis, F.N., Gouma, D.E. First report of *Pseudomonas viridiflava* causing a bacterial blight of artichoke bract leaves. Plant diseases, (2012): 96 (8):1223-1224 APS journals.
8. Vidal-Valverde, C., Frias, J., Sotomayor, C., Diaz-Pollan, C., Fernández, M., & Urbano, G. Nutrients and antinutritional factors in faba beans as affected by processing. Zeitschrift für Lebensmittel-Untersuchung und –Forschung,(1998): 207, 140–145.
9. Wilkie, J.P., Dye, D.W., and Watson, D.R.W. Further hosts of *Pseudomonas viridiflava. N.Z.J.* Agriculture research (1973):21:153-177.
10. Nene, Y. L. Multiple disease resistance in grain legumes, Annu. Rev. Phytopathol.(1988): 26: 203

Deportment of Botany,
Raj Rishi Govt. College, Alwar (Raj.)
email : *26manjumeena@gmail.com

5. Development of Environmental Principles, Its Legal Impacts and Governance of SDGs

Dr. Anita Gupta

Abstract

The present research study has been carried out with the view to scrutinise the development of environment principles by Indian Judiciary and in implementing the Sustainable Development goals. The present article is directed towards researching on two points (1) the article examines the reason for the tardy procedure of implementation of environment principles developed by Indian Courts. As, the problem which can be foreseen is environment principles are not governed by an independent regulatory body and has to seek for government's permission (Ministry of Environment Forest and Climate Change (MoEF)) for implementation of any measures/rules for the protection of environment despite the country has developed framework of the environment laws and; (2) That the aberration to environment principles and implementation of environmental laws and protection of environmental rights has been hampered as the information about the environment protection is not disseminated to the public, NGOs, or even official bodies. The underlying reason is that the hampering of implementation of environmental rights and its governance in the society is because the Indian Environment Laws doesn't provide for freedom of information for the governance of environment protection. After all, it may lead to the disclosure of industrial secrets of the industries to the competitors or the secrets within the authorizing body. Thus, due to this intricacy, environmental laws and their governance are lacking.

Keywords : Sustainable Development Goals, Monitoring, Environment Principles, Access to Freedom, Information

Introduction

The protection of the environment in India protection is evolving for ages and is still developing. The development of environment jurisprudence has been evolving as the growth of science and technology is increasing, thus the need to develop environment laws becomes a necessity. Therefore, the growing environmental hazards empower an obligation of environmental protection. Further, the growth and development of the environmental jurisprudence in India have been made through various precedents and principles opined by the Indian judiciary for the protection of the environment. The courts in India have played an important role in developing the environment jurisprudence by providing various principles for the protection of the environment. The judicial activism was carried by the cases filed by famous environment activist Mr. MC Mehta. Mr. Mehta has tremendously contributed to developing the environmental jurisprudence by filing various cases and PILs such as the protection of Taj Mahal from pollution[1] also, contributing in making recognize the "right to clean environment" as the "right to life", thus, helping in protecting people's right of a safe environment. Further, he has contributed to controlling industrial hazards and vehicle pollution[2]. Thus, has aided the country in laying down principles under environment jurisprudence. The article finally illustrates that despite the evolution of principle the implementation of environmental jurisprudence is slow and tardy due to which the significant growth in environment protection is limited.

Significance of the Study

The present study shall be conducive in gaining the attention of authorities towards the proper implementation of the developments made in environmental jurisprudence by Mr. Mehta and judiciary. As it help the government in recognising to formulate an independent regulatory body for the governance of environment laws and will help in achieving the UN's Sustainable development goals.

---

[1] *M.C. Mehta v. Union of India and others (Taj Mahal Case)*, 1987 AIR 1086

[2] *M.C. Mehta v. Union of India and others (Vehicular Pollution Case)*,1991 SCR (1) 866

Further, it will be helpful is making people aware of the evolved environment principles and worked done by Mr. Mehta and courts for the environment protection so that people and society are aware of environment rights and shall also implement in their day-today activities which shall help in protecting the environment and will help in attaining the clean surroundings.

The work shall also gain the attention of the officials, NGO's in claiming for the accessibility of information pertaining to the environment principles, which shall help in the proper governance of the principles.

Meaning of Environmental Jurisprudence

The term "Environmental jurisprudence"[3] is an anthology of regulations, laws curtailed by the aid of human governance which has been discovered from the thought that the individuals are a part of big globe and every individual has a their own sections in that globe wherein they have to ascertain that, they as community are accustomed for the development of the Environment as a "whole". Thereby, the large society of individuals will solely be doable and flourish if they adjust themselves as section of this globe and ascertain their working according the developmental regulations of this Universe. Moreover, the underlying principle of Environment jurisprudence is to dredge up the working of human governance system which shall additionally consist of ethics, laws, institutions, insurance policies and practices. In furtherance to, it also enshrines on the *"internalisation of and on non-public practice in dwelling in accordance with Environment jurisprudence as a way of life"*[4]. The doctrines, regulations etc. as provided under environmental jurisprudence has been derived from various

---

[3] Justice Ashok A. Desai, *Environmental Jurisprudence*, 39 Journal of the Indian Law Institute, 472-474 (1998), https://www.jstor.org/ stable/43953292.

[4] *Lalit Miglani vs State Of Uttarakhand And Others*, Writ Petition (PIL) No.140 of 2015

exclusive disciplines of research like primary sciences, earth science and common Law principles.[5]

Framework of Environmental Principles in India

The Legislative Framework

1. The Provisions Under the Indian Constitution

   The provisions contained under the Indian Constitution is environment friendly and serves as a cooked platter for the framing the environmental laws and policies in the country. Precisely, the 42nd Amendment to the constitution initially highlighted the importance of environment conservation and its development. The Environment Friendly articles under Indian Constitution are such as-

   a. Under Fundamental Rights: Articles including 21, 32 and 226
   b. Under Directive Principles of the State Policy: Articles including 47, 48A and 49
   c. Under Fundamental Duties: Article 51A(g)

2. Punishment for Violation of Environment under Criminal laws

3. Environment Protection under Special acts like Indian Forest Act, 1927, Wild Life (Protection) Act, 1972, Environment Protection Act, 1986, Air (Prevention and Control of Pollution) Act, 1981, Water (Prevention and Control of Pollution) Act, 1974, Public Liability Insurance Act, 1991, the National Environmental Tribunal Act, 1995 etc.

4. Various other Environment Policies like, National Environment Policy 2006, National Forest Policy, and National Agriculture Policy etc.

The Administrative Framework

1. Ministry of Environment and Forests (MoEF): The Indian ministry which provided for the development, conversation and regulative measures for the environment.

2. Various enforcement agencies like Central Pollution Control Board, National River Conservation Authority, National

---

[5] Indrajit Dube, Environmental Jurisprudence - Polluter's Liability (LexisNexis Butterworths (ISBN 978-818038-152-2) 1) (2007).

Afforestation & Eco Development Board, Department of Wasteland Development etc.

Contribution of MC Mehta towards Development of Environmental Principles

The Public Interest Litigation filed by Mr. Mehta has laid down the foundation for the development of environmental jurisprudence in India as they have helped in laying down principles pertaining to environment which includes-

i. The right to clean and healthy environment is a part of fundamental rights[6].

ii. The violation of fundamental right empowers the financial compensation by the Courts as a remedy.

iii. The evolvement of Polluters' Pay Principle by the Courts[7].

iv. The public resources have "high ecological value" and have to be sustained[8].

Role of Indian Judiciary towards Environmental Principles

In 1976 the 46th Amendment to the Constitution laid down explicitly that environmental protection is part of the Constitution fiat followed by the enactment of the Environment Protection Act, 1986. These were the most notable efforts of the legislative and executive over the last two decades towards inclusion of principles to safeguard the environment in the legal jurisprudence in India. Even though the initiatives of the legislative and executive, the efforts of the judiciary have overtaken them by careful rational of the Supreme Court. The Apex Court has been offering more means, qualitative as well as quantitative, to deal with the issues faced by the environment. The laws made by the State are not being followed efficiently by the State itself, leading the judiciary to step in and come up with a new method to ensure compliance of such laws

---

[6] Oleum Gas Leak Case, *supra* note 19.

[7] *Indian Council for Enviro-Legal Action v. Union of India,* 1996 3 SCC 212. See also, *Vellore Citizens Welfare Forum v. Union of India & Ors,* (1996) 5 SCC 647

[8] Mirka Laurila-Pant et al., *How to value biodiversity in environmental management?*, 55 Ecological Indicators , 1-11 (2015).

driven implementation of the set principles in India. Along with this, the Courts of India have also done their part to ensure efficiency of the environmental jurisprudence and social justice by interpreting the provisions of various statues as well as the Constitution of India in a very liberal manner. The Apex Court's "Green Bench" established the principles of sustainable development and absolute liability under the domain of environmental considerations. The Bench also came up with modus operandi such as spot visits and expert committees.

Doctrine of Sustainable Development

World commission on Environment and Development (WCED) in its "Brundtland Report"[9] emphasised on the concept of sustainable development. As per this report sustainable development indicates the "development that meets the needs of the present without compromising the ability of the future generations to meet their own needs"[10]. The courts need to balance the development taking place and conservation of the environment. The Supreme Court dealt with the issue of environment and development for the first time ever in the 1980s in the case of *Rural Litigation and Entitlement Kendra v. State of UP*[11]. The Court held that it is to be remembered always that the environment is the permanent asset of the mankind and is not to be exhausted in one generation. In the Vellore Citizens Welfare Forum case[12], the Supreme Court observed that the concept of sustainable development has been accepted as a feasible practice to eradicate poverty and improve the overall quality of life while living within the living capacity of the eco-system supporting us.

---

[9] Jarvie, M., 1987. *Brundtland Report, 1987.* World Commission on Environment and Development (WECD).

[10] International Institute of Sustainable Development, Sustainable Development (IISD), https://www.iisd.org/about-iisd/sustainable-development .

[11] *Rural Litigation and Entitlement Kendra v. the State of U.P.*, AIR 1985 SC 652

[12] *Supra* note 7.

People's Attitude and Awareness towards environment Principles

The law around environment in India has less importance on the people of the country. Across the world, most of the people are aware of the gravity of the degradation of the environment but are less active in taking initiative for protection of environment and they consider this to be an obligation of the State. After studying 24 countries[13], a mix of developed and developing countries and conducted a survey with 24,000 persons. It was found that the people considered environmental issues to be one among the top 3 problems of their countries. As far as India is concerned, a survey conducted by TERI in 2014[14] was based on the issue of whether the people were ready to make the concerned efforts towards the environment. The study found that people considered themselves to be just a part of a small group and that is the reason why they should not work hard enough. They feel their actions would not make a difference. It was further found that nearly 40% of these people felt that environment and development went ahead simultaneously[15]. In the same sample group of the survey, more than 30% of the people[16] were of the opinion that the priority of the government must be environment over development. In some other studies, it is found that the actions of the judiciary, through litigation and judgements, affected the opinions of persons with regard to the environment.

In spite of the high-pitched publicity by NGOs and governmental organisations, people lack to take initiatives for protection of the environment. The lack of combined effects of the persons is due to the fact that in India, people disown the responsibility to protect their environment causing a lack of interest in the minds of such persons and in the society as a whole.

Governance of SDG's

The enhancement of *"environmental rule of law"* and its accreditation to justice for resolving the environmental dispute is

---

[13] Riley E. Dunlap et al., *Of Global Concern*, 35 Environment: Science and Policy for Sustainable Development , 7-39 (1993).

[14] TERI, Environmental survey (2014), New Delhi.

[15] *Ibid.*

[16] *Ibid.*

necessary for attaining the UN's 2030 agenda for Sustainable Development and the Sustainable Development Goals (SDGs) in particular SDG Goal 16, i.e. "to provide access to justice for all and build effective, accountable and inclusive institutions at all"[17]. In order to achieve this goal it must be ensured that every state has established specialised courts and environmental tribunals that shall deal completely with matters pertaining to environmental issues. In relation and implementation of SDG Goal 16 in India, the want for organising environmental courts in India arose in special instances and in one of kind times as including in various instances like, *M.C. Mehta Vs. Union of India*[18], *Indian Council for Enviro-Legal Action Vs. Union of India*[19] and *A.P. Pollution Control Board Vs. Professor M.V. Nayudu*[20] it was found and determined that as the instances of environmental issues are growing at a speedy rate which also involved contain evaluation of scientific data and records henceforth placing up environmental courts on a regional groundwork with a legally certified professionals would assist velocity the judicial process. The 186th report of the Law Commission of India[21] advocated the institution of environmental courts in India such as National Green Tribunal (NGT).

Challenges in Implementation

Compliance Monitoring

The polluting agencies are legally obligated to procure a CTE ("Consent to Establish") and CTO ("Consent to Operate") from their respective SPCB. According to the notification of MOEF[22], certain

---

[17] Pring C & Pring G, Environmental Courts & Tribunals: A Guide for Policy Makers (UNEP, UN Environment) (2016).

[18] *M.C. Mehta v. Union of India*, AIR 1987 SC 965

[19] *Indian Council for Enviro-Legal Action v. Union of India*, 1996 3 SCC 212

[20] *A.P. Pollution Control Board v. Professor M.V. Nayudu*, 1992 2 SCC 718

[21] Law Commission of India, Proposal To Constitute Environment Courts (2003).

[22] *Environmental Clearances*, Ministry of Environment and Forests, September (2006).

new projects or activities of the industrial nature or even any organizations require a "Prior Environmental Clearance". While the Pollution Control Board has the authority to shut down or order the removal of power or water supply of a facility that is in violation, the Board may only impose penalties by way of filing cases under the Water Act and Air Act and the EPA, which may be inclusive of fines and/or imprisonment of the offender[23]. In spite of this, approaching the courts through litigation has been proved as an ineffective way of enforcement. This is due to overburdening of the courts, lengthy procedures in litigation and overstraining of the resources of the State Board. To ensure compliance by the industries, PCBs carry out various activities such as:

i. Training and technical assistance to the industries
ii. Developing reports that indicate problems in the specific industry
iii. Rule of Compliance
iv. Preventive Measures
v. Circulating the "charter on corporate" responsibilities of the industries towards the protection of the environment in the category of the highly polluting industries, which request compliance voluntarily beyond the standards that are prescribed by law.
vi. Awareness campaigns.

Presently, the economic mechanisms play an ancillary role in the promotion of environmental compliance in the country. Some important economic mechanisms doing so include, rebate on Cess on water, guarantees via bank, subsidies on equipment for control of pollution and other monetary incentives[24].

Access to Freedom of Information

Inability to access information can prove to be a major roadblock in environmental planning and management if even the official bodies or NGOs are unable to do so. In order to facilitate the flow of

---

[23] Alexander Fischer, *Which Road to Social Revolution? Liberalization and Constitutional Reform in India*, South Asia Institute, University of Heidelberg (2007).
[24] "India's Forests", Ministry of Environment and Forests, Government of India (2009).

information, many countries are releasing the information they have. In the USA, Freedom of Information Act has been enacted. The European Union is following the footsteps of the USA.

Even though such information is crucial for the planning and management of the environment, many governors and MNCs are apprehensive to share information as there is a possibility of a leak of industrial secrets into the market if there is too much of disclosure. There are also situations wherein the authorities announce strategic needs and suspend disclosure.

Conclusion

The legacy prevailing in the country has marked a noticeable owed towards the conservation and welfare of the flora, fauna and its biodiversity. The country used to have a clear prison provision to curb the issue of environmental destruction and disruption which has further made stringent the Indian Judiciary by laying down various environment principles which has helped in profitable reaching in conservation of the environment. Various environment conservationists such as Mr. MC Mehta has also aided the country in procuring various rule, doctrines, principles for the welfare of the Environment. It was well recognised that right to safe and clean environment is a right of every individual and is circumscribed under the purview of human rights laws as well which is also provided and given importance under Article 21 of the Constitution of India. Despite that the underlying problem is monitoring and access to information to public in implementing the principles which were developed.

Associate Professor,
Department of Chemistry,
RR College, Alwar (Raj.)
email : dr.anitag03@gmail.com

6. Climate Change : Causes, Effects and Ways to curb It

Dr. Sudha Sukhwal Shringi

Introduction

Climate change has become the biggest challenge for the mankind. In the last 50 years the temperatures of our planet earth have risen by a degree or 2°C and the situation is very alarming. This change in climate if it continues in the same way and at the same speed the day is not far when the ice in north pole and south pole will melt due to high temperatures on earth and most of the land will be underwater.

Climate change that is happening over the years at a slow pace threatens our existence. Due to Climate change, there would be scarcity of food and water for people and survival will be tough. There will be heavy flooding across the planet and more chances of Tsunamis and earthquakes. We might face extreme heat and temperatures which we are seeing as of now. This year in UK the temperatures have risen considerably and few people have died of heat stroke. We will see more diseases and loss of life along with huge effect on economy. Few Species of Plant and animal might become extinct due to Climate Change.

Causes

Greenhouse effect is one phenomenon that safeguards earth from outside radiations and makes this planet habitable. Our planet earth is warming at a faster rate in present times than any recorded history. This speed of warming is a cause of great concern and if proper measures are not taken in time survival will be impossible.

Few of the main causes of this faster climate change are as discussed in this Paper

Population of earth was 3 billion in 1960 and as of 2020 the population of earth was 7.75 billion. In 2022 it would be near to 8 billion. Which is more than double in last 60 years. Now this increased population causes lot of loads on the earth's natural resources which are limited.

1. Industrialization and Modernization is another reason as all the industries and manufacturing plants generate energy by burning

fossil fuels and thus releasing harmful gases in earth's atmosphere. Out of the total fuel used in producing energy 85% is fossil and rest is Nuclear, Hydro and Renewable.

2. Generation of power causes earth's resources to deplete and thus speeding climate change or Global warming. Power is generated by burning fossil fuels such as Coal, Oils and Gas. There is emission from these fossil fuels which is poisonous and destroys earth's atmosphere.

3. Transportation: Most cars, trucks, ships, and planes run on fossilfuels. That makes transportation a major contributor of greenhouse gases, especially carbon-dioxide emissions. Road vehicles account for the largest part, but emissions from ships and planes continue to grow due to faster transport means.

4. Food Production: Producing food requires energy to run farm equipment or fishing boats, usually with fossil fuels. Growing crops can also cause emissions, like when using fertilizers and manure. Cattle produce methane, a powerful greenhouse gas. And emissions also come from packaging and distributing food.

5. De-Forestation: We have been cutting down trees to accommodate more population and build cities, industries, farms, pastures etc. Trees when cut release the carbon stored in them in the atmosphere resulting in more carbon dioxide in the atmosphere.

6. Powering Buildings: Globally, residential and commercial buildings consume over half of all electricity. As they continue to draw on coal, oil, and natural gas for heating and cooling, they emit significant quantities of greenhouse gas emissions.

7. Consuming too much: Your home and use of power, how you move around, what you eat and how much you throw away - all contribute to greenhouse gas emissions. So does the consumption of goods such as clothing, electronics, and plastics.

Effects

Now we shall elaborate the effects of above Causes, which have been taking place over the years, on our planet earth

1. Increased drought: Water is becoming scarcer in more regions. Droughts can stir destructive sand and dust storms that can move

billions of tons of sand across continents. Deserts are expanding, reducing land for growing food. Many people now face the threat of not having enough water on a regular basis.

2. Hotter temperatures: Nearly all land areas are seeing more hot days and heat waves; 2020 was one of the hottest years on record. Higher temperatures increase heat-related illnesses and can make it more difficult to work and move around. Wildfires start more easily and spread more rapidly when conditions are hotter.

3. A warming rising Oceans: The ocean soaks up most of the heat from global warming. This melts ice sheets and raises sea levels, threatening coastal and island communities. More carbon dioxide makes the ocean more acidic, which endangers marine life.

4. More Severe Storms: Changes in temperature cause changes in rainfall. This results in more severe and frequent storms. They cause flooding and landslides, destroying homes and communities, and costing billions of dollars.

5. Loss of species: Climate change poses risks to the survival of species on land and in the ocean. These risks increase as temperatures climb. Forest fires, extreme weather, and invasive pests and diseases are among many threats. Some species will be able to relocate and survive, but others will not.

6. Not enough food: Changes in climate and increases in extreme weather events are among the reasons behind a global rise in hunger and poor nutrition. Fisheries, crops, and livestock may be destroyed or become less productive. Heat stress can diminish water and grasslands for grazing.

7. Poverty and displacement: Climate change increases the factors that put and keep people in poverty. Floods may sweep away urban slums, destroying homes and livelihoods. Heat can make it difficult to work in outdoor jobs. Weather-related disasters displace 2.3 crore people a year, leaving many more vulnerable to poverty.

8. More health risks: Changing weather patterns are spreading diseases such as malaria. Extreme weather events increase diseases and deaths, and make it difficult for health care systems to keep up. Other risks to health include increased hunger and

poor nutrition in places where people cannot grow or find sufficient food.

Ways to Curb

The action which needed to be taken for controlling these effects are very urgent and various governments are working on the same. Few of the immediate actions which can be taken at our end so as to avoid the catastrophe are as under. Everyone can help limit climate change. From the way we travel, to the electricity we use and the food we eat, we can make a difference. Start with these 8 actions to help tackle the climate crisis.

1. Walk, cycle, or take public transport: The world's roads are clogged with vehicles, most of them burning diesel or petrol. Walking or riding a bike instead of driving will reduce greenhouse gas emissions – and help your health and fitness. For longer distances, consider taking a train or bus and carpool whenever possible.

2. Save energy: At home much of our electricity and heat are powered by coal, oil, and gas. Use less energy by lowering your heating and cooling, switch to LED light bulbs and energy-efficient electric appliances, washing your laundry with cold water, or hanging things to dry instead of using a dryer.

3. Be Vegetarian: Vegetables fruits, whole grains have less carbon footprint on our environment and thus are not harmful to our climate. Whereas animal products release more carbon for per kg production and are thus more harmful. So it's best to turn to vegetarian food and focus on growing and processing more plant based foods.

4. Stop Food and resource wastage: It should be completely avoided as it consumes lot of energy to produce that number of resources, food or facility, when the resource is wasted all the energy used to produce goes waste and this waste when buried in landfill produces Methane gas that is harmful to our atmosphere.

5. Change your home's source of energy: Almost all the homes are supplied electricity by the company which in turn gets the electricity produced by using Hydro or fossil fuel. We can install solar or wind source on our rooftop and reduce the load on electricity produced by fossil fuel.

6. Reduce, reuse, repair & recycle: Electronics, clothes, and other items we buy cause carbon emissions at each point in production, from the extraction of raw materials to manufacturing and transporting goods to market. To protect our climate, buy fewer things, shop second-hand, repair what you can, and recycle.

7. Switch to alternative means of transport like electric or hydrogen vehicle. Indian government is heavily promoting electric vehicles and giving many incentives for encouraging use of same. This would stop the use of fossil fuels and thus reduce the carbon footprint.

The below charts show how humans have increased their footprints over the years and how fast the resources being depleted. Also, in second graph the consumption of earth's resources country wise is shown USA alone consumes 5 times the earth's resources. This data is from Global footprint Network.

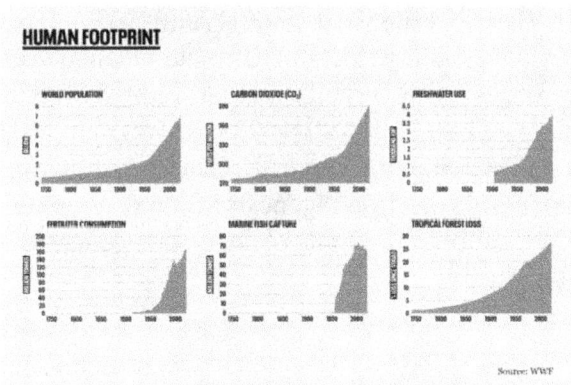

HUMAN FOOTPRINT

Source: WWF

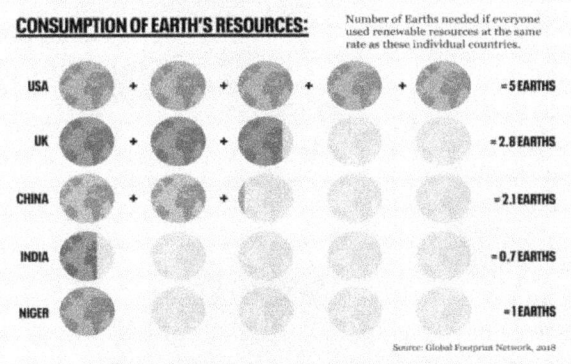

CONSUMPTION OF EARTH'S RESOURCES:

Number of Earths needed if everyone used renewable resources at the same rate as these individual countries.

USA	= 5 EARTHS
UK	= 2.8 EARTHS
CHINA	= 2.1 EARTHS
INDIA	= 0.7 EARTHS
NIGER	= 1 EARTHS

Source: Global Footprint Network, 2018

Conclusion

Earth's resources are limited and human wants are unlimited. For safeguarding our home we need to use the limited resources judiciously and switch to a lifestyle which is in sync with environment. Stop use of plastics, use clean fuel, tap energy from nature, Solar and Wind. There have been lots of efforts from United nations and countries for awareness about the climate change but the speed at which degradation is taking place is much faster than the steps taken to curb the menace.

References :

1. Climate Change Causes Effects and Solutions Author(s): John T. Hardy Publisher: Wiley, Year: 2003 ISBN: 0470850191,9780470850190,9780470864937
2. Climate: Causes and Effects of Climate Change Author(s): Dana Desonie Series: Our Fragile Planet Publisher: Chelsea House Publications, Year: 2008 ISBN: 9780816062140,0816062145
3. "Causes of Climate Change." Causes of Climate Change. Environmental Protection Agency U.S., n.d. Web. 06 May 2016.
4. https://www.un.org/en/climatechange/science/causes-effects-climate-change

Associate Professor,
Rajrishi College Alwar,
Rajasthan

7. Environment Accounting : The Accounting for The Nature

Dr. Suresh Kumar Rajora

Abstract

As the public concern over environmental degradation has increased, business firms are under compulsion to grant more consideration to the natural environment. Now business firms are under more pressure from stakeholders to disclose information about the impact of their environmental actions. Consequently, there's a growing trend among leading companies to report their environmental performance. In this scenario environmental accounting and reporting has emerged as a crucial tool to assess the impact of such actions on the society and environment. There are many ways in which information are often disclosed to the stakeholders. However, disclosures in annual reports are considered mutually of the foremost effective medium of communicating corporate environmental information. Disclosure of environmental issues in the Annual Report may be a fundamental requirement for an organization so as to satisfy the knowledge needs of its stakeholders, which include shareholders, creditors, employees, consumers, government and society at large. Inclusion of voluntary information like environmental disclosures, not only adds value to the annual reports, but also reflects the extent to which corporate unit is anxious with transparency in its activities. However, the way companies disclose environmental related information varies from company to company and from country to country. Many studies have shown that the majority companies in India have an interest in disclosing only mandatory information in their reports and there's lack of voluntary disclosures on this count. Most of the businesses disclose information which isn't only inadequate but misleading also. In fact, there's no standard way for presenting and interpreting these issues. Besides the qualitative level of this type of disclosure in terms of relevance, reliability, clarity, comparability, timelines and credibility, is usually not satisfactory. Although some studies on environmental reporting have proliferated in recent years, still this is often a state of research which must be explored thoroughly.

Keywords : Environment, Disclosure, Degradation, Depletion, Biodiversity.

Introduction

Various environment issues like heating, air, noise and pollution caused by industrial activity has led to the degradation and depletion of natural resources and biodiversity which has heightened the priority for the preservation of the environment and also the need for the implementation of environmental accounting theory and practice worldwide. The advantage of industrialization, economic process and development of the society mustn't be at the value of degrading the environment. These days, protection of environment has become a key issue everywhere the world. Several factors and forces are answerable for destruction of environment. Of these, growing hazardous industrialization might be a serious culprit. Environmental accounting is also a useful and sometimes necessary tool to be told more about the influences of environmental input/output of a company's activities on its bottom line and on the natural environment. Environmental accounting has become vital in the recent past. Today, in some companies, it's become an integral a component of monetary reports. Consequently, environmental accounting helps companies and other organizations boost their trust and confidence and are associated with receiving an honest assessment. This article explains the concept of Social Responsibility Accounting and Environment Accounting, its emergence, objectives and benefits of Environmental Accounting, guidelines and dimensions together with corporate Environmental Reporting.

Concept of Social Responsibility Accounting and Environment Accounting

Social Accounting also termed as Corporate Social Responsibility Accounting or Non- Financial Accounting could be a medium of communicating social and environmental effect of an organizational activity to a selected interest in a society. It's the potential to reveal the link between pursuing economic profit and therefore the pursuit of social and environmental objectives. As per D. Crowther "Social Accounting may be defined as the way of reporting on a corporation economic activity, the determination of these to whom the organization is accountable and also the identification of suitable measures and reporting techniques". It's wont to express the measuring and therefore the measuring of social and economic sustainability. According to Gray, the final objectives of social responsibility accounting are to work out and measure the net social contribution of the organization on a periodic basis and to judge the social performance of organizations by identifying whether the organization's strategies and objectives are per the social priorities. Globalization is one factor which shows that Social Accounting is becoming important. International trade has increased in 21st century resulting in the new aspect of relationship between business and society. When the organization increases their economic activity, it leads to environmental and social consequences and so the question of corporate social responsibility arises. Environmental accounting is largely a subset of social accounting, which focuses on the value structure and environmental performance of an organization. Environmental accounting is an inclusive field of accounting. It provides reports for both internal use, generating environmental information to assist make management decisions on pricing, controlling overhead and capital budgeting, and external use, disclosing environmental information of interest to the general public and to the financial community.

Environment Accounting – The Greener Side of Accounting

Going by the best definition, Environmental Accounting includes environment related costs and expenditure, the environment benefits of the products/activity and also the details regarding the sustainable operations taken by the organizations. Environmental accounting ensures the sustainable development of the entity's activity, the analysis of the prices and also the benefits generated by the impact of the environment on the activity, the event of the practices and policies concerning the control of pollution. Environmental accounting is employed so as to present the social and environmental responsibility as environmental costs. Environmental accounting provides a typical framework for organizations to spot and account for past, present and future environmental costs to support managerial decision-making, control and public disclosure. Environmental Accounting enables organizations to trace their environmental data and other greenhouse emission (GHG) emissions against reduction targets, and facilitates environmental reporting to produce sustainability for social, economic and environmental protection.

Environmental accounting is important for a corporation implementing the concept of sustainable development because it facilitates to require into consideration ecological activities of a company in economic measurement accounting can help achieve the target of corporations and other stakeholders in reducing the prices and decreasing the pollution respectively. Environmental accounting ensures the sustainable development of the entity's activity, the analysis of the prices and also the benefits; the event of the practices and policies concerning the control of pollution make sure the minimizing of the costs; action plans for recycling of waste and scraps. Environmental accounting consists of three key things: environmental conservation cost (monetary value), environmental conservation benefits (Physical units), and therefore the economic benefit related to environmental conservation activities (monetary value).

Objectives of Implementing Environmental Accounting

Environmental Accounting is required to fulfill lots of demands from different stakeholders. However, for educational reasons, the next basic objectives are often identified on the logical ground:

1. To identify, collect and analyze the information about the raw-material, energy consumption and environmental aspects of a commercial activity which can correspondingly help the business in better deciding profitability further as protection of the environment.
2. To supply information regarding the economic and environmental performance of a business entity which results in a far better relationship between business and therefore the external environment (I.e. interest groups)

3. By making environmental disclosures, companies may show their commitments and responsibility towards the environmental aspects and thus appear to be conscious of new factors.
4. It manages the acquisitions, consumption and sales of materials, including waste; contributes to a higher management of energy and water costs, etc.
5. Environmental Accounting helps in providing the relevant information to the moral investors which helps in building a positive image for the corporate thereby helping them to draw in more funds from the investors and therefore the groups.
6. Environmental Accounting helps to attenuate costs and therefore the negative impact on the environment, presenting facts about: the provision process, from an environmental perspective; the merchandise and therefore the responsibility of the producer; distribution and control costs, supply process, pricing policy etc.
7. Implementing environmental accounting helps in identifying distinct environmental costs, making provisions for risks and other costs.

Environmental Accounting Approaches

1. **Monetary Environmental Management Accounting (MEMA):** Monetary environmental management accounting (MEMA) is intended for internal use; it's normally voluntary and isn't needed for external stakeholders. It provides basis for financial accounting, environmental management systems like ISO 14000, and other environmental performance evaluations.

2. **Physical Environmental Management Accounting (PEMA):** Physical environmental management accounting (PEMA) helps in assessing the amount of environmental impact produced by the corporate. The data produced in PEMA is employed in alternative ways, for instance, it will be used for CO_2 equivalent trading, which might produce extra income for the corporate.

3. **External Monetary Environmental Accounting (EMEA):** External monetary environmental accounting is extremely kind of like financial reports but it requires the nominal presentation of the data in an exceedingly specific format to get specific results. The data are often used for various purposes like to guage the consequence of varied environmental taxes (e.g. CO_2 taxes),

pollution subsidies etc.

4. **External Physical Environmental Accounting (EPEA):** External physical environmental accounting helps the corporate in improving "green image"; it provides information to external stakeholders which help the corporate to boost the transparency of environmental performance undertaken by them.

Environmental Accounting Related Issues

Environmental issues can have a control on financial statements prepared on an accounting in some ways. The introduction of environmental laws and regulations may involve an obligation to acknowledge impairment of assets and consequently a desire to write-down the carrying value. A failure to position legal requirements concerning environmental matters, like emissions or waste disposal, may require accrual of remediation works, compensation or legal costs. For example a failure to accommodate pollution control laws may end in fines and penalties for an entity. For example, energy costs are considered an environmental cost because the employment of fossil fuels could also be a source of dioxide and pollution. Some entities may need to acknowledge environmental obligations as liabilities in the financial statements. As an example, obligations associated with solid waste landfill closure and aftercare and restoration obligations associated with mining operations.

Environmental Accounting Issues	Proposed Solutions
Definition of Environmental costs and expenses	Environment costs that don't cause future expected benefits.
Environmental costs recognition and measurement issues	Materiality, measurability and certainty
Capital problem or revenue allocation	Capitalize if it's intended to stop or reduce future environmental damage or to conserve resources
Capitalization of environmental costs incurred subsequent to the	Capitalize either (i) if the prices ends up in a rise in expected future economic benefits or (ii) if the

acquisition of a capital asset	prices are considered to be a value of expected future benefits
Accounting for future environmental expenditure	Where an entity includes a legal obligation to incur future costs, the prices involved represent an environmental liability.
Accounting for the impairment disclosures	Reduce the carrying amount of assets instead of introduce a liability
Environmental accounting policy disclosers	All significant accounting policies referring to financial statements items to be disclosed.

An entity may should disclose a possible environmental obligation as a contingent liability where

(a) The possible obligation depends on the possible occurrence of a future event, or
(b) The amount of this obligation cannot be reasonably estimated, or
(c) An outflow of resources to settle the duty isn't probable.

In the course of meeting the relevant principle requirements, some additional disclosures in the notes to the financial statements is additionally required.

Conclusion

Environmental accounting is incredibly important issue. As economic development moreover as environmental protection is equally important but contradictory issue therefore a careful assessment of the advantages and costs of environmental damages is important to seek out the tolerance limit of environmental degradation and also the required level of development. For that there's need for correct framework which may provide guidelines on the difficulty of environmental cost, environmental liability, environmental assets, capitalization of such cost and liability and reporting framework. Again environmental costs have impact on reported profit in the plan likewise as product pricing. Study of corporate reporting practices reflects that there's an increasing tendency among the company managers to disclose some information in their annual report back to inform about their efforts to shareholders and public normally. It's also clear that the majority of such environmental information reported by the businesses is found to be nonfinancial. Such information is mere description of the efforts made by the corporate. The knowledge on amount of cash spent for such initiatives and its material effect on financial results is grossly missing in such information. Again there's wide variation noticed in the type of reporting and theme the businesses selected to report. This could increase other dimension of the matter of lack of comparability and verifiability. So it's felt that such information should be integrated with financial accounting information to own reliability. For integration it's necessary for monetary measurement of environmental cost and benefits. But all cost and benefit to the environment can't be suitably measured in unit of measurement, a minimum of at micro level. Internal cost, like investment made by the company sector for minimization of losses to Environment by development, process development are often possible for monetary measurement but cost of externalities like degradation and destruction like wearing away, loss of bio diversity, pollution, pollution, sound pollution, problem of solid waste, depletion of nonrenewable natural resources i.e. loss emerged thanks to over exploitation of non-renewable natural resources like minerals, water, gas, deforestation etc. and therefore the environmental assets created by business like afforestation, bio-diversity conservation, water preservation etc cannot be suitably measured in monetary terms. Further, it's very hard to make a decision that what proportion loss has occurred to the environment thanks to establishment of a selected business unit. This makes obstacles in the total integration of environmental accounting in the framework of existing GAAP. However, it's possible to disclose internal cost and advantage of environmental measures that's undertaken by a business unit and its material effects in reported profit by disclosing the way of recognition.

References

1. Ahmed, N. N. N. and Sualiman, M. (2004). Environmental disclosures in Malaysian annual reports: A Legitimacy theory perspective. International Journal of Commerce & Management, 14(1), 44-58.
2. Al-Tuwaijri, S., Christensen, T., & Hughes, K. (2004).The relations among environmental disclosure, environmental performance, and economic performance: A simultaneous equations approach. Accounting, Organizations and Society, 29 (5), 101-135.
3. Banarjee, S.B. (2001), "Corporate environmental strategies and actions", Management Decision, Vol. 39 No. 1, pp. 36-44.
4. Chatterjee, B., & Mir, M. Z. (2008): The current status of environmental reporting by Indian companies. Managerial Auditing Journal, 23(6), 609–629
5. Cormier, D. and Magnan, M. 1999. Corporate Environmental Disclosure Strategies: Determinants, Costs and Benefits. Journal of Accounting, Auditing and Finance: 429-51.
6. Deegan, C. 2002. The Legitimising Effect of Social and Environmental Disclosures - a Theoretical Foundation. Accounting, Auditing & Accountability Journal 15 (3): 282-311
7. Environmental Accounting Guidelines (2005): Ministry of the Environment Japan, February 2005
8. Environmental Financial Accounting and Reporting at the Corporate Level: A Report of UNCTAD Secretariat, Fifteenth session Geneva, 11-13 February 1998
9. Gamble, G.O., Hsu, K., Kite, D. and Radtke, R.R. 1995. Environmental Disclosures in Annual Reports and 10Ks: An Examination. Accounting Horizons: 34-54
10. KPMG. 2002. Environmental Management Accounting: A Case Study for AMP. Australia: Environment Australia, ICAA, and EPA Victoria.
11. Rob Gray & Jan Bebbington (2001) : Accounting for the Environment: SAGE Publications Ltd: London
12. Schaltegger, S.; Muller, K.; and Hindrichsen, H. 1996. Corporate Environmental Accounting. New York: Chichester.

13. Shukla Dr. Anita &, Nidhi Vyas (2013): Environmental Accounting & Reporting in India (A comparative study of Bharat Petroleum Company Limited & Oil & Natural Gas Company Limited): Pacific Business Review International : Volume 5 Issue 7 (January 2013)

Assistant Professor,
Department of Accountancy and Business Statistics,
Government College Jaipur (Raj.)
email : skrajora014@gmail.com

8. कॉविड-19 महामारी सतत विकास एवं जलवायु परिवर्तन : पुरातन एवं नवीन दृष्टिकोण

श्रीमती मिथलेश सोलंकी

"आपदि प्राणरक्षा हि धर्मस्य प्रथमाङ्कुर: "

अर्थात आपदा ग्रस्त जीव की रक्षा करना ही धर्म है। महाभारत (शांति पर्व) अध्याय 13, श्लोक संख्या- 598।

कोरोना महामारी का कहर अब नया विषय नहीं रह गया है अपितु पुरी पृथ्वी का बच्चा बच्चा तक कोरोना से परिचित हो गया है। विश्व का कोई भी देश, कोई कोना कोरोना के विभत्स रूप से अछूता नहीं रह गया है। चीन के वुहान से जन्मा कोरोना विषाणु का कॉविड-19 प्रतिरूप इतना भयंकर रूप धारण करेगा इसका शायद ही किसी को अनुमान रहा होगा। इसकी विभिन्न लहरों ने लाखों लोगों की जाने ली। हम विकास कहकर अंधाधुंध कमाने के होड़ में आगे बढ़ रहे हैं उस पर इस महामारी ने लगाम लगा दी। संसाधनों का अत्यधिक दोहन, मुनाफा कमाने की होड़, विकसित तकनीकी जिसने आकाश को भी दूषित कर दिया है। नतीजे हमारे सामने आते जा रहे हैं। पृथ्वी का तापमान बढ़ना, असमान वर्षा वितरण, मौसम चक्र का संतुलन गड़बड़ाना यह सब निरंतर हो रहा है।

हाल ही में जारी वैश्विक सतत विकास रिपोर्ट 2022 को देखने पर पता चलता है की स्वास्थ्य संबंधी विविधता एवं शमानात्मक उपचारों में कमी, जलवायु, जैव विविधता, भू-राजनीतिक और सैन्य-संकट विश्व स्तर पर सतत विकास के लिए प्रमुख अवरोध है। एसडीजी इंडेक्स के विश्व औसत में वर्ष 2021 से लगातार दूसरे वर्ष भी गिरावट आई है। इसका मुख्य कारण महामारी का प्रभाव हो सकता है । भारी मानवीय क्षति के अलावा सैन्य संघर्ष, रूस-यूक्रेन युद्ध, अंतरराष्ट्रीय स्तर पर खाद्य सुरक्षा संकट, ऊर्जा की कमी, संसाधनों की होड़ आदि जलवायु और जैव विविधता संकट के कारण बढ़ रहे हैं। मानव जाति के उदय एवं विकास का इतिहास कई प्राकृतिक आपदाओं एवं महामारियों से भरा है समय-समय पर प्रकृति ने मानव के बढ़ते हौसलों एवं तेज रफ्तार पर लगाम लगाई है। महामारियों और प्राकृतिक आपदाओं द्वारा सभ्यताएं नष्ट होती रही हैं। भारतवर्ष के विभिन्न कालों में प्रकृति की सुरक्षा व सबका विकास संदर्भ ढूंढे जा सकते हैं इस पेपर का उद्देश्य ऐतिहासिक परिपेक्ष में उन सभी संदर्भों को प्रकाश में लाना है विभिन्न कालों में प्रकृति संरक्षण के उपाय सतत विकास के उद्देश्यों को लागू करना व वर्तमान उद्देश्यों का महामारी द्वारा

प्रभावित होना शामिल है। राजनीतिक संकट, युद्ध, राज्यों द्वारा प्रबंधन, सामाजिक सरोकार, अंतरराष्ट्रीय संबंध आर्थिक प्रगति विचारों ने मनुष्य को प्रभावित किया है। कहीं ना कहीं महामारियों ने मनुष्य की गति को रोका है या धीमा किया है प्रगतिशील सभ्यताओं को समाप्त किया है। सतत विकास के अवधारणा प्राचीन काल से ही भारतीय संस्कृति में विद्यमान है।

कीवर्ड्स : सतत विकास ,जैव विविधता,कोरोना महामारी,सामाजिक सरोकार,प्रगतिशील सभ्यताएं

परिचय

सतत विकास से हमारा अभिप्राय ऐसे विकास से है, जो हमारी भावी पीढ़ियों की अपनी जरूरतें पूरी करने की योग्यता को प्रभावित किए बिना वर्तमान समय की आवश्यकताएं पूरी करे। भारतीयों के लिए पर्यावरण संरक्षण, जो सतत विकास का अभिन्न अंग है, कोई नई अवधारणा नहीं है। भारत में प्रकृति और वन्यजीवों का संरक्षण अगाध आस्था की बात है, जो हमारे दैनिक जीवन में प्रतिबिंबित होता है और पौराणिक गाथाओं, लोककथाओं, धर्मों, कलाओं और संस्कृति में वर्णित है ।ट्रांसफॉर्मिंग आवर वर्ल्ड : द 2030 एजेंडा फॉर सस्टेनेबल डेवलपमेंट' के संकल्प को, जिसे सतत विकास लक्ष्यों के नाम से भी जाना जाता है, भारत सहित 193 देशों ने सितंबर, 2015 में संयुक्त राष्ट्र महासभा की उच्च स्तरीय पूर्ण बैठक में स्वीकार किया गया था और इसे एक जनवरी, 2016 को लागू किया गया। सतत विकास लक्ष्यों का उद्देश्य सबके लिए समान, न्यायसंगत, सुरक्षित, शांतिपूर्ण, समृद्ध और रहने योग्य विश्व का निर्माण करना और विकास के तीनों पहलुओं, अर्थात सामाजिक समावेश, आर्थिक विकास और पर्यावरण संरक्षण को व्यापक रूप से समाविष्ट करना है। सहस्राब्दी विकास लक्ष्य के बाद, जो 2000 से 2015 तक के लिए निर्धारित किए गए थे, विकसित इन नए लक्ष्यों का उद्देश्य विकास के अधूरे कार्य को पूरा करना और ऐसे विश्व की संकल्पना को मूर्त रूप देना है, जिसमें कम चुनौतियां और अधिक आशाएं हों।हम पृथ्वी को माता मानते है और सतत विकास सदैव हमारे दर्शन और विचारधारा का मूल सिद्धांत रहा है। सतत विकास लक्ष्यों को प्राप्त करने के लिए अनेक मोर्चों पर कार्य करते हुए हमें महात्मा गांधी की याद आती है, जिन्होंने हमें चेतावनी दी थी कि धरती प्रत्येक व्यक्ति की आवश्यकताओं को तो पूरा कर सकती है, पर प्रत्येक व्यक्ति के लालच को नहीं।

भारत सरकार द्वारा, न्यूयार्क में जुलाई, 2017 में आयोजित होने वाले उच्च स्तरीय राजनीतिक मंच (एचएलपीएफ) पर अपनी पहली स्वैच्छिक राष्ट्रीय समीक्षा (वीएनआर) प्रस्तुत करने हेतु लिया गया निर्णय इसका उदाहरण है कि भारत सतत विकास लक्ष्यों के सफल कार्यान्वयन को कितना महत्व दे रहा है। पर्यावरण को संरक्षित रखते हुए संपूर्ण विकास हेतु लोगों की आकांक्षाएं पूरी करने के लिए राष्ट्रीय

एवं राज्य तथा स्थानीय स्तर पर प्रत्येक व्यक्ति और संस्था द्वारा और अधिक प्रयास करने की आवश्यकता है।

समूची दुनिया लगभग डेढ़ साल से जारी कोरोना महामारी से त्रस्त है. सतर्कता और टीकाकरण से संक्रमण की रोकथाम की कोशिशें जोरों पर हैं. ऐसे उपायों के साथ हमें दीर्घकालिक नीतियों को अपनाकर ऐसी महामारियों से मानव जाति को सुरक्षित करने के ठोस उपायों पर ध्यान देने की जरूरत है. वायरस और बैक्टीरिया से होनेवाली बीमारियों का सीधा संबंध पर्यावरण के क्षरण से है. इसे रेखांकित करते हुए संयुक्त राष्ट्र पर्यावरण कार्यक्रम के भारत प्रमुख अतुल बगई ने कहा है कि कोविड-19 महामारी प्राकृतिक क्षेत्रों के क्षरण, प्रजातियों के लुप्त होने तथा संसाधनों के दोहन का परिणाम है. भारत समेत विभिन्न देशों को पारिस्थितिकी के क्षरण को रोकने और अब तक हुए नुकसान की भरपाई करने की कोशिश करनी चाहिए. पूरी दुनिया जलवायु परिवर्तन, प्रदूषण और जैव-विविधता के पतन के दुष्परिणामों को भुगत रही है. भारत उन देशों में शुमार है, जहां इन समस्याओं का असर सबसे अधिक है. प्राकृतिक आपदाओं की बारंबारता बढ़ने के रूप में एक नतीजा हमारे सामने है. महामारी में चिकित्सकों ने पाया कि प्रदूषण के प्रभाव से संक्रमण अधिक खतरनाक रूप धारण कर रहा है.

धरती का तापमान बढ़ने से गलेशियर तेजी से पिघल रहे हैं और उनका पानी समुद्री जल-स्तर बढ़ने का कारण बन रहा है. कई शोधों में यह इंगित किया गया है कि इन ग्लेशियरों में लाखों साल से दबे बैक्टीरिया और वायरस बाहर आ रहे हैं तथा जीव-जंतुओं के माध्यम से मनुष्यों तक पहुंच रहे हैं. वैज्ञानिक यह भी बता चुके हैं कि कई जीव वायरसों की संरचना कुछ दिनों में बदल सकती है. कोरोना वायरस के रूप बदलने के कई उदाहरण हमारे सामने हैं.

नये-नये रूपों में ये वायरस अधिक आक्रामक और खतरनाक होते जा रहे हैं. जैव-विविधता के ह्रास और अंधाधुंध विकास की वजह से हमारी रोगप्रतिरोधक क्षमता भी प्रभावित हो रही है. खाने-पीने की चीजों की उपलब्धता और गुणवत्ता तथा उनकी विविधता भी पर्यावरण से सीधे तौर पर जुड़ी हुई हैं. स्वास्थ्य की बेहतरी और जीवन शैली में सुधार सतत विकास की अवधारणा के अभिन्न अंग हैं. यदि हमारे जीने का ढंग प्रकृति के साथ साहचर्य व सामंजस्य की समझ से संबद्ध होगा, तो बर्बादी भी कम होगी और कचरे की भयावह समस्या भी नहीं आयेगी.

उल्लेखनीय है कि कूड़े-कचरे के समुचित प्रबंधन के अभाव में प्रदूषण की चुनौती गंभीर होती जा रही है. विभिन्न जानलेवा संक्रामक रोगों की जड़ में प्रदूषण है. प्राकृतिक संसाधनों के अनियंत्रित दोहन ने पर्यावरण संरक्षण प्रयासों पर पानी फेर दिया है. ध्यान रहे, जो नुकसान हो चुका है, उसे पूरा कर पाना लगभग असंभव है, इसलिए संरक्षण हमारी सबसे बड़ी प्राथमिकता होनी चाहिए. यदि हमने वैज्ञानिकों और विशेषज्ञों की बात नहीं मानी, तो बीमारियों और महामारियों से भी पीछा

छुड़ाना बेहद मुश्किल होगा. यह एक तथ्य है कि कोरोना महामारी अंतिम महामारी नहीं है. इसलिए हमें अभी से आगे के लिए मुस्तैदी से तैयारी करनी है।

मानवीय इतिहास के प्रारंभिक कालों में पर्यावरण लोगों के जीवन की गतिविधियों का हम हिस्सा था। प्राचीनतम स्रोतों से हमें ज्ञात होता है की वे जंगल, जमीन व प्राकृतिक संसाधनों के बहुत ज्यादा करीब थे। प्राचीन भारतीय पुरातात्विक स्रोतों के गहन अध्ययन, प्राचीन भारतीय ग्रंथ जैसे- अर्थशास्त्र, शतपथ ब्राह्मण, वेद, मनुस्मृति, वृहत संहिता, रामायण, महाभारत , राजतरंगिणी में वन पारिस्थितिकी और संरक्षण को विस्तार से दर्शाया गया है। सिंधु घाटी सभ्यता में नगर नियोजन और सामाजिक संरचना की कई विशेषताओं ने पर्यावरण के प्रति जागरूकता का पता उनके द्वारा प्रयोग किए गई मिट्टी के बर्तनों, सीलो,मूर्तियो ,एक सींग वाला वाला हिरन, बाघ,हाथी मुहरों में बेल विविध जीव विविधता को दर्शाता है।

संस्कृति व पारिस्थितिकी के बीच प्राचीन भारतीय समाज का संबंध बहुत गहरा था। विभिन्न जैविक भौगोलिकी का संरक्षण प्राचीन सभ्यताओं का महत्वपूर्ण घटक था। मानव ने धीरे धीरे पृथ्वी के ढांचे को बदलने की कोशिश की। मानवीय विकास की दौड़ ने पर्यावरण को बदल दिया। आग का विकास, पशुओं को पालतु बनाना, कृषि पद्धतियों ने महत्वपूर्ण प्रयोगों को बदलने पर मजबूर किया। वे प्रकृति एवं संसाधनों के अत्यंत करीब थे। हमारे पूर्वजों ने परिस्थिति की तंत्र व पर्यावरण को बचाने के काफी प्रयास किए, जो सतत विकास दर्शाता है। अनेक प्राचीन भारतीय दस्तावेजों में पर्यावरण,वन, जैव विविधता संरक्षण के दृष्टिकोण का पता चलता है।

प्राचीन भारतीय ग्रंथों में वन और जैव विविधता की अवधारणा

कौटिल्य का अर्थशास्त्र : कौटिल्य चंद्रगुप्त के मंत्री थे। उनके द्वारा लिखित पुस्तक में वर्षा, सिंचाई तकनीकी, मिट्टी के प्रकार, कृषि की उचित व्यवस्था को विस्तार से बताया है । उनकी पुस्तक में वन संरक्षण एवं प्रबंधन को भी महत्वपूर्ण स्थान दिया गया है। कर व्यवस्था के लिए बागानों, मनोरंजन के स्थानों को राजस्व के स्रोत के रूप में इसमें दिखाया गया है। भूमि के विभिन्न प्रकारों के बारे में जैसे-वन(अरण्य), ग्राम क्षेत्र(ग्राम्या), पर्वत, गीले या आंद्र क्षेत्र(औडका), शुष्क भूमि(भोमा), मैदान (समा) और असमान भूमि (विसावा) में बाटा गया है। साथ ही औसत वार्षिक वर्षा के अनुसार विभिन्न भागों में धरती को बाटा गया है। अर्थशास्त्र जीवित प्राणियों के प्रति अपनी चिंता को भी दर्शाता है। घरेलू व जंगली जानवर, पौधे व वनस्पति, दंड एवं दंड के प्रकार उनके द्वारा बनाए गए थे। जीवित प्राणियों को घायल करने पर दंड के प्रावधान थे। अनेक वन निर्देशकों की नियुक्ति की गई थी। पशु वध के लिए पर्यवेक्षक, मवेशियों, घोड़ों, हाथियों और चारागाहों के अधीक्षक ये अधिकारी वन्य जीवन की रक्षा करते

थे। पालतू जानवरों के लिए राशन की उचित व्यवस्था करते थे। चराई ,जंगली जानवरों के अवैध शिकार को रोकना, घरेलू पशुओं की उचित देखभाल करना इत्यादि। गैर कृषि भूमि का उपयोग कभी-कभी पशु चारागाहों के लिए भी किया जाता था, जहां जानवर पूरी तरह संरक्षित थे। इन अभयारण्यों में जानवरों को पकड़ना या मारना प्रतिबंधित था। पशुओं के प्रति क्रूरता रोकने के लिए ग्राम प्रधान व ग्राम समुदाय को जिम्मेदार ठहराया गया था। घोड़ो, हाथियों और गायों की देखभाल, प्रशिक्षण उपचार की उचित व्यवस्था थी।

राजा को वनों, हाथियों, सिंचाई कार्यों और खानों की रक्षा करने वाला स्वामी माना जाता था। अर्थशास्त्र मूल्यवान संसाधनों, वन उत्पादों का ठीक तरीके से उपयोग करने की सलाह देता है। पेड़ के किसी भी हिस्से को काटने पर अलग-अलग राशि का जुर्माना लगाया जाता था। सघन वन संसाधनों से भरपूर नदी के किनारे किसी के आश्रित स्थल हो सकता थे। अर्थशास्त्र में वर्णित पर्यावरणीय मुद्दे आधुनिक समय में बहुत ही प्रासंगिक है। 1972 में स्टाक होम पर्यावरण सम्मेलन में इनमें से कुछ बातों का उल्लेख भी किया गया था। भारत में 1974(प्रदूषण रोकथाम व नियंत्रण कानून), वन संरक्षण पर्यावरण कानून 1980, वन्यजीव संरक्षण अधिनियम 1972 हमें अर्थशास्त्र की बहुत सी बातों की याद दिलाते है।

मनुस्मृति : उत्तर वैदिक काल में लिखी गई मनुस्मृति में प्राकृतिक पर्यावरण की अखंडता को बचाने के लिए धर्म का सहारा लिया गया है। यह मानव न्याय शास्त्र का पहला नैतिक संग्रह है। मनुस्मृति में प्रदूषण की रोकथाम व पारिस्थितिकी जागरूकता के निम्न संदर्भ प्राप्त होते हैं-

1. जैव विविधता को सभी चल जीवित प्राणियों और आचार (अचल- पौधों का साम्राज्य),

2. प्रदूषण का अर्थ है अनैतिक कार्यों द्वारा पांचो प्राकृतिक स्थूल तत्वों का नष्ट होना।

3. सदुंषण से तात्पर्य स्वास्थ्य के विरुद्ध की गई कार्यवाही।

4. कंदमूल फल, जड़ेंदार फल सब्जियां, फूल,इमारती लकडियां, वृक्ष, फ़सल का आकर्षण बना रहे।इसको क्षति पहुंचाने के लिए मनुस्मृति दण्ड का प्रावधान करती है।

5. सभी प्रकार मछलियां मारने योग्य नहीं है। गधा,अश्व,मृग,ऊंट,हाथी की हत्या पाप है।

चरक संहिता और सुश्रुत संहिता

यह दोनों प्राचीन भारतीय इतिहास के महत्वपूर्ण चिकित्सा विज्ञान के दस्तावेज है। इन पुस्तकों में अलग-अलग अध्याय हैं। इनमें रोगों, रोगों के प्रकार उनके

57

उपचार औषधिय पौधों के प्रकार, औषधिय पौधों के संसाधनों की उपयोगिता के बारे विस्तार से दर्शाया गया है। विभिन्न महामारियों के इलाज, प्राकृतिक संसाधनों द्वारा इलाज़ के सन्दर्भ है, जो वर्तमान कोविड 19 महामारी में प्राकृतिक औषधी के सेवन इम्यूनिटी रोग प्रतिरोधक क्षमता को बढ़ाते हैं जिससे शरीर स्वस्थ रहता है। मिट्टी, जलवायु के प्रकार वनस्पति के द्वारा इलाज संभव है।

वेद

वेद हिन्दू धर्म के पवित्र ग्रंथ है। चार वेद ऋग्वेद, सामवेद, यजुर्वेद, अथर्ववेद।इन संहिताओं से तीन प्रकार के अतिरिक्त साहित्य जुड़े हुए थे। ब्राह्मण(अनुष्ठान की चर्चा), आरण्यक (जंगल में अध्ययन की गई पुस्तके), उपनिषद (दार्शनिक लेख)। इनमें से आरण्यकों में जंगलों की चर्चा की गई है।वृहदारण्यक उपनिषद इनमें महान वन पाठों की चर्चा की गई है।

आर्य लोग सिंचाई आधारित मौसमी कृषि करते थे। जैविक खाद का प्रयोग करते थे। प्रत्येक गांव में मवेशियों के लिए चारागाह होता था। आर्य पशुपालक थे। पशु उत्पादों दूध, मांस खाल, बाल पर निर्वाह करते थे। पशुपालक होने की वजह से एक स्थान से दूसरे स्थान पर चरवाहा जीवन व्यतीत करते थे। ग्रामीण व्यवस्था आर्य अपने पशुओं को लेकर चिंतित थे गवीशी, गोविष्टी आदि शब्दों के माध्यम से पता चलता है। वेदों में चार प्रकार के जीवों का उल्लेख मिलता है- अडंज (अंडे से पैदा), जीवज (गर्भ से पैदा), स्वेदजा (नमी से पैदा), उद्विजा (पृथ्वी से पैदा)। वेदों में विभिन्न ऋचाओं द्वारा वनस्पतियों व मनुष्यों से जीवो की रक्षा का पोषण-संपोषण का उल्लेख मिलता है। इनमें कहा गया है की प्राकृतिक शक्तियों की पूजा की जानी चाहिए। मीठी हवा, पानी, नदियों का सुखद वातावरण, सूर्य, चंद्रमा, गाय, मिट्टी के कणों की मिठास, फल को संरक्षित करना चाहिए। वनों के संरक्षण एवं विकास वनीकरण की अवधारणा इस समय विकसित की गई प्रकृति की तुलना माता, मित्रों, देवताओं से की जाती थी। जल को पवित्रता का प्रतीक माना जाता था। पानी व अग्नि को उन्होंने सामाजिक रीति रिवाजों के साथ पवित्रता की सूचक के रूप में जोड़ा। ऋग्वेद में सिंचित कृषि, जलाशय, नदियों, तालाबों को का वर्णन है। यह सब पारिस्थितिकी और पर्यावरण के आयामों को दर्शाती है। गांव में जानवरों के कल्याण के लिए प्रार्थनाएं की गई। पेड़ों झाड़ियों, फैली शाखोंओ, जड़ी बूटियों, झाड़ी धार पौधों, पर्वतारोही लताओ व पौधों का वर्गीकरण किया गया है। पेड़, जड़, पुष्प, शाखाएं, फल, फूल इन सब को उपचारात्मक शक्ति माना गया। वैदिक देवता धन्वंतरि जो बीमारियों का इलाज करता था। ऋग्वेद में वर्णित किया गया की विकास की प्रक्रिया में पौधे जानवर विशेष कर मनुष्य से पहले थे। उपनिषद में विकासवाद के विचार को उसी आत्मा के रूप में

व्यक्त किया गया था। आकाश से वायु, वायु से अग्नि, अग्नि से जल, जल से पृथ्वी और पृथ्वी से जड़ी बूटी,जड़ी बूटियां से भोजन और भोजन से व्यक्ति अस्तित्व में आया। मौखिक परंपरा में भारत में प्रकृति और पर्यावरण पर विचार के प्राचीनतम साक्ष्य वेद ही हैं। वैदिक साहित्य में धरती माता, देवी भूमि को पृथ्वी के रूप में व्यक्त किया गया। **अथर्ववेद** में कहा गया है कि -है माता अपने महासागरों नदियों और अन्य निकायों के साथ आप हमें पानी, अनाज उगाने के लिए जमीन देते हो, जिस पर हमारा अस्तित्व निर्भर करता है। कृपया हमें इस रूप में दे, इतना दूध, फल, पानी, अनाज जितना हमें खाने पीने की जरूरत है। अर्थात इस वक्त मनुष्य सिर्फ अपने संपोषण करने जितना ही मांग रहा है आज की आंधी दौड़ जैसा नहीं।

छान्दोग्य उपनिषद : सभी नदियां अपना जल समुद्र में बहा देती है, बादल समुद्र से वाष्प ग्रहण करते हैं, आकाश वाष्प को उड़ाकर उसे वर्षा के रूप में छोड़ देता है, यह जीवन विज्ञान चक्र का पुराना संदर्भ है।

इषोपनिषद में सतत् विकास और संरक्षण की अवधारणा है। इसमें कहा गया है की इस दुनिया में सभी चलित व गैर चलित(वनस्पति) शामिल हैं। प्रभु द्वारा प्रदत्त अपने संसाधनों का संयम से प्रयोग करें। दूसरों की संपत्ति ना हड़पे। हमें और दूर तक जाना है।

वेदों के अधीन उपवेदो में एक आयुर्वेद गहन ज्ञान को प्रदर्शित करता है जीवित प्रजातियां और पर्यावरण के बीच अंतर संबंध को दर्शाता है। पेड़-पौधे ,देसी वनस्पतियां और जीवो के लिए भुगतान करना चाहिए। पलाश, अर्जुन,यश, लक्ष्य, हरिद्रा जैसे औषधिय पौधे आदि का व्यापक रूप से उपचार के लिए उपयोग किया जाता था। हिंदू विचार यह है की पूरा विश्व एक जंगल है। जैसा है वैसा बनाए रखने के अक्षुण्ण प्रयास किए गये।

रामायण, महाभारत, भगवतगीता और अभिज्ञान शाकुन्तलम्

महाभारत के अनुसार गुरुओं की राजधानी हस्तिनापुर गाने जंगल में बसी थी गुरु और panchalon का साम्राज्य भी गंगा की तराई में फैला हुआ था देवी पुराण के पाठ 14 के अनुसार नो डरावने जंगल उसे समय हुआ करते थे। कुरू जंगल, निमिषा उत्पालरन्या उत्तरी गंगा के भागों से ढकें थे। जब पांडवों को आधा राज्य प्राप्त हुआ उन्होंने अपनी राजधानी इंद्रप्रस्थ को बनाया। उन्हें राजधानी बसाने के लिए जमीन की जरूरत पड़ी। उन्होंने अग्नि देवता की मदद से जंगलों को जलाया। कृष्ण व अर्जुन खंडवा जंगल गए थे, जो यमुना नदी के किनारे हैं । और जहां आज दिल्ली बसा हुआ है। अग्नि ब्राह्मण के देवता के रूप को दर्शाता है,जिसने शहरीकरण के विकास में प्रमुख भूमिका निभाई। रामायण में भी एक संदर्भ प्राप्त होता है। जब परशुराम राम को लेने

अयोध्या आए थे। माता कौशल्या को डर था कहीं घने जंगल में शेर, हाथी, चीते आदि कहीं राम को नुकसान ना पहुंचा दे। जंगल-भूमि सीता के आनंद का स्रोत थी। कमल के तालाब, गीज़,बतख, शहद सुगंधित उपवन, हिरनों के झुंड उन्हें मिले। जब वे अपना घर बना रहे थे। उन्होंने सबसे पहले वर्तमान में विलुप्त हो चुके काले हिरन की बाली दी। लक्ष्मण ने मांस को पकाकर, उबाल कर ईश्वर को समर्पित किया। आर्यावर्त की भूमि काले मृग के साथ संयोजित थी। विंध्य पर्वत के उत्तर में। रामायण में वर्णित अर्जुन, जटा पुष्प, कर्निकर(हिबीस्कस) आदि सीता के प्रिय वृक्ष थे। अशोक वृक्ष के नीचे रावण की कुटिया में सीता रही थी।

सदियों से जंगल धीरे धीरे साफ होने लगे। जैसे-जैसे मनुष्य की जनसंख्या बढ़ी, शहरीकरण बढ़ा, जंगल कम होने लगे। पारिस्थितिकी बदलने लगी। यह गति एक समान नहीं थी। जमीन की मांग बढ़ती गई और जंगल साफ होने लगे। अभिज्ञान शाकुन्तलम् संदर्भ से ज्ञात होता है की दुष्यंत शिकार पर गए थे और उसने अनेकों जानवरों को मार डाला लोगों के झुंड द्वारा प्रकृति पर अपनी शक्ति का प्रदर्शन किया गया साथ ही इसमें आश्रम और प्रकृति के सौंदर्य को भी दर्शाया गया है। शकुंतला हिरनों से, प्रकृति से बहुत प्यार करती दिखलाई गई है। पवित्र उपवन, छोटे-छोटे जंगल अनेक देवताओं को समर्पित थे। अलग-अलग भागों में उत्तर पूर्वी, पश्चिमी घाटों में सदाबहार बन पाए जाते थे। गांव के देवी-देवता अनादि काल से यहां संरक्षक थे। इन जंगलों में पौधों की दुर्लभ प्रजातियां, अल्प ज्ञात पेड़-पौधे, जीव-जंतु निवास करते थे। हनुमान द्वारा हिमालय पर्वत पर जड़ी बूटी लाना भी इस ओर इंगित करता है। इस समय ऐसे अनेक वैद्य थे जो दुर्लभ जड़ी बूटियां से इलाज करते थे। वैशाली, कुशीनारा, चंपा भारत के प्राचीन शहरों में इन दुर्लभ पेड़ों की लकड़ी के उत्पाद ग्रामीण समुदाय द्वारा इस्तेमाल किए जाते थे। बरगद, साल वृक्ष के नीचे ही बुध और महावीर को आत्मज्ञान हुआ था। आज भी पीपल, बरगद अन्य वर्षों को पूजा जाता है। भागवत गीता में कृष्ण ने दुनिया की कल्पना एक बरगद के वृक्ष के समान की है। जिसकी असीमित शाखाएं हैं। जिसमें पशु, मनुष्य, देवता सभी प्रजातियां निवास करती है। भारत और अफ्रीका में पीपल व बरगद का संरक्षण इतिहास में बहुत पुराना है।

वैष्णव धर्म में कृष्ण का जीवन पर्यावरण का सबसे बड़ा उदाहरण है। हमेशा उन्होंने प्रकृति की रक्षा की, गोवर्धन पर्वत को उठाया। जीव-जंतुओं की रक्षा की, गायों पेड़ों की रक्षा की, ग्रामीण जीवन की रक्षा की, उन्होंने कहा की सभी प्राणी जन्म लेते हैं, मरते हैं, सुख-दुख भोगते हैं। कर्म ही धर्म है, इसलिए इंद्र की पूजा करने की आवश्यकता नहीं है। पर्यावरण की रक्षा करना ही आपका कर्तव्य है। पहाड़, जंगल,गाय की पूजा करना, नाग काल्या को हराकर यमुना जल को साफ करना सभी प्राकृतिक

संसाधनों के प्रति उनके प्रेम को दर्शाता है। वृंदावन अपने कदम्ब वृक्ष, पीपल वृक्ष, अमलाकी व लताओं के लिए प्रसिद्ध थे। लेकिन वर्तमान में वहां ना के बराबर है। कृष्ण जंगल में जाकर बांसुरी बजाते, झूला झूलते, सारे वर्णन भागवत गीता में मिलते हैं। वैदिक साहित्य में भी ऐसे बहुत से साक्ष्य ऋषिगण जंगलों में निवास करते थे। पशु-पक्षियों की रक्षा करना, स्वच्छ निर्मल जल का सेवन, प्रकृति के बीच में तुच्छ साधनों से अपना जीवन जीना यह संदर्भ प्राप्त होते हैं। मनुष्य जन्म चार आश्रमों में विभक्त था। विद्या आश्रम में शिक्षा अध्ययन करना । वानप्रस्थ व संन्यास के समय भी मनुष्य प्रकृति के करीब था। अपनी स्वयं की खोज मनुष्य जंगल में आकर करता था। कुछ साहित्य पारिस्थितिकी संतुलन के लिए बहुत जागरूक थे। तमिल गृंथों में संगम कल में तिन्नई अवधारणा, ईसाइयों के समय रची गई इको जॉन। जो समाज की सांस्कृतिक, सामाजिक संरचना से संबंधित है।

प्राचीन भारतीय इतिहास के पुरातात्विक व साहित्यिक सोतों द्वारा सतत विकास व जैव विविधता का पता चलता है। साथ ही किस प्रकार मनुष्य ने इसे बिगाड़ा। जलवायु परिवर्तन ने किस प्रकार सभ्यता को नष्ट किया। इसका उदाहरण हम सिंधु घाटी सभ्यता में देख सकते हैं। सिंधु घाटी सभ्यता विकसित जल निकास प्रणाली, शहरीकरण के लिए जानी जाती थी। जैव विविधता के प्रमाण उसके सीलों, मूर्तियां में मिलते हैं। हिंदुओं का धर्म अभी भी इसी सभ्यता से सिख ले रहा है। लगभग 70 वर्ष पूर्व आरेल स्टीन, जॉन माार्शल आदि ने आधुनिक पुरातात्विक साक्ष्य के आधार पर यह अनुमान लगाया की सभ्यता का पतन जलवायु परिवर्तन के कारण हुआ। पर्याप्त वर्षा, उपजाऊ जमीन ने इसे मानव रहने योग्य बना दिया। यहां शहरीकरण हुआ, ईंधन पर्याप्त मात्रा में था। हिमालय के जंगलों से नदी में तैरती लकड़ियां ईंटों के लिए प्रयुक्त की जाती थी। चारों तरफ नहरों का जाल था। कृषि और विदेशी व्यापार भी होता था। इस शहरों में वनों की कमी का प्रमुख कारण ईंटों को पकाना हो सकता है। जिसने मोहनजोदड़ो को समुद्र से बंद कर दिया। जिससे जल स्तर में वृद्धि हुई। जो मोहनजोदड़ो के विनाश का कारण बनी। अपर्याप्त रख रखाव, बांध, सिंचाई आदि ने सभ्यता के पतन को तेज किया। कृषि मानकों का गिरना, प्रशासन का आंतरिक विघटन, योजना का अभाव,अस्वच्छता, पुरानी ईंटों का उपयोग उदासीनता को दर्शाता है। महामारियों की बात की जाए तो पता चलता है कि जल निकास प्रणाली के प्रदुषित होने से हैजा जैसी बिमारियों ने डेरा जमा लिया। सिंधु नदी ने अपनी दिशा बदल ली। बंजर जमीन, वर्षा और नमी के कारण कीटाणुओं का संक्रमण हुआ। बड़ी संख्या में लोग बीमारियों का शिकार हुए। शहर के शहर तबाह हुए। मोहनजोदड़ो में जल निकास प्रणाली भूमि के अंदर थी। बाढ़ के दिनों में यह पानी में मिल जाती थी। गंदा पानी   दस्त का काम करता था। यह बीमारियां पूरे शहरों में फैलती गई। मोहनजोदड़ो से प्राप्त कंकाल इसके प्रमाण है। भोजन की तलाश में लोग दक्षिण व

लोथल, सौराष्ट्र की ओर बढ़ने लगे। पूर्व की ओर लोगों का प्रसार हुआ। हड़प्पा सभ्यता से 7 स्तरीय खुदाई के प्रमाण प्राप्त हुए हैं। यह सभ्यता सात बार बनी। पारिस्थितिकी असंतुलन के कारण बिगड़ी, बर्बाद हुई।राजस्थान के सांभर डीडवाना, लूणकरणसर में पुरापाषाण कालीन साक्ष्य प्राप्त हुए हैं। यमुना व सतलुज के मार्गों का पूर्व और पश्चिम की ओर स्थानांतरण। सतई वह उपसतही जल की कमी (घग्गर घाटी) में। प्रकृति - वनस्पति दोनों पर प्रतिकूल प्रभाव पड़ा। लोगों को स्थानांतरण के लिए मजबूर होना पड़ा।

मध्यकालीन भारतीय इतिहास में अरब यात्री इब्नबतूता ने भी घने जंगलों का वर्णन अपने ग्रंथ रेहला में किया है।वह दक्षिण में भी गया था।1325-51 में वह लिखता है कि माबर अभियान में मुहम्मद तुगलक की अधिकतर सैना महामारी से मर गई थी।17वी सदी में प्लेग भारत के विभिन्न हिस्सों में फैला। जहांगीर ने तुजुके जहांगीरी में वर्णित किया है मेरे शासन के दशवे वर्ष में प्लेग फैला व उसने हिन्दू मुस्लिम सभी को तबाह किया।

अंग्रेजों के आगमन के बाद पर्यावरण को बहुत नुकसान पहुंचा। उन्होंने जंगल जमीन को अपने फायदे के लिए वसूल किया। ट्रेनों के विस्तार ने गांव-गांव जंगल जंगल में उनके शोषण को पहुंचाया और परिस्थिति को नुकसान पहुंचा। पहले गांव समुदाय जैव विविधता और पर्यावरण की रक्षा करता था लेकिन अंग्रेजों के आ जाने से और रेलों के विस्तार से जैव विविधता व पर्यावरण को भयंकर नुकसान उठाना । तेज़ रफ्तार, भौतिकता, संसाधनों के अंधाधुन बंटवारे ने मनुष्य की विकास की डोर को बहुत ज्यादा तीव्र कर दिया। आज हालत बदतर होते जा रहे हैं। पर्यावरण सम्मेलन आयोजित हो रहे हैं लेकिन फिर भी कोई उचित उपाय नहीं सूझ रहा है।

कोविड-19 महामारी का सतत विकास लक्ष्यों की प्राप्ति पर प्रभाव

- यूएनडीपी के अनुसार वैश्विक मानव विकास (शिक्षा, स्वास्थ्य और जीवन स्तर) का वर्तमान स्तर गिरकर 1990 के स्तर पर पहुच जायेगा। "दुनिया ने पिछले 30 वर्षों में कई संकटों को देखा हैं। प्रत्येक ने मानव विकास को कड़ी चुनौती दी दी है, लेकिन कुल मिलाकर वैश्विक स्तर पर वर्ष-दर-वर्ष विकास दर भी अर्जित हुई है। कोविड-19 महामारी, स्वास्थ्य, शिक्षा और आय के लिए तीन गुना चोट पहुचाकर इस विकासात्मक प्रवृत्ति को बदल सकता है। "

- स्वास्थ्य : सतत विकास लक्ष्यों के तहत दुनिया में 2030 तक हर किसी के लिए स्वास्थ्य सेवा सुनिश्चित करने के लिए प्रतिबद्धता व्यक्त की गयी थी। हाल के वर्षों में इस क्षेत्र में प्राप्त उपलब्धि (शिशु और मातृ मृत्यु दर में गिरावट, एचआईवी / एड्स पर नियंत्रण और मलेरिया से होने वाली मौतों को रोकना) पर खतरे की आशंका है। कोविड-19 महामारी से स्वास्थ्य सेवाओं में व्यवधान के कारण ना

केवल इन बिमारियों के बढ़ने की आशंका है बल्कि इसने टीकाकरण अभियानों पर भी विराम लगा दिया है।

- **भूखमरी :** कोविड-19 महामारी ने वैश्विक खाद्य आपूर्ति श्रृंखलाओं में कमजोरियों को उजागर करते हुए खाद्य आपूर्ति श्रृंखलाओं को छिन्न-भिन्न कर दिया है।

- **निर्धनता :** भारत और चीन ने तेजी से आर्थिक प्रगति करते हुए लाखों लोगों को गरीबी से बाहर निकाला है। SDG 1 निर्धनता को दूर करने हेतु समर्पित है लेकिन वर्तमान संकट ने इस लक्ष्य को और अधिक चुनौतीपूर्ण बना दिया है।

- **गुणवत्तापरक रोजगार :** लगभग 1.6 बिलियन लोग अनौपचारिक अर्थव्यवस्था में काम करते हैं जोकि वैश्विक कार्यबल का लगभग आधा है। अंतर्राष्ट्रीय श्रम संगठन की रिपोर्ट के अनुसार अपनी आजीविका के समाप्त होने के तात्कालिक खतरे से जूझ रहे हैं। ILO की रिपोर्ट के अनुसार, महामारी शुरू होने के बाद से छह में से एक से अधिक युवा अपनी नौकरी खो चुके हैं।

- **गुणवत्तापरक शिक्षा :** कोविड-19 महामारी के कारण गुणवत्तापरक शिक्षा खासकर ग्रामीण क्षेत्रों में एक बहुत बड़ा चुनौती थी हालांकि डिजिटलीकरण ने कुछ हद तक इसे संभव बनाया परंतु जहां नेटवर्क उपलब्ध नही है वहां यह सर्वसुलभ नहीं है।

- **मजबूत संस्थाएं :** कम से कम 18 राष्ट्रीय चुनाव और जनमत संग्रह पहले ही स्थगित हो चुके हैं जिससे इस क्षेत्रों में अशांति का खतरा बढ़ सकता है। सरकारों पर डिजिटल सेवाओं और सामाजिक सुरक्षा प्रदान करने के साथ सामाजिक अधिकारों को आगे बढ़ाने, मानव अधिकारों और कानून के शासन को बनाए रखने के सन्दर्भ में काफी दबाव हैं। कमजोर और अस्थिर सरकारों के सन्दर्भ में स्थितियां और भी विकट हो जाती है।

- **डबल हेलिक्स (The double helix) :** वैज्ञानिकों ने वर्षों से चेतावनी दी है कि अनियंत्रित वनों की कटाई, अवैध वन्यजीव व्यापार और जानवरों से मनुष्यों के बीच प्रसारित होने वाली बीमारियां एक बेकाबू महामारी को जन्म देगी। कोविड-19 महामारी ने इस दिशा में मानवीय हस्तक्षेप के कम होने से प्रकृति जहाँ एक और पुनः वापस अपनी अविरल स्थिति में दिखी लेकिन लॉकडाउन ने प्रकृति संरक्षण की गतिविधियों को भी प्रभावित किया। एक डबल हेलिक्स की तरह, SDGs और COVID-19 महामारी की प्रतिक्रिया आपस में जुड़ी हुई है और इन्हें अलग-अलग दृष्टिकोण से देखकर इससे नहीं निपटा जा सकता है। इसलिए हरित

अर्थव्यवस्थाओं में निवेश के द्वारा लोगों और ग्रह के बीच संतुलन को स्थापित करते हुए देशों को ऐसे संकट से उबरने में मदद प्रदान कर सकती है।

सतत विकास लक्ष्यों की प्राप्ति की दिशा में पुनः कैसे आगे बढ़ें?

- कोविड-19 महामारी की चुनौतियों से निपटने तथा समयबद्ध तरीके से सतत विकास लक्ष्यों को हासिल करने के लिए नीतियों में आमूल-चूल परिवर्तन की आवश्यकता है। इसके लिए सरकार को ऐसी नीति/नीतियाँ बनानी होंगी जिसमें तात्कालिक लक्ष्यों के साथ-साथ दीर्घकालिक लक्ष्यों की भी पूर्ति हो सके।

- इसके अतिरिक्त, नीतियों में समावेशी और जवाबदेह शासन प्रणाली, कोविड-19 जैसी महामारियों से भविष्य में निपटने हेतु लचीलापन, सशक्त संस्थाएं, सार्वभौमिक सामाजिक सुरक्षा व स्वास्थ्य बीमा, मजबूत डिजिटल बुनियादी ढांचा इत्यादि आवश्यक परिवर्तनों का हिस्सा होना चाहिए।

- एशिया और प्रशांत के कई देश विकास हेतु समावेशी दृष्टिकोण साथ नई रणनीति विकसित कर रहे हैं; जैसे- दक्षिण कोरिया ने हाल ही में दो केंद्रीय स्तंभों के आधार पर एक नयी नीति की घोषणा की है : डिजिटलीकरण (digitization) और डिकार्बोनाइजेशन (decarbonisation)।

- भारत ने हाल ही में सबसे बड़े सौर ऊर्जा संयंत्र के संचालन की घोषणा की है। चीन जीवाश्म ईंधन उद्योगों की तुलना में नवीकरणीय ऊर्जा क्षेत्र में अधिक रोजगार पैदा कर रहा है।

- सभी देशों को सामाजिक सुरक्षा, शिक्षा और स्वास्थ्य के साथ खाद्य सुरक्षा के लिए ऐसी आपूर्ति श्रृंखला को निर्मित करना होगा तो संस्थागत अवरोधों से न केवल स्वतंत्र हो बल्कि इनकी प्रकृति भी समावेशी हो।

- अत्यधिक पैड पौधे लगाकर। संसाधनों की मितव्ययिता।

- सौ साल में पहली बार, दुनिया एक सामान्य लक्ष्य पर केंद्रित है: कोरोनोवायरस की समाप्ति। हालाँकि "सामान्य रूप से वापस आना" संभव नहीं है लेकिन कोविड-19 महामारी संकट ने हमें दिखाया है कि हम लोग इस ग्रह और एक दूसरों से कितनी गहराई से जुड़े हैं। कोविड-19 ने हमें अपने मूल्यों को फिर से पुनः प्राप्त करने और विकास के एक नए क्षेत्र को डिजाइन करने के लिए बाध्य कर रहा है जो एसडीजी 2030 की परिकल्पना के रूप में आर्थिक, सामाजिक और पर्यावरणीय प्रगति को संतुलित करता है।इस दिशा में एकीकृत समाधान एकमात्र तरीका है जिसमें हम 2030 लक्ष्यों को पूरा करने में देशों की मदद करने के साथ-साथ एक हरियाली और अत्यधिक समावेशी भविष्य बनाने में सक्षम होंगे।

- इतिहास गवाह है कि महामारियों ने युद्ध को जन्म दिया है प्रथम विश्व युद्ध, द्वितीया विश्व युद्ध वर्तमान रूस क्रिमीया युद्ध यह सतत विकास की राह में बहुत बड़ी अडचन साबित हो सकता है।

- देशों के भीतर और अंतरराष्ट्रीय स्टार पर असमानता चरम पर हैं। टीकाकरण की सर्व उपलब्धता, उत्कृष्ट स्वास्थ्य सेवाएं, चिकित्सा की आसान पहुंच व अन्य सभी क्षेत्र में। महामारी ने बच्चों की शिक्षा, बाल श्रम को बढ़ावा, बाल विवाह, घरेलू हिंसा, महिला असुरक्षा, बेरोजगारी के साथ वैश्विक पर्यटन को भी ठेस पहुंचाई है। महामारी ने अमीर गरीब सभी को अपने कब्जे में जकड लिया। हालांकि महामारी का जलवायु परिवर्तन से सीधा संबंध नहीं है ,फिर भी अपशिष्ट प्रबंधन, रासायनिक कचरा, मास्क, किट इसका बड़े पैमाने पर प्रयोग से जैव विविधता खतरे में है। लेकिन साथ ही महामारी के संकट के दौरान सरकारों के सुशासन, लचीलापन, अनुकूलन क्षमता, नवाचारों के लिए किए गए प्रयासों, अंतरराष्ट्रीय सहयोग ने एक उज्जवल कल की तस्वीर पेश की है। हम मानव इतिहास में एक महत्वपूर्ण मोड पर है। आज हमारे द्वारा लिए गए निर्णय और कार्य आने वाली पीढ़ियों के लिए महत्वपूर्ण परिणाम होंगे।

कोरोना से मिलने वाली सबक यह है की पूंजीवाद ने जो हमें जीवन जीने के मायने दिए हैं अत्याधुनिक जीवन शैली, दिखावे का जीवन जो एक झटके में ही तबाह हो गया। वह सिर्फ साधारण खानपान, प्राकृतिक जीवन शैली , नेचुरोपैथी की ओर लेकर आ गया ।अभी भी समय है की हम अपनी प्राथमिकताओं को छोड़कर सतत विकास की ओर ध्यान दें । हम विनाश लीला से सतत विकास की डगर पर चले और महामारी से बचने से पहले उस महामारी से निपटे जो मुनाफाखोरो ने अपने लाभ के लिए हमारे ऊपर लाद रखी हैं। भले ही मनुष्य अपने को पृथ्वी का सर्वश्रेष्ठ प्राणी समझता हो । परंतु प्रकृति के लिए मनुष्य और किसी कीड़े में कोई फर्क नहीं है । जन्म ,प्रजनन और मृत्यु सबके लिए यही प्रक्रिया नियत है। प्रकृति बार-बार मनुष्य को इसका एहसास भी कराती हैं। कोरोना संकट के पैदा होने और उसके विस्तार का कारण और इसका शिकार मनुष्य ही है । कोरोना ने सर्वशक्तिमान होते जा रहे मनुष्य को एक आईना भी दिखाया है।

सन्दर्भ ग्रन्थ सूची :

[1] भट्टाचार्य एस., चौधरी पी ., मुखोपाध्याय ए., जर्नल ऑफ एंशीयट इंडियन हिस्ट्री 24 (2008) 97-106।

[2] इलियट एच एम,द हिस्ट्री ऑफ़ इंडिया ऐज टोल्ड बाय इट्स ओवन हिस्टोरियन,भाग 6पेज316-320

[4] ऐनॉन, इरिगेशन इन इंडिया थ्रू द एजेस। सिंचाई और बिजली पर केंद्रीय बोर्ड, नई दिल्ली ,भारत (1965)।

[5] चरक संहिता ,भाग 3

[6] कांगले आरपी , द कौटिल्य अर्थशास्त्र। दूसरा प्रकाशन। मुंबई विश्वविद्यालय, भाग I और II (1986)।

[7] रंगराजन एलएन, कौटिल्य- अर्थशास्त्र। पेंगुइगुन क्लासिक्स, भारत (1992)।

[8] बुहलर जी ।, कानूननू और मनु।नु इन: मैक्स मुलर, एफ। (एड।), द सेक्रेड बुक ऑफ द ईस्ट। क्लेरिं डन प्रेस, लंदन में ऑक्सफो र्ड (1886)।

[9] पाध्य एस., दास एस., महापात्र आर., जर्नल ऑफ ह्यूमन इकोलॉजी 19(1) (2006) 1-12।

[10] मजूमदार जी पी , प्राचीन और मध्यकालीन भारत में वनस्पति विज्ञान। इन: रे, पी ., सेन, एस.एन. (एड्स.), द कल्चरल हेरिटेज ऑफ इंडिया , वॉल्यूम.VI

[11] रे पी ., प्राचीन और मध्यकालीन भारत में प्राणी शास्त्र। इन: रे, पी . सेन, एसएन (संपा .) द कल्चरल हेरिटेज ऑफ इंडिया , खंड VI। रामकृष्ण मिशन इंस्टीट्यूट।

[12] ब्लूमफील्ड एम., वेद का धर्म: भारत का प्राचीन धर्म, ऋग्वेद से उपनिषद तक। निकरबॉकर प्रेस, न्यूयॉर्क, यूएसए (1908)।

[16] थापर आर., केनोयर जेएम, देशपां डे एमएम, रत्ननगर एस, भारत: ऐतिहासिक शुरुआत और आर्यन की अवधारणा । नेशनल बुक ट्रस्ट, नई दिल्ली,(2007)

[17] वत्नुची एम., वेद में पारिस्थितिक रीडिंग। डीके प्रिंट वर्ल्ड , नई दिल्ली , भारत (1994)।

[18] अग्रवाल ए., नारायण एस., डाइंग विजडम। भारत की पारंपरिक जल संचयन प्रणालियों का उत्थान, पतन और क्षमता । (भारत के पर्यावरण की स्थिति

[19] भट्टाचार्य सायन, International Letters of Social and Humanistic Sciences

सहायक आचार्य, इतिहास

राजकीय कला कन्या महाविद्यालय, कोटा

email : Mithleshsolanki.angel3@gmail.com

9. पर्यावरण प्रदूषण एवं यज्ञ

लक्ष्मी यादव

याग, यज्ञ, यजन अथवा इष्टि संस्कृत भाषा की यज् धातु से निष्पन्न हुए हैं।

यज्+अञ प्रत्यय =याग:

यज्+क्त:प्रत्यय =यज्ञ:

यज्+ल्यूट प्रत्यय=यजनम्

यदि यज् धातु से स्त्री वाचक क्तिन प्रत्यय जोड़ दिया जाए तो इष्टि: शब्द बनता है। इस प्रकार मात्र प्रत्यय भेद से शब्दों में भेद है अन्यथा याग, यज्ञ, यजन एवं इष्टि सभी एकार्थक हैं। चूंकि यज् धातु का प्रयोग यजन अर्थ में होता है अत:यज्ञ का सामान्य अर्थ है ।

"यज्" धातु से नङ् प्रत्यय करने पर यज्ञ शब्द बनता है।

यजयाचयत् विच्छ प्रच्छ रक्षोंनङ्

3/3/60 अष्टाध्यायी

"धातव: अनेकार्था" अर्थात धातु के अनेक अर्थ होते हैं। इस यज्ञ शब्द के अनेक अर्थ होते हैं।

यज् धातु का प्रयोग देवपूजा, संगतिकरण, दान इन तीन अर्थों में किया जाता है।

"यज देवपूजा संगतीकरण दानेषु"

भारतीय संस्कृति यज्ञमूलक है। ऋग्वेद के पुरुष सूक्त में यज्ञ द्वारा ही सृष्टि निर्माण बताया गया है।

यत्पुरूषेण हविषा देवा यज्ञमतन्वत।
वसन्तो अस्यासीदाज्यं ग्रीष्म इध्म: शरच्छिद्वि:॥

10/90/6 ऋग्वेद

तदनुसार वह सृष्टि यज्ञ भौतिक नहीं, मानसिक था। संकल्पात्मक अथवा प्रतीकात्मक था उस यज्ञ में वसन्त ऋतु ही आज्य ,ग्रीष्म ऋतु काष्ठ और शरद ऋतु हविष्यान्न था। इस प्रकार विराट पुरुष ने यज्ञ द्वारा ही सृष्टि का विस्तार किया था। किसी भी असाध्य /दूस्साध्य अथवा असंभव कार्य को संपन्न करने का सामर्थ्य यज्ञ से ही प्राप्त होता है ऐसा वर्णन मनुस्मृति में मिलता है।

67

भगवान प्रजापति ने भी सृष्टि रचना से पूर्व सामर्थ्य प्राप्ति के लिए गंगा तट पर उत्कृष्ट याग किया था फलत: उस तीर्थ का नाम ही प्रयाग पड़ गया। भारतीय उपनिषदों में भी इसी वेद मत का समर्थन मिलता है। वस्तुतः यह सृष्टि ही यज्ञमयी है। ग्रहमण्डल, देवता, मानव यह सब के साथ प्रकृति प्रतिक्षण यज्ञ करती है। सूर्य यज्ञ कर रहा है। इस प्रकृति में यज्ञ ही सर्वश्रेष्ठ कर्म है।

"यज्ञो वै श्रेष्ठतमं कर्म "

1/7/1/5 शतपथ ब्राह्मण

सृष्टि के समस्त कर्मों में यज्ञ ही सर्वश्रेष्ठ कर्म है।

" यज्ञ: कर्म समुम्भव: "

3/14 श्रीमद्भागवतगीता

भारतीय संस्कृत साहित्य का प्राचीनतम धर्म ग्रंथ वेद है। वेदों में ऋग्वेद सर्वाधिक प्राचीनतम है। ऋग्वेद में कर्मकाण्ड, ज्ञान काण्ड, उपासना काण्ड तीनों का वर्णन किया गया है। किंतु इन तीनों में प्रधान स्थान कर्मकाण्ड को ही प्राप्त है। अतः वेदों में यागादि क्रियाकलापों का बहुलता से वर्णन किया गया है। यज्ञ ही वेदों का मुख्य विषय है। मुख्य विषय होने के कारण यज्ञ में वेद मंत्रों का प्रयोग किया जाता है। वेद मंत्रों के बिना यज्ञ नहीं हो सकते अर्थात यज्ञ को बिना वेद मंत्रों के ठीक-ठीक प्रयोग करना संभव नहीं है।

पर्यावरण प्रदूषण और यज्ञ

पर्यावरण से अभिप्राय हमारे चारों ओर फैले उस वातावरण एवं परिवेश से है, जिससे हम घिरे रहते हैं। प्रकृति में मौजूद समस्त जैविक व अजैविक घटक पर्यावरण की संरचना में सहायक हैं अर्थात भूमि, जल, वायु, वनस्पति, जन्तु, मानव और सूर्य प्रकाश पर्यावरण के घटक हैं। ब्रह्मांड में संभवत: पृथ्वी ही एकमात्र ऐसा खगोलीय पिण्ड है जहां जीवन के अनुकूल प्राकृतिक दशाएं पायी जाती हैं, इसी कारण यहां जीवो का विकास संभव हो सका है। पृथ्वी पर जीवन की निरंतरता बनी रहे इसके लिए पर्यावरण/ प्रकृति के घटकों का एक निश्चित अनुपात में संतुलित रहना आवश्यक है, तभी हमारे तथा हमारी आने वाली पीढ़ियों के लिए यह प्रकृति सुरक्षित रह सकती है।

समस्त प्रकृति और मानव सृष्टि के आरंभ से ही यज्ञ कर रहे है। सूर्य यज्ञ कर रहा है, कैसे? समुद्र रूपी यज्ञ कुंड में अपनी किरणों का हवन करके। जिससे बादल बनते हैं एवं वर्षा होती है, वर्षा से उत्पन्न होता है, अन्न से प्राणी उत्पन्न होते हैं। चंद्रमा औषधि

(जड़ी बूटी) रूपी कुंड में हवन करता है जो जड़ी बूटियां इस यज्ञ से पैदा होती हैं वे रोगनाशक तथा बलवर्धक हैं। एक किसान भी निरंतर यज्ञ करता है, क्षेत्र रूपी कुण्ड में बीजान्त का हवन करता है जिससे हरी-भरी फसलें उत्पन्न होती हैं। उपनिषदों में अग्नि, वायु, वरुण, सूर्य एवं पृथ्वी आदि समस्त देवों को प्रतिक्षण यज्ञरत बताया गया है।

अन्नादभवंति भूतानि पर्जन्यादन्नसम्भव:।
यज्ञाद्भवति पर्जन्यो यज्ञ: कर्म समुद्भव:॥

3/14 श्रीमद भगवत गीता

अग्नौ प्रास्ताहुतिः सम्यगादित्यं उपतिष्ठते ।
आदित्याज्जायते वृष्टिर्वृष्टेरन्नं ततः प्रजाः ।।

3/76 मनुस्मृति

अग्नौदास्ताहुतिः ब्रह्मन्नादित्यमुपगच्छति।
आदित्याज्जायते वृष्टिवृष्टेरन्न- ततः प्रजा ।।

263/11 महाभारत शान्तिपर्व

अग्नि में डाली गई आहुति सूर्य मंडल को प्राप्त होती है, सूर्य से जल की वृष्टि होती है, वृष्टि से अन्न उत्पन्न होता है तथा अन्न से समस्त प्राणी जन्म लेकर जीवन धारण करते हैं। आदि मानव पूर्णत: प्रकृति पर निर्भर था। अतः मानव और प्रकृति में एक सामंजस्य था, किंतु आधुनिक युग में मानव की आवश्यकताएं चरम पर हैं, जिसकी पूर्ति के लिए मानव ने प्रकृति का निर्दयता पूर्वक दोहन शुरू कर दिया है परिणाम हम सबके सामने है! "पर्यावरण प्रदूषण" जो आधुनिक सभ्य समाज की देन है। प्रदूषण के कारण ही पूरा ब्रह्मांड संकट में है। लेकिन हमारी प्राचीन धार्मिक परंपराएं इतनी महत्वपूर्ण हैं कि समूचे जन जीवन को सुख समृद्धि प्रदान करने के साथ ही यह विज्ञान सम्मत भी हैं उदाहरण स्वरुप यज्ञ को ही ले। यह एक ठोस वैज्ञानिक प्रक्रिया है जो हमारे जीवन का अभिन्न अंग है।

महर्षि दयानंद ने भी कहा था "यदि पर्यावरण की शुद्धि एवं सुखों की वृद्धि चाहते हो तो नित्य, प्रातः सांय प्रत्येक घर में यज्ञ करो" यज्ञ एक व्यापक शब्द है और इसका रूप भी व्यापक है। श्रीमद भगवद गीता में भगवान श्री कृष्ण अर्जुन को कर्म योग समझाते हुए दान, पुण्य, सेवा, उपकार, रक्षा आदि सत्कर्मों को यज्ञ की संज्ञा देते हैं।

यज्ञ की परंपरा प्राचीन काल से रही है।ऋषि वनों में रहकर प्रातः सांय दैनिक हवन किया करते थे। अनेक प्रकार के श्रोत व स्मार्त यज्ञो का प्रचलन था। धार्मिक अनुष्ठान के समय वृक्षों में भगवान का वास मानकर पीपल आदि वृक्षों की पूजा की जाती थी तथा उनकी काष्ठ से हवन किया जाता था। जिससे पर्यावरण शुद्ध होता था। मध्य काल में यज्ञों में अनेक विकृतियां आ गई तथा यज्ञ कर्म लुप्त प्राय हो गए।

यज्ञ आज केवल धार्मिक कर्मकांड तक ही सीमित नहीं रह गया है, यह शोध का विषय बन गया है। अमेरिका तथा भारत में यज्ञ पर अनेक शोध हुए हैं और प्रायोगिक परीक्षणों से पाया गया है कि वृष्टि, जल एवं वायु की शुद्धि, पर्यावरण संतुलन एवं रोग निवारण में यज्ञ की अहम भूमिका है।

चेचक के टीके के आविष्कारक डॉ. हैफकिन का कथन है कि **"घी जलाने से रोगों के कीटाणु मर जाते हैं।"**

फ्रांस के वैज्ञानिक प्रो. ट्रिलबर्ट कहते हैं **"जली हुई शक्कर में वायु शुद्ध करने की बड़ी शक्ति है ,इससे टीबी, चेचक,हैजा आदि बीमारियों के जीवाणु शीघ्र नष्ट हो जाते हैं।"**

अंग्रेजी शासन काल के दौरान मद्रास के सैनिटरी कमिश्नर डॉ कर्नल किंग आई एम एस ने कहा कि **"घी व चावल में केसर मिलाकर अग्नि में जलाने से प्लेग से बचा जा सकता है।"**

आज अत्याधिक धूम्रपान तथा अंधाधुंध पेट्रोलियम पदार्थों के प्रयोग से बढ़ता प्रदूषण तथा विषैली गैसें चिंता का विषय है जिस का प्रतिकार यज्ञ है।

सुप्रसिद्ध वैज्ञानिक डॉक्टर स्वामी सत्यप्रकाश ने भी कहा है **"यज्ञ में बहुत स्वास्थ्यप्रद उपयोगी ओजोन तथा फार्मल्डिहाइड गैसें उत्पन्न होती हैं। ओजोन ऑक्सीजन से भी ज्यादा लाभकारी एवं स्वास्थ्य वर्धक है यह ठोस रूप में प्रायः समुद्र के किनारे पाई जाती हैं जिसे हम अपने घर में ही यज्ञ द्वारा पा सकते हैं।"**

हमारे प्राचीन ऋषि-मुनियों ने वैज्ञानिक आधार पर शोध करके सामग्री व संमिधाओ का चयन किया था। यथा बरगद, पीपल, आम, बील, पलाश,शमी, गूलर, अशोक,पारिजात, आंवला, मौलश्री की संमिधाओ का घी सहित यज्ञ हवन में विधान किया था जो आज विज्ञान सम्मत है क्योंकि यज्ञ का उद्देश्य पंचभूतों की शुद्धि है, जो हमारे पर्यावरण का अंग है।

यज्ञ विज्ञान का नियम है कि जब कोई पदार्थ अग्नि में डाला जाता है तो अग्नि उस पदार्थ के स्थूल रूप को तोड़कर सूक्ष्म बना देती है इसलिए यजुर्वेद में अग्नि को "धुरसि" कहा गया है। महर्षियों ने इसका अर्थ दिया है कि भौतिक अग्नि से पदार्थों के सूक्ष्मातिसूक्ष्म होने पर उनकी क्रियाशीलता उतनी ही बढ़ जाती है। यह एक वैज्ञानिक सिद्धांत है यथा अणु से सूक्ष्म परमाणु और परमाणु से सूक्ष्म इलेक्ट्रॉन होता है। अतः यह क्रमानुसार एक दूसरे से अधिक क्रियाशील व गतिशील हैं। यज्ञ में यह सिद्धांत एक साथ काम करता है यज्ञ में डाली गई समिधा अग्नि द्वारा विघटित होकर सूक्ष्म बनती है वहीं सूक्ष्म पदार्थ स्थूल सामग्री से अधिक क्रियाशील एवं गतिशील होकर विस्तृत क्षेत्र को प्रभावित करता है। जिस घर में हवन होता है, यज्ञ अग्नि के प्रभाव से वहां की वायु गर्म होकर हल्की होकर फैलने लगती है और खाली स्थान में यज्ञ से उत्पन्न हवा पहुंच जाती है। इसमें विसरणशीलता का वैज्ञानिक नियम काम करता है। अतःहम देखते हैं कि जिस स्थान पर यज्ञ होता है, वहां कई दिनों तक समिधा की महक विद्यमान रहती है।

पर्यावरण प्रदूषण आज की विकट समस्या है। इसका कारण हमारी भोगवृत्ति प्रकृति तथा दूसरा प्राकृतिक पदार्थों का अमर्यादित दोहन तथा दैनिक जीवन में अमर्यादित आचरण भी है। आज का बढ़ता तापमान, औद्योगिकीकरण, वृक्षों की कटाई पॉलीथिन का उपयोग, जल, वायु, मृदा प्रदूषण चरम पर है जिसके कारण प्राणियों की रक्षक हमारी ओजोन परत में छेद होने लगा है। अतः हमें इस अमर्यादित आचरण पर अंकुश लगाने की आवश्यकता है तथा यज्ञ को पुनर्जीवित करना है।

उद्योगों कल कारखानों से गंदगी निकल कर पृथ्वी को प्रदूषित कर रहे हैं बेतरतीब वाहनों से निकलता धुआं अर्थात कार्बन मोनोऑक्साइड से अनेक बीमारियां यथा सिर दर्द, आंखों में जलन, अस्थमा, टीबी आदि से लोग परेशान हैं। संपूर्ण जैवमंडल विनाश के कगार पर है। ओजोन परत के छेद के कारण सूर्य के प्रकाश की प्रचंड गर्मी अर्थात पराबैंगनी किरणें कई रोगों को उत्पन्न कर रही है जैसे चर्म रोग, अंधापन, कैंसर आदि। ऐसे में इस समस्या के समाधान हेतु प्रयासों के साथ क्या हम एक छोटा सा प्रयास " यज्ञ" के रूप में नहीं कर सकते हैं ।

यज्ञ से ही संपूर्ण सृष्टि का निर्माण व पालन पोषण होता है।

अन्नाद्भवन्ति भूतानि पर्जन्यादन्नसम्भवः ।
यज्ञाद्भवति पर्जन्यो यज्ञः कर्मसमुद्भवः ॥

श्रीमद्भगवदगीता 3/14

यज्ञ से पर्यावरण में संतुलन उत्पन्न होता है जिससे ग्लोबल वार्मिंग जैसे भयानक विनाश से बचा जा सकता है। क्योंकि यज्ञ द्वारा अनेक बीमारियों को नष्ट करने के साथ ही पर्यावरण प्रदूषण भी कम किया जा सकता है।

यज्ञ से बादलों का निर्माण होता है तब स्वास्थ्य वर्धक तथा भूमि को उपजाऊ बनाने वाली वर्षा होती है जिससे अन्न उत्पादन में वृद्धि होगी।यज्ञ से समय पर वर्षा होगी, जिससे सूखा से निपटा जा सकता है।

वर्षा होने पर उष्णता में कमी आएगी तथा ग्लोबल वार्मिंग कम करने में सहायता होगी तथा पर्यावरण सुरक्षित, संरक्षित होगा। अत: आओ हम सब मिलकर एक प्रयास पर्यावरण प्रदूषण को कम करने के लिए करें । कदम बढ़ाए तथा अपने भविष्य तथा वर्तमान को सुधारें। आओ हम सब एक कदम "यज्ञ" की ओर बढ़ाएं व पर्यावरण को बचाने में सहायक बनें।

शोधार्थी,
राज ऋषि भर्तृहरि मत्स्य विश्वविद्यालय, अलवर,
राजस्थान

10. 'आर्सेनिक' प्रदूषित जल : दुष्प्रभाव एवं परिणाम

डॉ. मीनाक्षी चौधरी

धरती पर पानी का संकट गहरा रहा है। पोखर, तालाब, कुएं व नदियां सूख रही हैं। भूजल स्तर गिरता जा रहा है। मौसम का मिजाज बदल रहा है। जलवायु परिवर्तन से प्राकृतिक आपदा के खतरे बढ़ गए हैं। दो दशक पहले तक गांवों में कुएं के पानी का इस्तेमाल होता था। आज अधिकांश कुएं ठप हो चुके हैं। नदियां मैली होती जा रही हैं। दूषित जल की वजह से नदियों के जलीय जीवों पर खतरा मंडरा रहा है। गर्मी आते ही हैंडपंप का पानी सूख जाता है। पानी की पहली परत प्रदूषित हो चुकी है। आयरन, आर्सेनिक, फ्लोराइड युक्त पानी धरती के प्राणियों के लिए कहर बनता जा रहा है। शुद्ध पेयजल का संकट गहराता जा रहा है। देश की बड़ी छोटी नदियों में मल, मूत्र, दूषित जल व औद्योगिक कचरा डाला जा रहा है। धरती के प्राणी दूषित पानी पीने को मजबूर हैं।वह दिन दूर नहीं जब धरती के प्राणी बूंद-बूंद पानी को तरसेंगे। विश्व बैंक की रिपोर्ट के अनुसार भारत में तकरीबन 60 प्रतिशत बीमारियों का कारण अशुद्ध पानी है। जल प्रदूषित होने का मुख्य कारण मानव द्वारा औद्योगिक कचरे को जलधाराओं में प्रवाहित करना है।

फैक्टरियों से निकलने वाले अवशिष्ट जल प्रदूषण का प्रमुख कारण है। रासायनिक तत्व पानी में मिलकर जलजनित बीमारियों को जन्म देते हैं। कैल्शियम, मैग्नीशियम, सोडियम, पोटेशियम, आयरन, मैग्नीज, क्लोराइड, सल्फेट, कार्बोनेट, तेल, फिनोल, वसा, ग्रीस, मोम, घुलनशील गैसें आदि जल के वास्तविक गुण को प्रभावित करती हैं। पृथ्वी पर कुल 71 प्रतिशत जल उपलब्ध है जबकि इसमें से 97.3 प्रतिशत पानी खारा होने के कारण पीने के योग्य नहीं है। भारत में ग्राउंडवाटर का 90 प्रतिशत पानी खेती में प्रयोग किया जा रहा है। जल विशेषज्ञ रणजीव कहते हैं कि कम वर्षा होने, पानी के संरक्षण की दिशा में उदासीनता, भूगर्भ जल के अति दोहन की वजह से जल का संकट गहराता जा रहा है। आज मानव भौतिक सुख के चक्कर में अपनी पुरानी परंपराओं को भूलता जा रहा है। पहले गांव में पोखर, कुएं व नदियां जीवित थीं तो जल स्तर ठीक था। मनुष्य की करतूत के कारण जल का स्तर नीचे खिसकता जा रहा है। धरती की चिंता किसी को नहीं है। बड़ी-बड़ी इमारतें बनाने के चक्कर में पानी का ज़बरदस्त दोहन हो रहा है। धीरे-धीरे भूजल स्तर में कमी आती जा रही है।

73

Sustainable Development and Climate Change

आर्सेनिक युक्त पानी वर्तमान में कई राज्यों के लिए संकट हन गया है। आर्सेनिक धातु के समान एक प्राकृतिक तत्व है जो पृथ्वी की भूगर्भ में खनिज व चट्टानों में पाया जाता है। यह घातक व बिषैला होता है। चट्टानों में आर्सेनिक कार्बनिक पदार्थ के रूप में पाया जाता है। भूमि कटान इत्यादि के माध्यम से नदी के तलछट में एकत्रित होता रहता है और रिसकर भूजल में मिल जाता है। मिट्टी और तलछट में भी सूक्ष्म जीव उपस्थित रहते है जो आर्सेनिक युक्त यौगिक उत्पन्न करते है और यह यौगिक जल में घुलनशील होता है। भूमिगत जल में आवश्यकता से अधिक आर्सेनिक की मात्रा होने के कारण उनके सेवन से होने वाली बीमारियों को आर्सीओनिक कहा जाता है।

आश्चर्य है कि बिहार जैसे प्रांत में सरकार ने सिंचाई योजना के तहत 7.5 लाख नलकूप लगाने की घोषणा की है। जबकि सरकार को ज्ञात है कि खेती के लिए नलकूप का इस्तेमाल पानी का संकट पैदा करता है और इससे आर्सेनिक भी जल के साथ ऊपर आ जाता है। वर्षा कम होना और खेती में नलकूप का प्रयोग पानी के स्तर व संतुलन को बिगाड़ रहा है। बावजूद इसके सरकार भी जल संरक्षण को नजरअंदाज कर रही है।

विश्व स्वास्थ्य संगठन डब्ल्यू.एच.ओ. ने पीने के पानी में आर्सेनिक की प्रति लीटर मात्रा 0.01 मि.ग्रा.तय की हुई है, जबकि भारत सरकार ने 0.05 मि.ग्रा.तक आर्सेनिक का मानक तय किया हुआ है। पीने के पानी में इससे अधिक आर्सेनिक होना स्वास्थ्य के लिए जान लेवा सिद्ध हो सकता है।

वैज्ञानिक डॉ.एन.सी.घोष के मुताबिक करीब 10 हजार वर्ष पहले मिट्टी पथरीली थी और धीरे-धीरे जियोजेनिक कारणों से कुछ पत्थर मिट्टी में परिवर्तित हो गए। इन पत्थरों के कण लौह तत्व से मिलकर भूजल में घुलनशील होकर आर्सेनिक में तबदील हो गए। डॉ घोष बताते हैं कि कि समूची गंगाघाटी की धरती के नीचे आर्सेनोपायराइट)आयरन आर्सेनिक सल्फाइड (के रूप में आर्सेनिक दबा हुआ है जो पानी में घूलनशील नहीं होता है। पर भूजल के अत्यधिक दोहन और ऑक्सीजन के प्रवेश करने से भूगर्भ का वातावरण बदलता है। आर्सेनोपायराइट का विखण्डन होकर आयरन और आर्सेनिक अलग हो जाता है और आवेशित रूप में आ जाते हैं। आवेशित अवस्था में आर्सेनिक जल में घूलनशील है और भू-जल में आर्सेनिक घुलने लगता है। इसलिये भूजल में आर्सेनिक की मात्रा बढ़ती गई है।

आर्सेनिक दरअसल धरती की कोख में पड़ा है। प्राकृतिक कारणों से अलग-अलग जगहों पर वह अलग-अलग रूपों और मात्रा में बिखरा हुआ है। वह पानी में घूलने लगा। गंगाघाटी में चापाकलों और नलकूपों के माध्यम से भूजल दोहन बड़े पैमाने पर होने से यह आर्सेनिक समस्या बन गया। भू-जल दोहन से धरती के भीतर के पर्यावरण में बदलाव हुआ। भूजल स्तर घटने से ऑक्सीजन को भूजल भण्डार में जाने का मौका मिला। ऑक्सीजन के सम्पर्क में आर्सेनिक के पुराने रूपों का विखण्डन हुआ और

घूलनशील अवयवों में बदल जाने से पेयजल के साथ वह शरीर में प्रवेश तो कर जाता है, पर मल या मूत्र के माध्यम से शरीर से बाहर नहीं निकलता, वहीं पड़ा रहता है। यही संकट का कारण है।तटवर्तीय मैदानी इलाकों में बसे लोगों के लिए गंगा जीवनरेखा रही है। गंगा ने इलाकों की मिट्टी को सींचकर उपजाऊ बनाया। इन इलाकों में कृषक बस्तियां बसीं। धान की खेती आरंभ हुई। गंगा घाटी और छोटानागपुर पठार के पूर्वी किनारे पर धान उत्पादक गांव बसे। बिहार के 85 प्रतिशत हिस्सों को गंगा दो 1.उत्तरी एवं 2. दक्षिणी (हिस्सों में बांटती है। बिहार के चौसा,(बक्सर (में प्रवेश करने वाली गंगा 12 जिलों के 52 प्रखंडों के गांवो से होकर चार सौ किमी की दूरी तय करती है। गंगा के दोनों किनारों पर बसे गांवों के लोग पेयजल एवं कृषि कार्यों में भूमिगत जल का उपयोग करते है।

आर्सेनिक के चट्टान समूची गंगा और ब्रह्मपुत्र की घाटी की तलहटी में है जो दक्षिण में राजमहल की पहाड़ियों, उत्तर में दार्जिलिंग पहाड़ी और पूर्वोत्तर में शिलांग पठार से घिरा है। इसका एक तिहाई हिस्सा बंगाल में पड़ता है। बाकी उत्तर प्रदेश का पूर्वी इलाका, बिहार का उत्तरी इलाका, नेपाल का दक्षिणी इलाका और बांग्लादेश का पश्चिमी इलाका में आता है। गंगा बेसिन में 60 मीटर गहराई तक जल आर्सेनिक से पूरी तरह प्रदूषित हो चुका है। गंगा के मैदानी इलाकों में बसा गंगाजल को अमृत मानने बाला समाज जल में व्याप्त इन हानिकारक तत्वों को लेकर बेहद हताश और चिंतित है। गंगा बेसिन के भूगर्भ में 60 से 200 मीटर तक आर्सेनिक की मात्रा थोडी कम है और 220 मीटर के बाद आर्सेनिक की मात्रा सबसे कम पायी जा रही है। वैशाली के बिदुपूर में विशेषज्ञों ने पानी की जांच की तो नदी से पांच किमी के दायरे के गांवों में पेयजल में आर्सेनिक की मात्रा देखकर वे दंग रह गये। हैंडपंप से प्राप्त जल में आर्सेनिक की मात्रा 7.5 एमजी/एल थी । विश्व स्वास्थ्य संगठन के मानक के अनुसार 0.010 एमजी/एल है जबकि गंगा बेसिन में बसे लोगों के आहार श्रृंखला में आर्सेनिक की मात्रा 50 गुणा अधिक है। भूजल में आर्सेनिक की समस्या पर लगातार शोधरत डॉक्टर एके घोष ने कहा कि पूरी गंगा घाटी में यह समस्या है। गंगा के दोनों ओर पाँच किलोमीटर में समस्या अधिक गम्भीर है। गंगा से दूरी बढ़ने पर उसकी मात्रा कम मिलती है। लेकिन आर्सेनिक की उपस्थिति नेपाल तराई के क्षेत्रों में भी है।गंगा नदी बेसिन में आर्सेनिक खनिज हिमालय से आते हैं और गंगा की बेल्ट में जमा हो जाते हैं। हालांकि सभी नदियां सुरक्षित हैं, लेकिन उसके चारों ओर का क्षेत्र खासकर गंगा की शुरुआती धारा प्रदूषित है। धारा प्रवाह बदले जाने के बाद अब बाई ओर का छोर दायां बन गया है और यही वह क्षेत्र है जहां भूजल में आर्सेनिक की मिलावट है।

75

जाहिर बात है कि ग्राउंड वाटर में आर्सेनिक की मात्रा विद्यमान होती है, तो इसका इस्तेमाल प्राणियों पर जहर जैसा ही काम करेगा। लोग जानते हुए भी दूषित पानी पीने को मजबूर है। संयुक्त राष्ट्र के मुताबिक प्रत्येक साल तकरीबन 1500 घन किमी पानी बर्बाद हो जाता है। जादवपुर यूनिवर्सिटी के स्कूल ऑफ एनवायरमेंट स्टडीज के एसोसिएट प्रोफेसर व आर्सेनिक पर ही पीएचडी करने वाले प्रोफेसर डॉ . तरित रायचौधरी कहते हैं -गंगा, ब्रह्मपुत्र और मेघना नदी के मैदानी क्षेत्र आर्सेनिक से प्रभावित हैं। पश्चिम बंगाल भी इसी क्षेत्र में है। वे आगे कहते हैं-आर्सेनिक मानव निर्मित नहीं है बल्कि भौगोलिक-रासायनिक प्रतिक्रिया के चलते तलछट में आर्सेनिक जमा हो गया और जब भूगर्भ से ट्यूबवेल के जरिए पानी निकाला जाने लगा तो पानी के साथ आर्सेनिक भी बाहर आने लगा।संयुक्त राष्ट्र के मुताबिक प्रत्येक साल तकरीबन 1500घन किमी पानी और बर्बाद हो जाता है। दुनिया में 3.1 प्रतिशत मौतें अशुद्ध जल के कारण होती हैं। अशुद्ध पानी पीने से हर साल डायरिया के चार अरब मामलों में 22 लाख मौतें होती है।पृथ्वी पर भूजल पर आश्रित 24 प्रतिशत स्तनधारियों व 12 प्रतिशत पक्षी प्रजातियों के विलुप्त होने का खतरा मंडरा रहा है, जबकि एक तिहाई उभयचरों की स्थिति चिंताजनक बताई जा रही है। विश्व के 14 करोड़ लोग आर्सेनिक युक्त पानी पीने को मजबूर हैं।

गंगाघाटी में पेयजल का साधन पहले कुआँ था। सिंचाई के लिये भी कच्चे कुएँ बनते थे। कुओं की देखरेख सामूहिक तौर पर किया जाता था। जिन कुओं से पीने और दूसरे घरेलू कामों के लिये पानी लिया जाता था, उन्हें बाढ़ और नाले का पानी जाने से बचाया जाता था। बरसात के बाद उसमें उत्पन्न होने वाले रोगाणुओं की सफाई के लिये नीम के पत्ते या चूना डालने की विधि थी। पर कुएँ सभी लोगों को आसानी से उपलब्ध नहीं थे। फिर भी 70 के दशक तक कुएँ का उपयोग ही अधिक होता था। पर सतही प्रदूषण से उसके पानी में रोगाणु उत्पन्न हो जाते थे। इससे जलजनित रोग होते थे। शिशु और बाल मृत्युदर अधिक थी। रोगाणु मुक्त पेयजल की जरूरत थी। बाढ़ग्रस्त इलाके में कुओं को सतही दूषण से बचाना कठिन था। बाढ़ का पानी प्रवेश करने पर उसके साथ आई सिल्ट से भी कुओं में बालू-मिट्टी भर जाता था। फिर यहाँ करीब चालीस साल पहले सिंचाई में भूजल का इस्तेमाल आरम्भ हुआ। लोग संशय से भरे थे। इसे 'नरक से आने वाला पैशाचिक पानी' भी कहा गया। लेकिन भूजल के इस्तेमाल का दायरा बढ़ता गया। इसमें सन 67-68 में अकाल का बड़ा योगदान था। तालाब और कुआँ खुदवाने की अपेक्षा नलकूप लगाना आसान और सस्ता था। ताबड़तोड़ चापाकल और नलकूप लग गए। इससे बाल व शिशु मृत्यु दर में तो काफी कमी आई, भू-जल का

उपयोग बढ़ता गया। पानी सर्वसुलभ होने का असर खेती पर पड़ा। अब धान की दो फसलें हो सकती थीं। लेकिन इस पानी में जहर आर्सेनिक छिपा था। इसका पता बहुत बाद में चल पाया। भूजल के अत्यधिक उपयोग से धरती के भीतर छिपा आर्सेनिक पानी में घुलकर बाहर आने लगा।उधर कुओं का उपयोग बन्द हुआ, उनकी संख्या तेजी से घटती गई। इस तरह भू-जल का पुनर्भरण बुरी तरह बाधित हुआ। डॉ .घोष ने बताया कि खुले कुएँ के पानी में आर्सेनिक नहीं मिलता। कारण है कि उसमें वर्षाजल भी एकत्र होता है जिससे जलस्तर कभी इतना नीचे नहीं जा पाता कि धरती के भीतर के वातावरण में ऑक्सीजन के सम्पर्क से आर्सेनिक के यौगिकों का विखण्डन हो।

आर्सेनिक तब तक इन चट्टानों से अलग होकर पानी में नहीं मिल सकता जब तक यह रासायनिक माध्यम में घुलनशील नहीं हो जाये। सिंचाई के काम में भूजल के अत्यधिक दोहन ने इस प्रक्रिया को गति प्रदान किया। भूगर्भ विज्ञानियों के अनुसार, भूजल के अत्यधिक दोहन से भूजल का स्तर घट गया। जलस्तर घटने से वे जलकुण्ड सूख गए जिनमें आर्सेनिक था। जलस्तर घटने से खाली जगह में ऑक्सीजन ने प्रवेश किया। वह ऑक्सीजन उन चट्टानों में प्रवेश करता है और पाइराइट का ऑक्सीडाइजेशन होता है। इस प्रक्रिया में निकले अम्ल को आर्सेनिक यौगिक के साथ प्रतिक्रिया करके उसे जल में घुलनशील बना देता है।

दरअसल 1990 के दशक में केंद्र और राज्य सरकारों ने पूरे देश में ज्यादा से ज्यादा लोगों तक पीने योग्य पानी पहुंचाने के लिए हैंडपंप)नलकूप (लगवाने शुरू कर दिए। डॉक्टरों ने भी अपने मरीज़ों को कुएँ का पानी नहीं पीने और साफ पानी के लिए नलकूप का पानी इस्तेमाल करने के लिए कहना शुरू कर दिया। लगभग एक दशक बीत जाने के बाद पता चला कि नलकूप के पानी में आर्सेनिक की मात्रा खतरनाक स्थिति को पार कर चुकी है। कई शोध हुए तो पता लगा कि कुएँ का पानी सेहत के लिए सबसे अच्छा होता है। नलकूप में आर्सेनिक की मात्रा ज्यादा क्यों होती है और कुएँ का पानी सेहत के लिए क्यों अच्छा है, इस सवाल के जवाब में दीपांकर कहते हैं कि कुएँ का पानी खुला होने की वजह से धूप और हवा)ऑक्सीजन (के संपर्क में रहता है। दूसरी बात यह है कि कुएँ के पानी में मौजूद आयरन)लौह तत्व (के संपर्क में आकर आर्सेनिक नीचे चला जाता है।

आर्सेनिक पर आधा दर्जन से अधिक शोध कर चुके प्रो .रायचौधरी भूजल के इस्तेमाल के सम्बन्ध में कहते हैं, 'पहले लोग सतह पर मौजूद पानी का इस्तेमाल किया करते थे लेकिन सतह पर मौजूद पानी में कई तरह की गन्दगी होने के कारण पेट सम्बन्धी रोग होने लगे तो लोगों ने भूजल का इस्तेमाल करना शुरू कर दिया। यह 70 के दशक की बात होगी। ट्यूबवेल के जरिए लोगों ने पानी निकालना तो शुरू कर दिया

लेकिन पानी कितना भीतर से निकालना चाहिए यह लोगों को पता नहीं था। ये तो रही पीने के पानी की बात लेकिन एक अन्य शोध में ऐसे चौंकाने वाले तथ्य सामने आये हैं जो सिरदर्द और बढ़ा सकते हैं। यह शोध वर्ष 2002 में एक अन्तरराष्ट्रीय जर्नल फूड एंड केमिकल टॉक्सिकोलॉजी में छपा था। इस शोध में प्रो .रायचौधरी के साथ ही कई विदेशी प्रोफेसर शामिल थे। इस शोध के अनुसार, आर्सेनिक युक्त पानी द्वारा सिंचाई किये जाने के कारण आलू, साग-सब्जियों, चावल, गेहूँ आदि खाद्यानों में भी आर्सेनिक पाये जा रहे हैं। रायचौधरी ने कहा, 'हाल के शोध में भी यह बात सामने आई है कि आर्सेनिक युक्त पानी से सिंचित खाद्यानों में आर्सेनिक है।'

पश्चिम बंगाल, बिहार, उत्तर प्रदेश, झारखण्ड, छत्तीसगढ़, असम, नागालैंड, मणिपुर, त्रिपुरा, अरुणाचल प्रदेश ,पंजाब आदि राज्यों में आर्सेनिक का प्रभाव पाया गया है। ज्यादा प्रभावित राज्य पश्चिम बंगाल, बिहार, उत्तर प्रदेश और झारखण्ड हैं। जिनके अनेक गांवों में भूजल में आर्सेनिक तत्व पाए जाने की पुष्टि वैज्ञानिकों ने की है।हाल ही में आई एक रिपोर्ट के अनुसार गंगा के दोनों ओर स्थित बिहार के 15 जिलों के भूजल में आर्सेनिक के स्तर में खतरनाक बढ़ोतरी हुई है, जिसके कारण इस इलाके में रहने वालों के लिये कैंसर का खतरा बढ़ गया है। IANS की रिपोर्ट के अनुसार गंगा किनारे के दोनों तरफ़ के भूजल में आर्सेनिक की भारी मात्रा पाई गई है।

बिहार के भूजल में आर्सेनिक घूलने का पता सबसे पहले 2002 में भोजपुर जिले के गाँव में चला। 2009 में 16 जिलों में तथा 2015 में 17 जिलों में आर्सेनिक के मामले दर्ज किये गए हैं। पर्यावरण विज्ञान के प्राध्यापक डॉ अशोक कुमार घोष का तो मामना है कि केवल दो जिलों -भभुआ और रोहतास को छोड़कर समूचे बिहार के भूजल में आर्सेनिक है। उनका आकलन है कि बिहार के 87 प्रतिशत क्षेत्र का भूजल आर्सेनिक से दूषित हो गया है। 2011 में किए गए सर्वे के मुताबिक बिहार के 18 हजार 431 गांव ऐसे हैं, जहां शुद्ध पेयजल की उपलब्धता नहीं है। इसमें से 1112 गांव आर्सेनिक व 3339 गांव फ्लोराइड एवं 13 हजार 980 गांव आयरन युक्त पानी पीने को मजबूर है। भूजल में आर्सेनिक की मात्रा मौसम के अनुसार घटती-बढ़ती भी है। इसलिये भूजल की नियमित जाँच आवश्यक है। परन्तु बिहार में पानी की जाँच करने की व्यवस्था ही पर्याप्त नहीं है। बिहार के पड़ोसी राज्य झारखंड के 68 गांव असम में 9 ब्लॉक, मणिपुर में 4 जिले और छत्तीसगढ़ के 4 गांव ऐसे पाए गए है, जिनमें भूजल आर्सेनिक के कारण प्रदूषित हो चुका है।उड़ीसा के 13216 और 475

गांव भी आयरन और आर्सेनिक से प्रभावित हैं। उत्तर प्रदेश में तीन जिलों के 7 ब्लॉकों के 69 गांवों के भूजल में आर्सेनिक पाए जाने की पुष्टि वैज्ञानिकों ने की है। ये इलाका बलिया, गाजीपुर तथा वाराणसी के आस-पास का है।

हाल ही में यूनिसेफ की मदद से उत्तर प्रदेश सरकार ने एक सर्वे करवाया, जिसमें उत्तर प्रदेश के बीस से अधिक जिलों का भूजल "आर्सेनिक" प्रदूषित पाया गया है। सर्वे की प्राथमिक रिपोर्ट के मुताबिक लगभग 31 जिले और ऐसे हैं जहाँ यह खतरा हो सकता है, हालांकि उनकी विस्तृत जानकारी अभी सामने आना बाकी है। यूनिसेफ द्वारा यह अध्ययन प्रदेश के 20 जिलों के 322 विकासखण्डों में किया गया, जहां आर्सेनिक अपनी मान्य मात्रा 0.05 माइक्रोग्राम प्रति लीटर से कहीं अधिक पाया गया। शोध बताते हैं कि यह इन क्षेत्रों में 100-150 पार्ट प्रति बिलियन तक पानी में आर्सेनिक पहुंच चुका है। बलिया और लखीमपुर जिले सबसे अधिक प्रभावित पाये गये। सुरक्षा के लिहाज से सैकड़ों की संख्या में हैण्डपम्प सील कर दिये गये हैं। बहराईच, चन्दौली, गाज़ीपुर, गोरखपुर, बस्ती, सिद्धार्थनगर, बलरामपुर, सन्त कबीर नगर, उन्नाव, बरेली और मुरादाबाद, जिलों में भी आर्सेनिक की अधिक मात्रा पाई गई है, जबकि रायबरेली, मिर्ज़ापुर, बिजनौर, मेरठ, सन्त रविदास नगर, सहारनपुर और गोण्डा आंशिक रूप से प्रभावित जिले हैं। मथुरा में बैराज के कारण यमुना का रुका जल स्थानीय भू गर्भ के लिए खतरा बन रहा है तो मथुरा के आसपास के कुछ स्थानों पर बोरिंग के दौरान लाल रंग का पानी निकलने लगा है। कोलकाता के जादवपुर विश्वविद्यालय में रिसर्च स्कूल ऑफ एन्वायरमेंटल स्टडीज के निदेशक प्रोफेसर दीपांकर चक्रवर्ती ने 'शुक्रवार' को बताया, 'बलिया और भोजपुर का शाहपुर इलाक़ा एशिया के सर्वाधिक आर्सेनिक ग्रस्त इलाकों में से एक है।' पिछले दो दशकों के दौरान इस इलाके में कम-से-कम 2000 लोगों की मौत आर्सेनिक युक्त पानी पीने से हो चुकी है।

दिल्ली के मेडिकल संस्थान एम्स की जांच के अनुसार दिल्ली के दक्षिण-पश्चिम में दो सौ किलोमीटर के दायरे में आर्सेनिक का एंडमिक क्षेत्र विकसित हो रहा है। इस क्षेत्र को आर्सेनिक के मामले में विश्व के दो सर्वाधिक प्रभावित क्षेत्रों में से एक कहा गया है। रिपोर्ट के मुताबिक इसका एक कारण बांग्लादेश से आने वाली गहरी अंत : नलिका तो है। गोकुल बैराज से भी जो जल जमीन के नीचे जा रहा है, वह भयंकर रूप से आर्सेनिक को अपने साथ भू गर्भ में ले जा रहा है तथा यमुना जल में भारी मात्रा में केमिकल कचरा तथा बस्ट बोरिंग इसका दूसरा बड़ा कारण माना जा रहा है।

अभी तक यह माना जाता था कि गंगा नदी के आसपास के इलाके में ही आर्सेनिक युक्त भू-जल की समस्या है। लेकिन पंजाब कृषि विश्वविद्यालय द्वारा किये गये एक अध्ययन में यह चौंकाने वाला खुलासा हुआ है कि पंजाब का लगभग 80 प्रतिशत भूमिगत जल पीने लायक नहीं रह गया है। इस जल में आर्सेनिक की मात्रा का स्तर काफ़ी बढ़ चुका है। पानी में आर्सेनिक की मात्रा का सुरक्षित मानक स्तर 10 ppb होना चाहिये, जबकि अध्ययन के मुताबिक पंजाब के विभिन्न जिलों से लिये पानी के नमूने में आर्सेनिक की मात्रा 3.5 से 688 ppb तक पाई गई है। यह खतरा दक्षिण-पश्चिम पंजाब पर अधिक है, जहाँ कैंसर के मरीजों की संख्या में भी बढ़ोतरी देखी गई है। पंजाब कृषि विश्वविद्यालय के मृदा-वैज्ञानिकों के एक दल ने यह पाया कि फसलों और सब्जियों में रासायनिक खाद व कीटानाशक का प्रयोग अधिक नहीं किया गया है, लेकिन फ़िर भी पीने और अन्य उपयोग के लिये जो भू-जल दोहन किया जा रहा है उसमें घातक आर्सेनिक का अंश काफ़ी मात्रा में है। दक्षिण पश्चिम पंजाब के कई जिलों में भूजल का एक भी नमूना पीने लायक नहीं पाया गया। यहाँ आर्सेनिक की मात्रा 11.4 से 688 ppb तक पाई गई।

आर्सेनिक के जहर वाला पानी नमकीन हो जाता है, अगर आर्सेनिक मिले पानी को लंबे समय तक पिया जाए तो इससे कई भयंकर बीमारियां होनी शुरू हो जाती हैं। पानी में घुलित आर्सेनिक कैंसर के कई रूप, त्वचा कैंसर और किडनी फेल होने जैसी बीमारियों का कारक है। अमेरिका की संस्था "एजेंसी फ़ॉर टॉक्सिक सब्सटेन्सेस एंड डिसिजेज़ रजिस्ट्री" ने एक शोध के द्वारा आर्सेनिक का त्वचा और फ़ेफ़ड़ों के कैन्सर से सम्बद्धता को दर्शाया है। मथुरा के शंकर कैंसर चिकित्सालय के डॉ .दीपक शर्मा के अनुसार आर्सेनिक के प्रभाव से गाल ब्लैडर में कैंसर हो सकता है। वृंदावन पैलिएटिक केयर सेंटर के डॉ .संजय पिशारोड़ी के अनुसार आर्सेनिक और नाइट्रेट के कारण मनुष्य का इम्यून सिस्टम प्रभावित होता है। इससे समय से पहले वृद्धावस्था के लक्षण नजर आते हैं। इम्यून सिस्टम प्रभावित होने पर मस्तिष्क में कैंसर का खतरा बढ़ जाता है। आर्सेनिक से टाइप दो की डायबिटीज का भी खतरा बढ़ जाता है।

आर्सेनिक से प्रदूषित जल के सेवन से धमनियों से संबंधित बीमारियाँ होने और परिणामस्वरूप दिल का दौरा पड़ने और पक्षाघात के ख़तरे बढ़ जाते हैं। वैज्ञानिकों के अनुसार उन्होंने शरीर में आर्सेनिक के निरंतर प्रवेश का मस्तिष्क से जुड़ी धमनियों में सिकुड़न और अलिचलेपन से प्रत्यक्ष संबंध पाया है। अमेरिकन हार्ट एसोसिएशन में छपी अनुसंधान रिपोर्ट में आर्सेनिक और कई जल अशुद्धियों को रक्तवाहनियों से जुड़े रोगों का कारण बताया गया है। बांग्लादेश और चीन सहित दुनिया के विभिन्न देशों में चट्टानों में आर्सेनिक की मात्रा पाई जाती है। लंबे समय तक आर्सेनिक प्रदूषित जल के

सेवन से त्वचा संबंधी बीमारियाँ भी होती हैं, लेकिन कपड़े धोने या स्नान के लिए इस जल का उपयोग ख़तरनाक नहीं माना जाता है। पशुओं के साथ किये गए अध्ययन में पाया गया कि बीमार करने की क्षमता के बराबर आर्सेनिक के डोज गर्भवती मादाओं को देने से कम वजन वाले बच्चों का जन्म, गर्भस्थ शिशु में विकृति या उसकी मृत्यु हो सकती है।

बक्सर जिले का गाँव 'तिलक राय का हाता' सिमरी प्रखण्ड में गंगा के तट पर है।तिलक राय का हाता का सर्वेक्षण हुआ है। इसकी रिपोर्ट 2015 में प्रकाशित हुई। आर्सेनिकोसिस का फैलाव देखकर अध्ययनकर्ता चौंक गए। यहाँ के अधिकांश निवासियों में आर्सेनिकोसिस के लक्षण दिखते हैं। आर्सेनिकोसिस के लक्षण त्वचा, हथेली और पैर के तलवे पर पहले दिखते हैं। चमड़ी का रंग बदल जाता है। सफेद छींट जैसे दाग हो जाते हैं। तलवों में काँटे जैसे निकल जाते हैं। हथेली में चमड़े के नीचे काँटीदार स्थल बनने से तलहटी खुरदुरी हो जाती है। आन्तरिक अंगों पर असर बाद में दिखता है। यह असर कैंसर की शक्ल में होता है। आँत, लीवर, फेफड़े व दूसरे अंगों में कैंसर के मरीज मिले हैं। पेयजल में आर्सेनिक होने की वजह से बिहार के जिन गाँवों में कैंसर फैल रहा है, उनमें यह गाँव भी है आर्सेनिकोसिस के शिकार गरीब लोग ठीक से इलाज भी नहीं करा पाते।आर्सेनिक प्रभावित इलाके में चर्म रोग सबसे पहले दिखते हैं। इसके अलावा लोग हाईपर केराटोसिस ,मेलोनोसिस ,आँत की बीमारियाँ ,गैस्ट्रीक, लीवर सम्बन्धी रोग, पाचन और भूख की कमी जैसे रोगों का शिकार हो रहे हैं और साथ ही साथ इससे लोगों की प्रजनन क्षमता पर असर पड़ रहा है। पुरुषों मेंनपुंसकता)एजूसपरमिया (औरतों में बाँझपन, मासिक-चक्र में गड़बड़ी भी देखने को मिलती है।कई बार स्कूली बच्चों में भी आर्सेनिकोसिस के गम्भीर लक्षण दिखाई पड़ते हैं। कुछ बच्चों की हथेली और तलुवों में हाईपर केराटोसिस के लक्षण वैज्ञानिकों द्वारा देखे गए। जो लोग वर्षों से अधिक आर्सेनिक वाला पानी पी रहे हैं उनके रक्त में आर्सेनिक की अधिकतम मात्रा 664.7 पीपीबी दर्ज की गई तथा कइयों कि तो रक्त की संरचना भी बदल गई।

आर्सेनिक युक्त जल को अगर खुली धूप में 12-14 घंटे तक रख दिया जाए तो उसमें से 50 फीसदी आर्सेनिक उड़ जाता है। उसके बाद उस जल का इस्तेमाल पेयजल के रूप में किया जा सकता है। उबालकर आर्सेनिक को नहीं हटाया जा सकता, चूँकि यह वोलेटाइल पदार्थ नहीं है सो उबालने से इसकी सान्द्रता बढ़ जाने का ही खतरा रहता है। इससे बचने के लिए पीने के पानी व सिंचाई के लिए कुएँ, तालाब व अन्य

प्रकार के सतही जल का उपयोग अधिकाधिक किया जाए, वर्षा के जल का संग्रहण किया जाए। यदि नलकूप ही लगवाने हो तो उन्हें उचित गहराई तक खोदा जाए।

इसके अलावा अंतर्राष्ट्रीय स्तर पर किए जा रहे प्रयासों के तहत बंगाल कालेज ऑफ इंजीनियरिंग ने कम्युनिटी एक्टिव एलुमिना फिल्टर का निर्माण भी किया है जो पानी से आर्सेनिक निकालने में मददगार साबित हो सकता है। राष्ट्रीय वनस्पति शोध संस्थान के वैज्ञानिक भी इस समस्या से निजात दिलाने के रास्ते खोज रहे हैं संस्थान के वैज्ञानिकों ने उस जीन का पता लगा लिया है जो सिंचाई के बाद आर्सेनिक के स्तर को कम करने के साथ साथ उसे अनाज व सब्जियों में पहुंचने से रोकेगा। इस शोधकार्य में महती भूमिका निभाने वाले वैज्ञानिक डॉ .देवाशीष चक्रवर्ती ने कहा, "यह शोध प्लांट डिडेंस मैकेनिज्म को आधार बनाकर किया गया है"।

ब्रिटेन के बेलफास्ट स्थित क्वींस यूनिवर्सिटी के शोधकर्ताओं ने भी ऐसी किफायती तकनीक विकसित करने का दावा किया है, जिससे आर्सेनिक संदूषित जल की समस्या से निजात मिल सकती है। इस परियोजना के समन्वयक भास्कर सेनगुप्ता ने कहा,"क्वींस के शोधकर्ताओं द्वारा तैयार की गई यह तकनीक पर्यावरण के अनुकूल, इस्तेमाल में सरल, किफायती और ग्रामीण क्षेत्रों में उपलब्ध कराई जा सकने वाली दुनिया की एकमात्र तकनीक है। "यह तकनीक आर्सेनिक संदूषित भूमिगत जल के एक हिस्से को पारगम्य पत्थरों में रिचार्जिंग पर आधारित है। इन पत्थरों में जल धारण करने की क्षमता होती है। यह तकनीक भूमिगत जल में ऑक्सीजन स्तर को बढ़ा देती है और मिट्टी से आर्सेनिक निकलने की प्रक्रिया धीमी कर देती है। इस तकनीक से पानी में आर्सेनिक की मात्रा धीरे-धीरे कम होने लगती है। इस तरह के वैज्ञानिक दावों से उम्मीद बँधी है।

पानी से आर्सेनिक निकालने की एक और विधि है लेकिन वह विधि तभी कारगर हो सकेगी जब पानी में आयरन हों। वे गुजरे जमाने की बात करते हुए कहते हैं, 'पहले बड़े-बुजुर्ग रात को बर्तन में पानी रख दिया करते थे और सुबह वही पानी पिया करते थे, इसके पीछे वैज्ञानिक कारण था। दरअसल 12 घंटे तक पानी को रखने से आयरन के साथ आर्सेनिक व अन्य गन्दगी नीचे बैठ जाती थी और पानी साफ हो जाता था।'

एक अन्य भी एक उपाय है जिससे पानी से आर्सेनिक को हटाया जा सकता है। इस पर इंडियन इंस्टीट्यूट ऑफ टेक्नोलॉजी)आईआईटी विभाग के प्रो .शीर्षेंदु दे ने एक दशक से अधिक समय तक शोध किया है। यह है पानी के परिशोधन में लेटराइट सॉइल)लाल मिट्टी (का इस्तेमाल। प्रो .दे ने अपने शोध में पाया कि जहाँ लाल मिट्टी

होती है वहाँ पानी में आर्सेनिक की कोई समस्या नहीं देखी जा रही है। जब उन्होंने और गहराई से शोध किया तो पता चला कि लाल मिट्टी में आर्सेनिक को अवशोषित करने की क्षमता होती है। प्रो .शीर्षेंदु दे बताते हैं, 'वर्ष 2002 में हमने देखा कि गंगा-ब्रह्मपुत्र-मेघना के मैदानी क्षेत्रों में पानी में आर्सेनिक है लेकिन मिदनापुर, बांकुड़ा और अन्य जिलों में आर्सेनिक की समस्या नहीं है। इन जिलों में लाल मिट्टी पाई जाती है। तभी हमें पता चला कि लाल मिट्टी की वजह से ही यहाँ आर्सेनिक की समस्या नहीं है।' वे आगे कहते हैं, 'लाल मिट्टी में आयरन और एल्युमिनियम की मात्रा अधिक होती है जो आर्सेनिक को अवशोषित कर लेती है। मिट्टी का केमिकल ट्रीटमेंट कर हमने इस लायक बना दिया कि वह आर्सेनिक को शत-प्रतिशत अवशोषित कर ले।'

आईआईटी खड़गपुर की मदद से राजारहाट और मालदह में प्रायोगिक तौर पर लाल मिट्टी आधारित वाटर ट्रीटमेंट प्लांट स्थापित किया गया है। यहाँ से लोगों को न्यूनतम कीमत पर पानी मुहैया करवाया जा रहा है। आम लोग भी चाहें तो इस विधि का प्रयोग कर पानी से घातक आर्सेनिक को बाहर निकाल सकते हैं। प्रो .शीर्षेंदु दे ने कहा, 'गाँवों में रहने वाले लोग भी यह प्रयोग कर सकते हैं लेकिन इसके लिये उन्हें पहले लाल मिट्टी का केमिकल ट्रीटमेंट करवाना होगा।' दे के मुताबिक एक कम्पनी केमिकली ट्रीटेड लाल मिट्टी को बाजार में उतारने की तैयारी भी कर रही है।

आर्सेनिक प्रभावित इलाकों में रहने वाले लोगों को चाहिए कि वे सरकार से कोई उम्मीद न कर खुद पहल कर पोखरें खुदवाएँ और बारिश का पानी संचित कर उन्हें सिंचाई के काम में ले। सामाजिक कार्यकर्ताओं के साथ वैज्ञानिक और जागरूक नागरिक भी इस अभियान से जुड़कर समाज और देश के प्रति अपने कर्तव्य का निर्वाह कर सकते हैं।

संदर्भ ग्रंथ :

1. पर्यावरण ऊर्जा टाइम्स
2. www.hindi.indiawaterportal.org
3. www.thethirdpole.net
4. www.chauthiduniya.com

व्याख्याता,
राजकीय डूँगर महाविद्यालय, बीकानेर

11. Women and Sustainable Development - Women's Empowerment is a key Factor for achieving Sustainable Economic Growth

Dr. Aditi Sharma

Abstract
Women and girls make up more than half the world's population and they are on the frontlines, often more deeply impacted than men and boys by poverty, climate change, food and nutrition insecurity, lack of healthcare system, and global economic and environmental crises. Strengthening women's participating in political sphere is also a critical step towards empowerment of women. Women have a vital role in environment and development. Their full participation is therefore is essential to achieve sustainable development goals. Their contributions and leadership are central to finding a solution. With the new global 2030 roadmap and Sustainable Development Goals (SDGs) approved by UN Member States on 25 September 2015, we take a look at how women are affected by SDGs, as well as how women and girls can and will be key to achieving these goals. Ending all forms of discrimination against women and girls is not only a basic human right, but it also crucial to accelerating sustainable development. It has been proven time and again, that empowering women and girls has a multiplier effect, and helps drive up economic growth and development across the board. 25
Keywords : SDGs, Women, Sustainability, Discrimination, Human Rights.

Introduction
Sustainable development depends on an equitable distribution of resources for today and for the future. It cannot be achieved without gender equality. Women's empowerment is a key factor for achieving sustainable economic growth, social development and environmental sustainabilituy.

Sustainable development is broadly defined as development which meets the requirements of the present without compromising the

---

[25]https://www.researchgate.net/publication/327814277_Women_and_Sustainable_Development_Goals

ability of future generations to meet their own needs. Sustainable development should be a key principle of all policies and actions, which are broadly designed to create a society which is based on freedom, democracy and respect for fundamental rights, fostering equality of opportunity and solidarity within and between generations.

The sustainable development should be based on balanced economic growth and price stability, a highly competitive social market economy, aiming at full employment, a high level of education and social progress, and a high level of protection and improvement of the quality of the environment. Sustainable development should be a key objective for all national policies, and should aim at the continuous improvement of the quality of life on earth of both current and future generations. It is about safeguarding the earth's capacity to support life in all its diversity. It is based on the principles of democracy and the rule of law and respect for fundamental rights including freedom and equal opportunities for all. It brings about solidarity within and between generations. It seeks to promote a dynamic economy with a high level of employment and education, of health protection, of social and territorial cohesion and of environmental protection in a peaceful and secure world, respecting cultural diversity.[26]

Viewed in a broad spectrum, women have played a vital role in the global environmental movement. The World Commission on Environment and Development, in its report entitled Our Common Future, published in 1988, linked the environmental crisis to unsustainable development and financial practices that were worsening the North-South gap, with women a majority of the world's poor and illiterate.[27] Over the years, women have continued to speak out for policies and practices that do not threaten the health and well-being of future generations. They continue to fight for improved living standards and protection of the environment. In

---

[26] https://www.indiawaterportal.org/articles/women-and-sustainable-development-womens-empowerment-key-factor-achieving-sustainable

[27] https://www.peacewomen.org/UN/sustainable-development

almost all countries, women are disproportionately represented among the poor. And studies have found that the poor, in urban and rural areas of rich and poor countries, bear the greatest burden of environmental degradation and pollution. Women share the primary responsibility for nutrition, child care and household management in almost all countries. They are also active in environmental management. In most developing countries, women play a major role as farmers, animal tenders, and water and fuel collectors. Yet, despite their roles, women are not adequately represented in the decision-making processes related to the issues of environment and development at local, national or international levels.

Having their expertise, knowledge and perspective been overlooked for years, women are now demanding that their voices be heard. They recognize that an integrated approach to sustainable development is necessary since political, economic, social and environmental issues are closely interlinked. Women took active part in the Rio Earth Summit process and succeeded in obtaining a chapter on women and sustainable development and over one hundred references and recommendations pertaining to women in the final agreement, Agenda 21. The 1992 Rio Summit, together with the 1993 Human Rights Conference, the 1994 International Conference on Population and Development, the 1995 Social Summit and the 1995 Fourth World Conference on Women, have focused the work of the United Nations on the environment, population, human rights, poverty and gender, and the relationships between these issues.

In Rio, women were considered a "major group" whose involvement was necessary to achieve sustainable development. Today, there is a growing emphasis on "mainstreaming"- integrally incorporating women's concerns and participation in the planning, implementation and monitoring of all development and environmental management programmes to ensure that women benefit. The United Nations system is in the process of mainstreaming a gender-perspective in its work.

The Fourth World Conference on Women held in Beijing in September 1995, emphasized that empowerment, full participation and equality for women are the foundations for peace and sustainable development. The plan also acknowledges that sustainable development policies that do not involve women and men alike will not succeed in the long run.

Women and poverty

According to broad estimates, more than one in five people around the world live in conditions of extreme poverty on little more than $1 per day. In all developing regions except East Asia, the number of poor people has been rising since the 1980s. Studies indicate that the gaps between rich and poor are widening, and that the majority of the world's poor are women. Since the 1970s, the number of rural women living below the poverty line has increased by 50 per cent, in comparison with 30 per cent for men. Women accrue less income than men over their lifetime for a variety of reasons.28 They get paid less for the same work and are more likely to work less in order to reconcile their careers with child or elder care. These gaps in women's employment history reduce the amount of social security women gain. It also decreases the likelihood of receiving credit or loans. All these facts increase women's vulnerability to poverty, especially in old age. Governments must introduce policies, programmes and quota systems which correct this imbalance.

The United Nations Development Programme has defined sustainable development as development that not only generates economic growth but distributes its benefits equitably, that regenerates the environment rather than destroying it and that empowers people rather than marginalizing them. It is development that gives priority to the poor, enlarging their choices and opportunities and providing for their participation in decisions that affect their lives. Many women's groups are concerned that current patterns of economic development and globalization are increasing the gap between rich and poor, benefiting men more than women, and leading to increased environmental degradation. One

28 https://www.cambridge.org/core/journals/ethics-and-international-affairs/article/abs/transformative-equality-making-the-sustainable-development-goals-work-for women/ 45082 EE0136677 6987 CD3F96614775F2

report published by the Women's Environment and Development Organization (WEDO), "The imperatives of the global economy seem to be outrunning the post-Rio agenda five years later. How to bring them into closer step is the current challenge." Women are calling for gender-sensitive research in this area. They are also calling for increased access to resources - land, credit, education, technology and information--so that they can participate equally with men in key decisions that affect their lives and all life on planet Earth. Women have also raised demand that Governments establish new forms of economic accounting to include women's unpaid work and promote public policies that will reduce the disproportionate time women spend working, which is often twice as much as men.

Management of natural resources

Almost all developing regions, women are often the primary users and managers of land, forest, water and other natural resources. Women in rural areas of developing regions spend major parts of their day growing food, gathering fuel wood, cooking and carrying water. Women are responsible for most local food production in Africa and Asia. Consequently, they are responsible for the selection of seeds, fertilizers and pesticides and the maintenance of productive soil to nourish seedlings and plants. Women are also users, preservers and managers of biodiversity. Research on 60 home gardens in Thailand revealed 230 different species - many of which had been rescued from a neighboring forest before it was cleared. Indigenous women have a special relationship to natural resources. Their cultures and practices promote a balanced, respectful use and preservation of natural resources so that future generations can meet their needs. Yet most development schemes today ignore the needsand practices of indigenous peoples.

As consumers and producers, caretakers of their families and educators, women play an important role in promoting sustainable development through their concern for the quality and sustainability of life for present and future generations. However, due to discrimination, many women are unable to exercise their full potential in natural resource and environmental management, given their lack of training, status, land and property rights and capital.

Women and water

In rural areas in most developing countries, women are the managers of water resources - often walking miles to fetch water for basic household chores. In some parts of Africa, women and children spend eight hours a day collecting water. The proportion of rural women affected by water scarcity is estimated at 55 per cent in Africa, 32 per cent in Asia and 45 per cent in Latin America. Access to safe water is also an issue of increasing concern for urban women and families. Poor water access and quality affect not only women's crop and livestock production and the amount of labour they must expend to collect, store and distribute water, but also their health and that of their families. Water-borne diseases such as cholera, dysentery, typhoid, malaria and diarrhoea claim millions of lives each year. Parasitic diseases, such as onchocerciasis (river blindness), are also spread through contaminated water. However, despite their responsibility for water collection and sanitation management, women rarely participate in decision-making when the construction of facilities is planned. All too often they have no say about the location of a pump or the design of latrines. It is now recognized that the exclusion of women from the planning of water supply and sanitation schemes is a major cause of their high rate of failure. In order to improve health and quality of life for women, water and sanitation programmes must concentrate on reducing the time and energy women expend in water collection, and increasing women's participation in community decision-making regarding water and sanitation. Efforts must also be increased to ensure access to safe water. According to broad estimates, currently, more than one billion people in developing countries do not have access to safe water.

Conclusion

Women's contribution to sustainable development must be recognized. Women have a strong role in education and socializing their children, including teaching them care and responsibility with regard to the use and protection of natural resources. More should be done to increase women's voice in environmental decision making and to enable women to seize opportunities in the "green economy".

More capacity building programmes and training tailored to the needs of women are needed. In order to build women as catalyst for sustainable development, their role in family, community and society at large has to free from socio-cultural and religious traditions that prevent women participation. There is need for change of mindset, especially of the males who dominate the scene.

12. Assessment and Inventory of Herpetofaunal and Avifaunal Diversity in Urban Area of Ajmer, Rajasthan

Dr. UmeshDutt*[1] and Dr. Bharti Prakash[2]

Abstract

Small water bodies are important repositories of various groups of faunal biodiversity. They are exclusive habitats and provide the breeding and feeding grounds for various faunal species. Thus, they play a vital role in maintaining a variety of food chains and food webs in different ecosystems. Those species which are strictly dependent on water-bodies and their surrounding areas are known as wetland faunal species. Simultaneously species using waterbodies partially are known as wetland dependent faunal species. In vice versa condition certain species having distributions around water bodies but not having any major dependency on water bodies are categorized as terrestrial faunal species. During the last few years considerable studies on avifaunal diversity from different fresh water bodies of Ajmer have been carried out by researcherslike Dutt, and Prakash, (2018), Prakash, and Dutt, (2018), Meena et.al., (2018), and Dutt,(2019).. The main objective of the present study was to document the comprehensive database of faunal diversity around the human habitation to quantify the Herpetofaunal and Avifaunaldiversity in urban area of Ajmer, Rajasthan. For this several surveys were conducted during the study period (2017-2018) on various water bodies and surrounding areas. Overall 105 species of vertebrate fauna belonging to 3 classes (Amphibian, Reptile and Aves) were documented from study area along with population abundance status from different study sites. Various threats for vertebrate biodiversity at wetland areas of Ajmer district were identified and categorized and these factors have resulted in population decline of faunal species at study area in Ajmer.

Keywords : Faunal species, Wetland, Herpetofaunal, Abundance

Research Methodology : The present study of Herpetofaunal and Avifaunal diversity was studied in Ajmer urban area and nearby small fresh water bodies (ShrwanSagarTalab., Fool SagarTalab)

parts of district Ajmer of Rajasthan state. Ajmer, Rajasthan lies in between $26^0 16$'N $74^0 25$' E and $26^0 27$'N $74^0 42$' E and elevation 486 m (1.594ft) with an area of 8481 km^2. Site of interest are two small fresh water bodies known as the

ShrwanSagarTalab : is an annual water body, and nearby inhabitants are largely dependent on it for the basic daily needs along with cattle industries and farming purposes. It is drained by the rain water from nearby hillocks only. Most of months of the year it is filled with water but during theextreme summer (May-June) it becomes dry and gets refilled during the rains every year.

Fool SagarTalab : is also an annualwater body situated nearby distance of approximately 2.5 km. from ShrwanSagartalab. During 2007-2010 this annual water body did not receiveany drainage from surrounding hills due to blockage of drainage pathways and encroachments from certain agricultural practices. But during 2011-2012 due to good heavy rains this water body again git filled and till date it is filled with a good amount of water and preferably inhabited by various faunal species for variety of activities.

Objective : Present study objective was undertaken to document the comprehensive database of faunal diversity around the human habitation to quantify the Herpetofaunal and Avifaunal diversity in urban area of Ajmer, Rajasthan.

For covering the special emphasis study sites (water bodies and surrounding area) several surveys were conducted during the study period (2017-2018) (Survey duration August 2017 to July 2018) with the aim of providing a comprehensive database of Herpetofaunal and Avifaunal diversity.

Several techniques are available for generating species lists or information on species richness for a site. For the most part, field techniques are methods of general collecting, as historically practiced by various workers. Typically they involve searching for the collecting organism in all possible (appropriate microhabitats both during the day and night and result in modest habitats modification. These general collecting techniques have been used for both long term and short term sampling and often include both data retrieval and field work and thus is more eclectic.

For the compilation of this study random surveys were made for the assessment of the vertebrate faunal diversity of the mentioned study area. Survey was carried outday and night to find out the diurnal as well as nocturnal species. Survey was conducted to classify microhabitats and to also assess the distribution according to the microhabitats.

Surveys include the mainly Ad-hoc search method with the adjoining of Visual Encounter survey method and Transect method. Point count method was also used for the assessment the population of the organism of interest. Present study comprised with various field method exclusively and in combination also. Mainly used methods of the searching biodiversity for the present study are listed below:

Ad-hoc Search Method : In this methodology worker randomly search the desired habitats for the assessing thediversity and population status of the habitat of interest.

Visual Encounter Method : A Visual encounter method (VEM) is one which field personnel walk through an area or habitat for a prescribed time period systematically searching of organisms. Time is expressed as the number of person hours of searching in each area to be compared. The (VEM) is an appropriate technique for both inventory and monitoring based studies.

Quadrate Sampling : Quadrate sampling consists of laying out a series of small squares (quadrates) at randomly selected sites within a habitat and thoroughly searching those squares for organism.

Diversity Indices analysis using the Shannon Wiener , Simpson's index, and Jaccard and Sorenson index was attempted by (Hollenbeck and Ripple, 2007; Krebs, 1989 ; Bibi and Ali 2013; Lawania, *et al.* 2013) looking for distribution patterns among bird communities. Similar analysis was also carried out for measuring the species richness, evenness, in Ajmer by (Swarrop and Yadav 2017; Yadav and Swarrop 2017) (Prakash and Dutt 2018).

Classification of Microhabitats : Area under investigation was classified in the following microhabitats for the convenience of the study.

Wetland / Marsh (WM) : All ponds, lake, ditches, roadside water logged areas (temporary and permanent) were classified as wetlands or marshy area type of microhabitats.

Agricultural Fields (AF) : Area where the agricultural practices were going on were included as the agricultural microhabitat.

Forest Area (FA): Unequally distributed forest in Rajasthan state restricted to the southern and eastern part of state which categorized as Forest area microhabitat.

Urbanized Areas (UA) : All area near by human settlements was categorized as urbanized microhabitat. This type also includes the residential as well as industrial areas.

Population status of the organisms were categorized in different categories as:

Most Common (MC) ; Common (C); Not Common (NC); and Rare (R) on the basis of their population occurred during the various field surveys. Several diversity measures are available for assessment of species diversity in an area. Species abundance relations were also assessed in the form of the Evenness indices more specifically Similarity measures namely "Jaccard Index" and "Sorenson Index" were also assessed for the different sites.

> **Jaccard Index:** $Cj = j / (a + b - j)$ Where $j =$ the number of species common to both sites
> $a =$ the number of species in site A and
> $b =$ the number of species in site B
> **Sorenson Index:** $Cs = 2j / (a + b)$ Where $j =$ the number of species common to both sites
> $a =$ the number of species in site A and
> $b =$ the number of species in site B

Result and Discussion : Overall 105species of vertebrate fauna belonging to 3 classes (Amphibian, Reptile and Aves) were documented from study area along with population abundance status from different study sites of study area. Out of these observed 105 species, 5 species represented by class Amphibia (3 species found as

Most Common; 1 species found Common and 1 species observed as Rare); 6 species from Reptiles (1 species found Common; 3 species observed as Not Common and 2 species observed as Rare) and 94 species of Aves (12 species found as Most Common; 29 species found Common; 27 species observed as Not Common and 26 species observed as Rare. In combination or in general scenario out of 105 species, 15 species found as Most Common, 31 species found as Common, 30 species observed as Not Common and 29 species observed as Rare.

The class amphibian have maximum 60% of most common category followed by 20% of common and 20% of rare category and in class reptile maximum percentage 50% of not common category followed by 33.33% of rare and 16.66% of common category and in class aves have maximum percentage 30.85% of common category followed by 28.72% of not common category and 27.65 % of rare category.

Table.1. Percentage and number of species belong to 3 classes in study area.

	Most Coommon		Common	
	No of Species	% of Species	No of Species	% of Species
Amphibia	3	60%	1	20%
Reptile	0	0%	1	16.66%
Aves	12	12.76%	29	30.85%
	Not Common		Rare	
Amphibia	0	0%	1	20%
Reptile	3	50%	2	33.33%
Aves	27	28.72%	26	27.65%

Site-wise distribution and population status of observe species.
Study Site A : ShrawanSagar Talab : Over all 87 species of vertebrates belonging to three classes were documented from the study site A ShrawanSagar along with population abundance status. Out of these observed 87 species 5 species were represented by class Amphibia (3 species found as Most Common, 1 species found Common and I species found as Rare), 6 species from Reptiles (2 species found as Common. 1 species found as Not Common and 3

species observed as Rare) and 76 species from Aves (15 species found as Most Common, 28 species found Common, 21 species observed as Not Common and 12 species observed as Rare. In combination or in general scenario out of 87 observed species 18 species found as Most Common, 31 species found as Common, 22 species observed as Not Common and 16 species observed as Rare.

Site B : Fool SagarTalab : Over all 100 species of vertebrates belonging to three classes were documented from the study area along with population abundance status at Fool SagarTalab. Out of these observed 100 species, 5 species were represented by class Amphibia (3 Species found as Most Common, 1 species found as Common and 1 species observed as Rare) 5 species from Reptiles (3 species found as Common, 1 Species observed as Not Common and 1 species observed as Rare) 87 species from Avis (13 species found as Most common, 31 species found Common. 25 species observed as Not Common and 18 Species observed as Rare.

Similarity or Evenness Status among Various Study Sites : To assess the similarity or evenness of species occurrence among studied different sites A (ShrawanSagarTalab) and site B (Fool SagarTalab) the biodiversity indices "Jaccard Index" and "Sorenson Index" were assessed for assessment of species diversity at study area.

During the entire period of study the maximum species was observed from the Wetland / Marsh (WM) microhabitat (3% of birds species) followed by Agricultural Fields (AF) and Forest area Cover (FA) both microhabitats (25% of bird species). In contrast the minimum species represented by Urban settlements area (UA) microhabitat (19% of birds species). The higher amount of species diversity indicated the better quality and resource availability at that particular microhabitat. Jaccard and Sorenson index's increasing values indicates the similarity between two microhabitats. The Wetland / Marsh (WM) microhabitats have highest values (Jaccard= 0.8333, Sorenson= 0.9090) are much similar to each other.

Conclusion

> *Threats to anuran population of study areas :* Various threats for vertebrate biodiversity at wetland areas of Ajmer district were

identified and categorized into two groups mainly: (*Primary threats*) such as mining, deforestation, urbanization and other anthropogenic activities whereas (*Secondary threats*) includes such as soil erosion by air and water. Reduction in ground water level and desiccation of open water source such as pond, lakes and seasonal rivers or streams. These factors have resulted in population decline of faunal species at study area in Ajmer. Biodiversity at this area facing serious threats and needs special conservation efforts particularly in the areas and outside the protected areas.

➢ Most of water bodies and small ditches (breeding grounds / feeding grounds) transected by roads and some places by national highways this has caused heavy loss of biodiversity due to road accidents.

➢ Urbanization associated with deforestation has taken away the habitats of several species. The building and roads constructions at their natural habitats adversely affect the biodiversity at study area.

➢ Introduction of many crop species in the recent past of agricultural fields requires extensive use of fertilizers during monsoon period result washing out these chemicals in nearly land causes fluctuations in physicochemical properties of this study area.

Fig.1.Satellite Map showing the study area ShrwanSagarTalab& Fool SagarTalab in Ajmer district of Rajasthan

➤ **Conservation Strategies :** There is strong need of conservation of these types of areas there are important repositories of biodiversity. This study also supports that biodiversity is not a properties of protected areas only and India has a good spatial and temporal variations in occurrence of biodiversity at certain sites.

Reference :

✓ Bibi, F. and Z. Ali, (2013): Measurement of diversity indices of avian communities at Taunsa Barrage Wildlife Sanctuary, Pakistan. The journal of animal and plant Science, 23. (2). pp. 469-474.

✓ Dutt, U. (2019): (*Habitat Preference of Avifauna: Study of Wetlands of Ajmer, Rajasthan.*) Ph. D.ThesisMaharshiDayanandSaraswati University Ajmer.

✓ Dutt, U. and Prakash, B. (2018): Distribution and Assessment of Water-Bird and Water-Associated Birds Diversity from Two wetlands of Ajmer, Rajasthan. Int. J. ShrinkhlaEkShodhparakVaicharikPatrika Vol. 5(12) ISSN NO.: 2321-290X pp. 82-89.

✓ Hollenbeck, J. P. and Ripple, W.J.(2007): Aspen and Conifer Heterogeneity Effects on Bird Diversity in the Northern Yellowstone Ecosystem. Western North American Naturalist. 67(1): pp. 92-101.

✓ Krebs, C. J. (1989): Ecological Methodology. Harper-Collins Publishers, New York. pp. 654.

✓ Lawaniya, N. K. ; Sharma , D. D and Sharma ,V. (2013): Occurrence and Distribution of Avianfauna from certain wetlands of Hadauti plateau, Kota, Rajasthan. Int. Jou. of Environmental and Animal Conservation; Vol. 2(1). pp. 8-21.

✓ Meena, D., Yadav, D., Sharma,V., Senapati, T. and Kachhawa, S.B.J. 2018. Current Status of fresh water Avifaunal Diversity of TehsilKekri and nearby area of Ajmer District, Rajasthan India. Int. J. for Research in App. Sci. &Engi. Tec. (IJRASET) ISSN: 2321-9653: Vol. 6. pp. 1998-2004.

✓ Prakash, B. and Dutt, U. (2018): Assessment of Diversity Indices of Water-Birds in Fresh Water Lake of Ajmer (Rajasthan) *Int. J. ShrinkhlaEkShodhparakVaicharikPatrika* Vol. 5(10) ISSN NO.: 2321-290X Pp. 22-27

✓ Swarrop, R. and Yadav, I. (2017): Frequency and Status of Occurrence of Water-Birds at Anasagar Lake, Ajmer. Inter. J. for Res. in Applied Science & Engineering Tech. (IJRASET). ISSN: 2321- 9653; Vol. 5. Issue (10). pp. 1079- 1090.

✓ Yadav, I. and Swroop, R. (2017): Diversity, Abundance and Inter-specific Correlation in Water-birds at Anasagar Lake, Ajmer. Int. Jon. Sci. and Res. (IJSR)., Vol. 6(7). pp. 1306-1317.

Assistant Professor in Zoology,
Government College Begun, Chittorgarh
Associate Professor in Zoology ,
S.P.C. Government College Ajmer
email : umeshdutt1980@gmail.com,
dr.bharti.prakash@gmail.com

13. A Strategy for Sustainable Tourism Development : A Case Study of Jaisalmer District

Yashi Sharma

Introduction

Tourism is the largest developing industry of the world. Jaisalmer is famous in the world for its beautiful heritage and rich culture. It is situated in the heart of the "Great Indian Thar Desert". Jaisalmer was established by Mahawaral Jaisal Singh in 1155 A.D. Jaisalmer is known as the "Golden City" of India, because yellow sand stones used in every architecture and the sandy desert around give a beautiful yellow - golden look to the entire city. It is renowned and famous for its geoheritage and cultural heritage, The land of miracles, the religious faith and values, temples, culture, traditions, fairs and festivals, desert culture and life, desert topography, mesmerising sunsets and sunrises, majestic fort, havelis, royal palaces, historical monuments, beautiful architecture with amazing artwork and fine designs, beautiful lake, colourful ethnics, folk dance and music, art and handicrafts, authentic cuisines, heritage, a land of brave kings and queens their stories, brave soldiers and many more. The world admires and appreciates and thousands of tourists both domestic and foreign visit every year. It has become one of the most pleasant and beautiful tourist places of India and has become one in the world and tourism industry has become one of the most important industries of Jaisalmer. There is another side which has concern towards the preservation of heritage. More tourism and people from different countries and cultures affect the originality of culture and environment and people of Jaisalmer. To protect and maintain a balance between resources and people sustainable tourism development is necessary so the future generations will also get to know about the great importance and value of their true geoheritage and rich cultural heritage.

Objectives

The main objectives of the study are as follows :

1. To understand the concept of sustainable tourism.
2. To evaluate the ways of proper planning and strategy for sustainable tourism development.

3. To study the need and importance of sustainable tourism in the study area.
4. The preservation of geoheritage and cultural heritage of Jaisalmer.

Hypothesis
The hypothesis of the study - tourism does not affect the environment and sustainable tourism development is not needed in the study area.

Methodology
The present study has been done with the help of various methods, qualitative and quantitative and statistical techniques have been used to collect and represent the data.

Methods :
Primary Data Collected Through :
• Personal observation of the study area.
• Personal interviews from people of Jaisalmer, domestic and foreign tourists, shopkeepers, guides, owners of monuments, owners of hotels and restaurants.

Secondary Data Collected Through :
• Books and booklets
• Articles, Journals and Newspaper
• R.T.D.C. reports
• Department of Tourism, Jaisalmer.

Statistical Techniques :
• Bar Graph and Diagram

Study Area
India

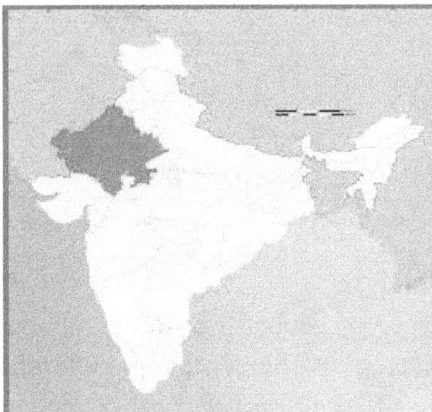

Rajasthan

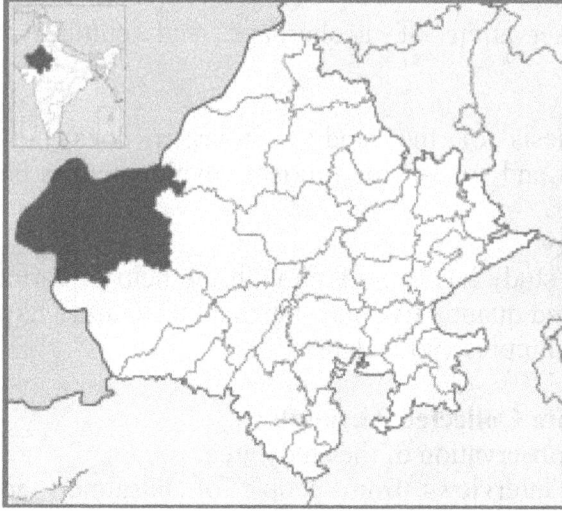

Jaisalmer

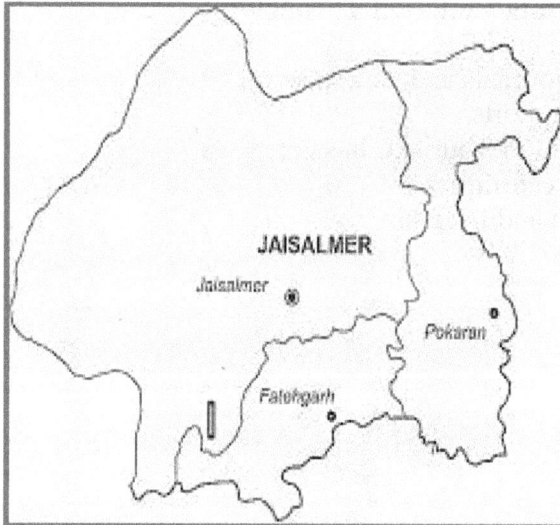

Discussion and Analysis

Jaisalmer is the place of geoheritage tourism. Geoheritage is geo + heritage, geoheritage involving the geomorphological feature, historical place or site, culture and cultural heritage and it can be scientific and aesthetic also. The United Nations World Tourism Organizations (UNWTO) defines Sustainable Tourism, "Tourism that takes full account of its current and future economic, social and environmental impacts, addressing the needs of visitors, the industry, the environment and host community." Sustainability between resources, tourists' pressure and environment both physical and socio - cultural, it has become a very important responsibility. Jaisalmer is a incredible beautiful desert place with amazing and mesmerising tourist destinations. Jasialme has great importance globally on the tourist map and world also as geographically, historically, culturally, economically. The culture and heritage has its own uniqueness and beauty. Thousands of domestic and foreign tourists visit every year. Fairs and Festivals and tourist season is on peak. Preservation and conservation of the geoheritage is important.

Pillars of Sustainable Tourism are :

- Balance between tourism,development and resources
- Optimum use of resources
- Socio - cultural and physical environment balance
- Long term beneficial with proper planning

Dimensions of Sustainable Tourism Development

- Responsible Tourism - social and self awareness both are equally important.
- Ecotourism - take good care of the environment and should not pressure the local resources of the study area.
- Geotourism - develop a responsible sense of place.
- Voluntourism - it is one of the most important one, giving back to the community.
- Development with optimum and proper planning

Types of Tourism in Jaisalmer :

1. Religious or Spiritual Tourism
2. Cultural Tourism
1. Heritage Tourism
3. Desert Tourism
4. Historic Tourism

5. Adventurous Tourism

6. Fairs and Festivals

7. MICE Tourism

Geoheritage and Cultural Heritage of Jaisalmer

"Our culture is our heritage." It is the richness and real beauty in a true manner. Jaisalmer is a desert district. The desert culture and desert life is a true beauty and unforgettable experience which stays in the hearts and touches the soul.

The Geoheritage of Jaisalmer are the Desert topography and long and widely spread beautiful Sand Dunes, the Wood Fossil National Park, Akal National Park.

The Cultural Heritage of Jaisalmer are the Temples, Fairs and Festivals, historical monuments - Fort, Havelis, Palaces, the Lake, Museum, Folk Dance and Music, Arts and Handicrafts, Khadi and Leather products, Traditional and ethnic clothes and jewellery, authentic cuisines, importance and value of their culture, traditions, their value and many more.

Decadal Growth in Tourist Arrivals in Jaisalmer from 1981 - 2011

Years	Domestic	Foreign	Total
1981	65908	7413	73321
1991	104610	38103	142713
2001	103109	46107	153233
2011	281159	122969	404128

Source : Tourist Department, Government of Rajasthan, Jaipur

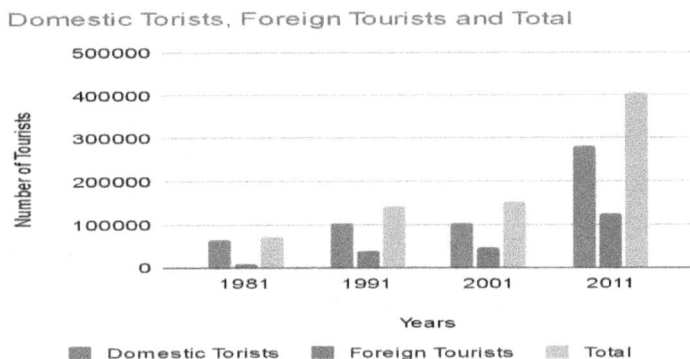

Fig.1. Representing the decadal growth in domestic and foreign tourists in Jaisalmer.

Tourist Arrivals in Jaisalmer from 2011-2020

Years	Domestic	Foreign	Total
2011	281159	122969	404128
2012	126490	73299	199789
2013	122883	73607	196490
2014	250716	91759	342475
2015	266175	84533	350708
2016	359497	90937	450434
2017	493755	122851	616601
2018	592695	136406	729101
2019	345524	91019	364543
2020	144899	26014	170913

Source : R.T.D.C.Reports and Annual Progress Reports of Rajasthan, Government of Rajasthan, Tourism Department Jaisalmer.

Domestic and Foreign

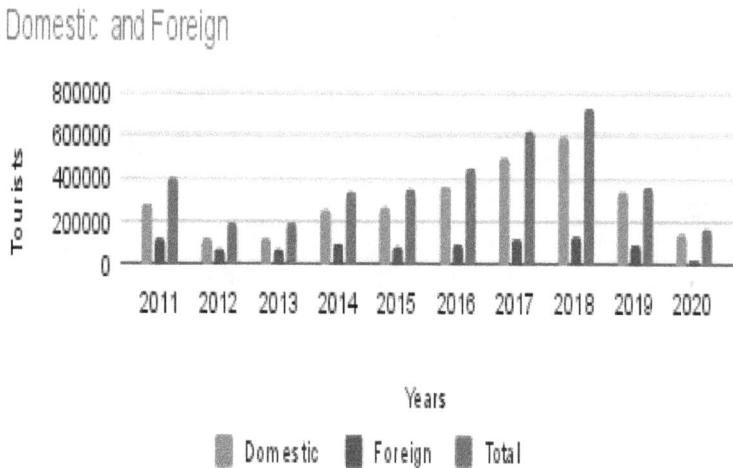

Years

█ Domestic █ Foreign █ Total

Fig.2 Representing the trends of tourists from 2010 - 2020.

Effects of Tourism on the Environment of Jaisalmer

Tourism has a great impact on the physical as well as socio - cultural environment. There are both positive and negative effects of tourism on the environment of Jaisalmer.

Effects on Physical Environment :

1. Development of roads, new constructions towards the Ghantiyali Mata Mandir and the Tanot Mata Mandir. There was pure desert earlier and from 10-20 years, desertification work has started and new trees and bushes are being planted by limiting the area of sand dunes.

2. Thousands of tourists coming every year increases the pressure on the desert topography. There are more than 50 desert villages developed on the main road side and nearby areas of sand dunes and specially in 'Sam village and Khuri village'. their height is going down and spreading. The desert villages were built by making sandy areas plain. The sand dunes are the real geoheritage beauty of Jaisalmer keeping them clean and tidy, and decentralization of tourists on different places inside and new desert villages can develop on the inner side from the main roads.

3. Earlier when the sand dunes shift with the wind and air pressure they come in the middle of the path, people then remove the sand

dunes from the way and move forward. For this to limit the area, plantation of trees and bushes have been started.

4. In tourist season the people and crowd increases in the city area and also in the outer areas specially the desert villages built near the Sam and Khuri villages. More crowds cause pressure on the local resources and noise pollution.

5. Continuous tourist pressure, camel, jeep safaris and other desert adventurous activities, mainly jeep safaris run up and down with speed on the opposite sides on the sand dunes, due to this the height of the sand dunes goes down and area spreads. Decentralization of tourism will also help to reduce pressure from particular areas and recover early.

6. Tourism affects the flora and fauna of the study area. People throw garbage, bottles, plastics and other things mixed into the sand dunes and can injure others and harm the environment. Keeping the places clean by not throwing things here and there, cleanliness is also very important.

7. Economically, tourism is a boom for Jaisalmer, hotels, restaurants, desert villages and other new construction are developing. But, to create new construction, the sand dunes and sandy areas turn into lined, which has an adverse effect on the desert topography. And the originality of the dense sand dunes become different.

Effects on Socio - Cultural Environment :

1. Cultural, traditions and values changing.

2. Originality and mentality of the people of Jaisalmer are changing from the influences of tourists coming from different places, people copying and applying their habits into their life. By adapting their language, lifestyle, food habits, etc. into their life..

3. Crime rate is increasing.

4. People provide their houses for tourists to stay on rent for their income and the old houses are suffering from overcrowding and extra pressure on the old as well as new construction.

5. Earlier the Fort and Havelis were not allowed to go on the top, and because of more tourists the drainage system started being affected, leakages and the construction is getting weaker this causing breaks and serious concern to the heritage constructions.

The delicate and fine art designs on the jharokhas, chhatris, pillars, gates, ceiling, flooring of the Temples, Fort, Havelis, Palaces, Lake side, and other important and beautiful historical monuments are very delicate and from pressure of tourists they are also getting weaker and they need special maintenance and care.

6. Educational level and standard of living has risen and people have become technically advanced with time and also influenced by tourists from different states and countries.

7. More working opportunities and options have opened in different fields.

Importance and Sustainable Tourism Development in Jaisalmer

Jaisalmer is. In table:1, the decadal growth in the domestic tourists were a bit less in 2001 and then increased again and the foreign tourists are continuously increasing, continuous increase in tourists till 2011 in total and a major increase in 2011. In table:2, domestic tourists and foreign tourists are fluctuating. The maximum number of domestic and foreign tourists arrivals are in 2018 in Jaisalmer. A fall in the number of tourists in 2020 is because of corona and will surely rise again. Jaisalmer is a beautiful place. It is a important to preserve and save the following will help to make proper strategy for sustainable tourism development in Jaisalmer :

1. Preserving Culture and Heritage and Respect for others' culture, traditions, values are very important.

2. Protection of historical monuments and their maintenance can be done to control the pressure of thousands of tourists every year, the monuments are hundreds of years old, this needs to be understood. Balance between resources and population, including tourists and the main local population of Jaisalmer, like over usage of water, systematic drainage, etc. are also important.

3. Social awareness through organisations, policies, programmes and Self awareness, Mutual understanding also, Cleanliness of tourists and other places is also very important. Providing more Security and safety. Strengthen good Governance for the betterment of tourism development in Jaisalmer.

4. Security and safety and Strength good Governance for the betterment of tourism development in Jaisalmer.
5. Development should be done but with taking care and responsibility toward the environment.

"Our culture is our heritage." It is the real richness in a true manner. Sustainable tourism is important to save the heritage and every small start will be helpful and the collective contribution toward this will give a good result. Proper planning and execution for tourism and tourism development. Every small step taken for a good reason will be a good start to bring a good change.

Conclusion

The study is important to understand the value and preserve the heritage of Jaisalmer. The hypothesis has proved wrong, tourism does affect the physical and socio - cultural environment and sustainable tourism development is very important in Jaisalmer to protect and save the beautiful heritage of Jaisalmer. By discussion and analysis, the study came to a conclusion that sustainable tourism is important in Jaisalmer and preservation and protection of the geoheritage and cultural heritage should be the responsibility. With the proper strategy, planning and execution good, The Golden City Jaisalmer will keep shine with sustainable tourism and welcome people by saying "PADHARO SA MHARE DESH " with smiles and pure hearts and keep spreading the divine golden beauty of the beautiful geoheritage and precious cultural heritage.

Reference

1. Boora. S. S. (2007) "Sustainability in Cultural tourism". Indian Journal of International Tourism and Hospitality
2. Research, Kurukshetra University Kurukshetra. Vol.-1. 108-117.
3. Brayley. R, Var, T. and Sheldon, P. (1990) "Perceived influence of tourism on social issues". Annals of Tourism Research, 17 (2).
4. Brunt, P. and Courtney, P. (1999) "Host perceptions of socio-cultural impacts". Annals of Tourism Research.

5. Shachley Myra (1996) "Community Impact of the Camel Safari Industry in Jaisalmer". Tourism Management.Vol. 17, NO3 PP 213-18.
6. Sharma. N. K., "Jaisalmer The Golden City", Jaisalmer, Rajasthan.
7. Tourism Statistics, Rajasthan Tourism Development Corporation (RTDC). Jaipur 2011.

Research Scholar,
Bhagwant University, Ajmer,
Rajasthan

14. Sustainable Dyeing in the Textile Industry

Dr. Rashmi Gupta

Humans have been coloring fabric for millennia with the use of synthetic and natural dyes, all dyes were made with natural pigments and oils. In this article, we will discuss the current issues related to textile dyeing & treatment, and explore new technologies and sustainable dyeing practices. There are many problems with current textile dyeing and treatment practices, and almost all of them are related to excess water consumption and pollution. The dyeing process of textiles varies depending on the type of fabric.

Most of the clothing we wear today is colored using synthetic dyes. The problem with these is that valuable raw materials, such as crude oil are needed during production and the chemicals added are toxic to the environment and our bodies. Even though natural dyes are less toxic than synthetic dyes, they still require agricultural land and pesticides for the plants that make up the dyes.

Labs across the world are discovering a new way to create color for our clothing: bacteria. Streptomyces coelicolor is a microbe that naturally changes color based on the pH of the medium it grows inside. By changing its environment, it is possible to control what type of color it becomes. Bacterial dyes use less water than conventional dyes and can be used to dye many different patterns with a vast range of colors, which are not toxic as synthetic dyes as well not harm nature as natural dyes.

Keywords : sustainable dyeing, Streptomyces coelicolor, conventional dyes, pigments

Introduction

The textile industry is the second most polluting industry in the world. Synthetic dyes contribute to a major part of this pollution, with nearly 20 percent of global water pollution being linked to textile dyeing processes. The main contributors to this problem are the use of non-biodegradable petroleum-based colorants to dye textiles, toxic agents to fix colorants on the textiles, and the release of large proportions of these colorants and fixation agents into the surrounding ecosystem.

There are many problems with current textile dyeing and treatment practices, and almost all of them are related to excess water consumption and pollution. Textile industries rank second in the world for polluting clean water. It releases some 72 toxic chemicals into the water from textile dyeing. Unfortunately, some of these chemicals cannot be removed. All the processes in the textile industry, from dyeing to rinsing use large amounts of water. For dyeing factories, it is easy to throw away the effluent water rather than clean it and re-using it. As a result gallons of wastewater are thrown away by mills every year, which contains harmful chemicals like formaldehyde, chlorine, lead, and mercury. These chemicals are dangerous for both living beings and the environment. Lots of chemicals go into different processes which turn cotton into cloth. Another chain of chemicals is used to dye the cotton and to fix these dyes.

In the wake of those closures and strict environmental regulations, industries are now looking into greener ways to color clothes. A viable alternative to synthetic colorants may be the natural colors extracted from biodegradable plant sources. However, toxic fixation agents still need to be used with these colorants. Altogether, the textile and fashion industries are now in search of alternative coloring methods. Here are a few of the more benign techniques innovative companies are using to color clothes.

1. Pigments from Microbes

As more consumers become aware of the harmful effects of current dyeing practices, new technologies make way for more cost-effective, resource-efficient, and **sustainable dyeing alternatives**. Innovation in dyeing technologies is creating natural pigments from microbes. Current dyeing innovations can help reduce water usage, replace wasteful practices with efficient and cost-effective ones, and attempt to completely transform the way in which it creates the pigments that give our clothing beautiful colors. some of tomorrow's apparel could potentially be bioengineered—that is, made from living bacteria, algae, yeast, animal cells, or fungi—

which would break down into nontoxic substances when eventually thrown away. Such methods could reduce waste and pollution.

2. Hybrid Pigments

This technology can be applied for dyeing cotton garments at low temperatures and also to wool in a more ecological process. Eco foot-Indigo, a hybrid pigment used in dyeing denim, avoids using toxic reducing agents that are traditionally used in converting indigo pigment to a water-soluble form. common reducing agents are considered environmentally unfavorable, as the sulfite and sulfate generated in the dyebath can cause various problems when discharged into the wastewater.

3. Huue

It makes sustainable, biosynthetic indigo blue meant for the denim industry. Their technology does not use petroleum, cyanide, formaldehyde, or reducing agents. This eliminates massive amounts of water pollution. Instead of using toxic chemicals, huue. uses sugar to make dye. They use proprietary bioengineering technology to create microbes that mirror nature's process and consume sugar to enzymatically produce dye.

4. Powder Dyes from Textile Fibers

This process for dyeing uses recycled clothing, fiber material, and textile scraps. It developed a sophisticated eight-step system (patent pending) in which all the fabric fibers are crystalized into an extremely fine powder that can be used as a pigment dye for fabrics and garments made of cotton, wool, nylon, or any natural fiber. Recycrom can be applied to the fabrics using various methods such as exhaustion dyeing, dipping, spraying, screen printing, and coating. Recycrom is applied as a suspension while most dyes are used as a chemical solution and hence can be easily filtered from the water, thus reducing the environmental impact.

5. Digital Printing

Intech Digital introduced a new "waterless" textile printing technology using BlackJet reactive pigment textile inks (nano pigment ink) to provide coloration. BlackJet textile inks use a pigment that is insoluble in the ink carrier, rather than a dye and contains resin binders that help the pigment particles adhere to the fabric. This technology uses a four-step process consisting of fabric pretreatment, digital printing with reactive pigment inks, and fabric heating for fixing the pigment onto the fabric, followed by a post-treatment process.

Future Challenges

These innovations are very promising and environmentally friendly, but there are still many barriers to overcome. The textile industry is a manufacturing industry working under pressure, there is cutthroat competition for garment prices. The innovative technologies highlighted here still require a lot of optimization in terms of achieving low-cost production and commercial viability while meeting customer demands.

Associate Professor,
Garment Production and Export Management,
Govt. G.D College for women, Alwar.
email : guptareshu67@gmail.com

15. Role of Physics for Achieving Sustainable Development

R. A. Kunale

Abstract

Physics generates fundamental knowledge needed for the future sustainable advance technology that will continue to drive the economic engines of the world. Physics contributes to the technological infrastructure and provides trained personnel needed to take advantage of scientific advances and discoveries.It improves our quality of life by providing the basic understanding necessary for developing new instrumentation and techniques for various fields like medical applications, such as computer tomography, magnetic resonance imaging, positron emission tomography, ultrasonic imaging, and laser surgery.

Introduction

Scientific research and discovery plays an important role in developing quality of human life. Physics has long been instrumental in responding to critical societal challenges and improving the quality of life worldwide. As we move towards an international year devoted to basic sciences for sustainable development we can celebrate by reflecting on some of these achievements[1]. Research in physics rapidly increases and it can help address in sustainable and ethical ways pressing societal challenges in all countries, such as access to clean water, affordable and clean energy, food security or health. These efforts can be calibrated against the UN Agenda 2030 and its Sustainable Development Goals1, which helps to answer the question posed above. Of course, basic or 'pure' physics has a position on the assembly line for building our technological base including providing the context in which innovative applications can actually be conceived and implemented in the first place. However, it also has an intangible benefit in satisfying our natural and evolutionary instincts for exploration, discovery and understanding [2].

1) Energy consumption
2) Food production

3) Water cleaning
4) Communication
5) Health

1) Energy Consumption

Energy consumption due to lighting has been radically reduced owing to the invention of the blue light-emitting diode (LED), for which the Nobel Prize was awarded in 2014 to Isamu Akasaki, Hiroshi Amano and Shuji Nakamura. For a community completely off the electricity grid, LEDs can help to end the use of unhealthy kerosene lamps, while not overtaxing portable power systems as the filament bulb did, enabling children and adults to safely read after dark. In high-income countries, where people unnaturally spend much of their time indoors, the same digital lighting can be tuned to help improve productivity and well-being by mimicking the diurnally varying spectrum of the Sun.

2) Food Production :

Fig 1. LED food prduction

Growing plants indoors, in the presence of LED lights and using multiple layers to maximize production.Tunable LED systems can address hunger by improving plant yield in indoor production sites, which are augmenting traditional farming to feed an ever-increasing population as shown in Fig 1 [3]. Food production can also profit from remote-sensing and imaging of crops, and spectroscopic devices can be used to measure oxygen content in packaged food, indicating whether its shelf life has expired.

3) Water Cleaning :
Solar-powered desalination stations can help produce drinkable water in many parts of the world, and ultraviolet LEDs can help clean it.

4) Communication :
Optical fiber is raising in communication due to its advantages as faster speed with less attenuation, less impervious to electromagnetic interference (EMI), smaller size and greater information carrying capacity. The unceasing bandwidth needs, on the other hand, are also yielding significant growth in optical fiber demands. The optical fibersare powering the Internet, increasing our connections globally as shown in Fig 2 [4].

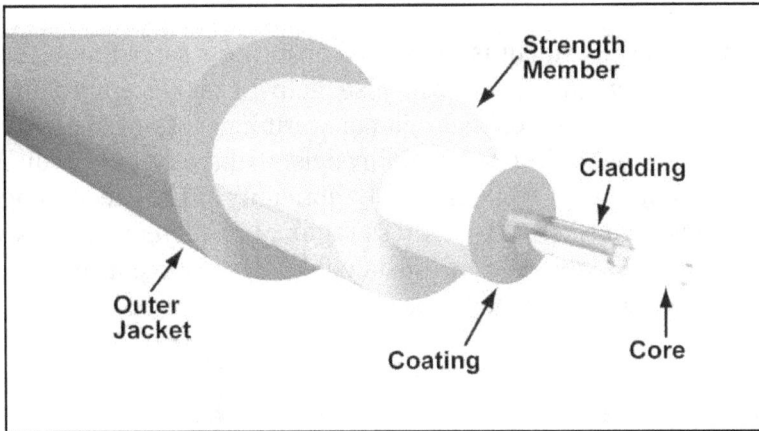

Fig. 2.Optical fiber Cable

5) Health
We can also find physics in the healthcare applications that have recently preoccupied our minds. Laser therapy uses an intense, narrow beam of light to remove or destroy cancer and abnormal cells that can turn into cancer. Tumor cells absorb light of different wavelengths (or colors) than normal cells do. So, tumor cells can be targeted by selecting the proper wavelength of the laser source as shown in Fig. 3[5].Photodynamic therapy, using lasers, is being employed in many regions of the world to treat certain types of cancer, and portable point of care devices, lab on chip platforms and remote patient monitoring are helping to improve the health of many people who are far away from hospitals.

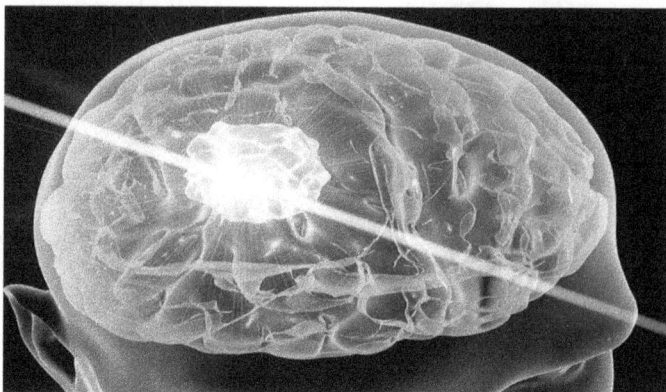

Fig. 3 Laser treatment for destroying brain tumor.

Conclusion:

Sustainable development is the key to ensuring a safer future for the forthcoming generations. It will also help to tackle environmental issues such as climate change, global warming, loss of species, and shortage of natural resources.Physicists directly or indirectly contributed to the wellbeing of humanity. The technological innovations are effective to address regional challenges. In this way physics play a key role in sustainable development in energy, medical, food and production.

References:
[1] www.iybssd2022.org.
[2] Niemela, J.J. Physics for a better world. Nat. Phys. 17, 871–872 (2021).
[3] https://depositphotos.com/383966918/stock-photo-plants-vertical-farms-grow-led.html
[4] https://community.fs.com/blog/the-advantages-and-disadvantages-of-optical-fibers.html
[5] https://medicine.wustl.edu/news/lasers-help-fight-deadly-brain-tumors/

**Kai. Rasikamahavidyalaya, Deoni,
Latur, Maharashtra**

16. Evaluation of Ethno-Botanicals of Sariska National Park, Rajasthan to control *Pseudomonas Viridiflava* causing Leaf Spot Disease of Cotton

Pawan Kumar Meena*,
Ashwani Kumar Verma
Laxmi Meena

Abstract

Antibacterial efficacy of fourteen different medicinal plant extracts of Sariska National Park were tested *in vitro* against *Pseudomonas viridiflava* causing infectious leaf spot disease in cotton plant. Plant extracts of methanol introduced at two concentrations of 50 and 100% w/v used to study their antibacterial efficacy. Results indicated that all 14 plants extracts showed prominent effectiveness to control the pathogen. The *Argemone mexicana* leaf extract was found more effective to inhibit *P. viridiflava* exhibited 2176.02 mm^2 IA at 100% and 50% concentration. Pure methanol extract (100%) revealed the highest antibacterial properties as compared to dilute form (50%). The present study concluded that the methanolic extracts of medicinal plants play a consequential role in eco-friendly disease management. Therefore, medicinal plant extracts can be used as antibacterial agents to replace synthetic bactericides.

Keywords : Antibacterial, Cotton, Medicinal plants, *P. viridiflava*, Sariska National Park.

Introduction

Cotton is the most important fiber crop worldwide; a total of 34 million hectares of land cotton is grown in more than 50 countries economically in the tropical and temperate regions. For optimum production adequate moisture with proper irrigation, dry and hot climatic condition are necessary for cotton crop. These climatic conditions are found in some specific countries including India, Australia, USA, China, and the Middle East. A seedy coat of cotton expands into tubular fiber and is spun into yarn. Globally total 50 species of cotton in which four spp. are only cultivated. Among these 4 cultivated crops two of these tetraploids (*G. barbadense* and *G. hirsutum*), and two (*G. herbaceum* and *Gossypium arboreum*) are diploids. Also the 50 spp. acknowledge as dicotyledonous genus *Gossypium* (Malvaceae family). *Gossypium* genus has 45 diploids which are divided into 3 subgenera *Gossypium, Houzingenia,* and *Sturtia* according to geographical groups (Khadi *et al.,* 1970).

Various bacterial pathogens cause numerous diseases in several plant species (Lindeberg *et al.,* 2009; Martín-Sanz *et al.,* 2013). Among them, Pseudomonas are known as one of the pathogens to cause bacterial diseases associated with several infections. Species of *Pseudomonas* (Gram-negative bacteria) are generally aerobic bacilli measuring 0.5 to 0.8 µm by 1.5 to 3.0 µm and due to presence of single polar flagellum it is motile. *Pseudomonas* genus having more than 140 spp., mostly are saprophytic (Iglewski, 1996). In addition, bacterial blight is a common disease of cotton caused by *Xanthomonas axonopodis* pathovar. The disease attacks the stem, leaf, and bolls of the cotton plant. On the stem it is known as a black arm; on the leaf as an angular leaf spot; and on the boll, as boll spot and boll rot. The trouble is disseminated by infected seeds. Generally the most noticeable symptom of the disorder form on the leaves, where spots occurred that is the appearance of water-soaked, at first dark green, bounded by small veins, and angular in form (Rolfs, 1914). Thus, plant pathogens not only reduce crop yield with infections but also affects the economic value of the cotton plant.

The use of synthetic chemicals is dangerous to human health and the environment, demand increases the use of biologically active products such as essential oils, plant extracts, and medicinal plants are a natural source of antimicrobials to control microbial pathogens. Plants are an essential form for the production of novel CTA (Chemotherapeutic agents) (Agrawal *et al.,* 2012; Agrawal *et al.,* 2010; Soltania and Aliabadib, 2013). Mostly extracts of herbal plant parts have been utilized for their anti-bacterial activity.

Hills of Aravallis Sariska tiger reserve has its self-importance and certain features endowed with special biodiversity (Dular, 2015). Sariska National park (SNP) is located in the Alwar district of Rajasthan between the longitude (27*5'-27*33'N and 76*17'-76*34'E) latitude. Undulating area and around or on the hills *Anogeissus pendula* (Dhok) is the dominant species. Steep rocky areas growing species namely *Opuntia elatior* (Prickly pear), *Boswellia serrata* (Salar) and *Lannea coromandelica* (Garjan). *Zizyphus mauritiana* (Bordi), *Acacia catechu* (Khair), *Butea monosperma* (Dhak) and *Kydia calycina* (Pulao) are grown in valleys (Meena, 2018). In Sariska Tiger Reserve approximately 403 cultivated indigenous plants and 86 families belonging to 271 genera. This also involves 4 plant species belongs to *Pteridophytes* under 3 genus and 3 families as well as one plant species relates to Gymnosperm. Sariska used total number of 110 spp. of plants which are belongs to 43 families and 88 genera as a medicinal healer of several disease like as diarrhea, jaundice, dysentery, fever, skin problems, rheumatism and diabetes etc. (Jain *et al.*, 2009). The aim of this study analysis the effectiveness of methanolic extracts of plants such as *Desmodium gangeticum* resin, *Butea monosperma* flower, *Tribulus terrestris* fruit, *Pongamia pinnata* leaf, *Eclipta prostrate* leaf, *Cassia fistula* leaf, , *Argemone Mexicana* leaf, *Bauhinia racemose* leaf, *Terminalia bellerica* fruit, *Catharanthus roseus* leaf, *Euphorbia caducifolia* stem latex, *Euphorbia nerrifolia* stem latex, *Abrus precatorious* seeds and *Gloriosa superba* rhizome to control the cotton plant bacterial pathogen *Pseudomonas virdiflava.*

Materials and Methods

Collection of Plant Sample

The infected plant materials (leaf, seed and fruit) were collected from the Thanagazi, Umrain, Behror, and Mundawar areas of the Alwar district of Rajasthan from the farmer's field and ethanomedicinal plants were collected from Sariska National Park Area Alwar of Rajasthan.

Preparation of Methanolic Extracts

The collected fourteen Sariska medicinal plant parts were air dried in room temperature, followed by pounded into fine powder using grinder. By using Soxhlet extraction apparatus 5gm plant sample was extracted with 50ml methanol for 10 to 12 hours. Methanolic solution was filtered via Whattman No. 1 filer paper. Filtrate was concentrated by using flesh Rotary vacuum evaporator under reduced pressure at 90°C temperature. Sample can be store at -18°C for further studies (Nahak and Sahu, 2017).

Test Microorganism

Methanolic plant extracts examined antibacterial activity against *Pseudomonas viridiflava* isolation from infected cotton plant parts.

Antibacterial Screening of Extracts

In vitro antibacterial activity of the crude methanolic extract of Sariska plants was studied through well diffusion method against isolated pathogen's (Perez *et al.,* 1990). In the bacteriological medium Mueller Hinton agar no. 2 (Hi Media, India) was used. The 100% concentration was prepared from crude methanol extract according to 10mg/ml with dimethyl-sulphoxide (DMSO). Further dilution of 50% conc. was made with DMSO (Soltania and Aliabadib, 2013). Both 100% and 50% concentration were used for the experiment. The Mueller Hinton agar was prepared and sterilized by autoclaving at 15 lbs pressure (121°C) for 15mins. After sterilized media preparation, Mueller Hinton agar plates were prepared in Laminar Air Flow. A standardized bacterial inoculum has 1.5×108 CFU/mL, 0.5 McFarland was poured into sterile petri plates and allowed to stand for 30 second. After incubation, remaining non-adhere pathogenic bacteria culture was decanted. Further, in the nutrient agar plate wells of 6 mm diameter were prepared carefully. The extracts of plants (90 µl) were injected into the well. The desired temperature of 37°C agar plates was incubated. Determination of antimicrobial activity of the extract against pathogens was done by measuring inhibition diameter prepared around the each well. Inhibition zones of the each extract were compared with Dimethyl sulfoxide using as negative control. Inhibition annulus (IA) of each extract was measured (Smale and Keil, 1966; Thornberry, 1959). IA = π (R_1-R_2) (R_1 + R_2) Here, R_1 is radius of inhibition zone + radius of filter paper disc, R_2 is radius of filter paper disc and π value is 3.14.

Table 1: Medicinal plant species selected for antibacterial activity

Plants	Local name	Family	Part used	Uses
Desmodium gangeticum	Salparni	Paplionaceae	Roots and seeds	postnatal complaints, diarrhoea, chronic fever, cough, vomiting, and asthma
Butea monosperma	Dhak	Paplionaceae	Seeds gum	Enhances Digestive System, Treats Hypertension, Combats Skin Infections
Tribulus terrestris	Gokhru	Zygophyllaceae	Fruit	stone in urinary bladder
Pongamia pinnata	Karanj	Fabaceae	Tree	For migraine used leaf juice as a nasal drops. Treatment of dandruff in scalp applied seed powder.
Eclipta prostrata	Bhrangra	Asteraceae	Plant juice	jaundice and hair tonic
Cassia fistula	Amaltas	Caesalpiniaceae	Fruit pulp	treatment of inflammatory swellings and as a cleaning agent for ulcers and wounds
Argemone mexicana	Kateli	Papaveraceae	Root	chronic skin disease
Bauhinia racemosa	Bidi	Caesalpiniaceae	Stem bark	Weakness
Terminalia belerica	Bahera	Combretaceae	Fruit pulp unripe fruit	Purgative
Catharanthus roseus	Sadabaha	Apocynaceae	Leaf and stem	Anti-cancer activity
Euphorbia caducifolia	Danda-thor	Euphorbiaceae	Stem latex	treatment of bleeding wound, cutaneous eruption and other skin diseases
Euphorbia nerrifolia	Sehund	Euphorbiaceae	Stem latex	treatment of swelling, for purgation, cough, rhinitis
Abrus precatorious	Chirmi/Ratti	Paplionaceae	Seeds	nervous disorder
Gloriosa superba	Bachnag	Colchicaceae	Rhizome	Paste apply forehead and neck cure asthma in children

Results and Discussion

Ethano-medicinal plants have several applications especially anti-microbial activity; therefore they can be used as therapeutic agent. Nowadays bacterial diseases are continuously increasing also increases in antibiotic resistance, which enhanced several disorders (Austin *et al.,* 1999). In higher plants found antimicrobial compounds which is useful in development of new medicines. Herbal based drugs have more effective to control bacterial diseases (Karthikeyan *et al.,* 2012).

The significant inhibition annulus 2176.02 mm^2, 1406.72 mm^2, 1271.1 mm^2 and 1142.96 mm^2 were recognized with pure methanolic extract of *A. mexicana* leaf, *D. gangeticum* resin, *A. precatorious* seeds, *C. roseus* leaf, *P. pinnata* leaf, *T. bellerica* fruit and *G.superba* rhizome against *P. viridiflava* pathogen followed by *A.mexicana, A. precatorius* IA 1476.58 mm^2 and 1142mm^2 respectively at 50%. 100% methanolic extract play important role as compared to 50% concentration.

Karthikeyan *et al.,* 2012 reported that the methanolic extract showed the highest antibacterial (24±2.3mm) against *S. mutants* thereafter extracts of *D. gangeticum* such as chloroform, aqueous and ethanol. Due to the presence of bio-active constituents such as sterols, essential oil, terpenoids and alkaloids, methanolic extracts consider as higher antibacterial properties which may be increased by the existence of methanol and higher potentiality extraction of methanol form a huge number of biological active compounds important for anti-microbial potential compared with chloroform, ethanol and aqueous extracts. Likewise Dave *et al.,* 2019 reported the methanolic extract of *Butea monosperma* exhibits maximum diameter of inhibition against various test microorganisms namely *B. cereus* (21±0.45mm), *B. subtilis* (22±0.5 mm) and *S. aureus* (17±0.5mm). Extracts of methanol showed better anti-bacterial activity towards the test pathogens in comparison to the other extracts like aqueous and acetone. Additionally, compared with acetone extract, the yield of methanol extract notably increased, which may be due to the highest solubility with *Butea monosperma* active compounds that responsible to the enhancement of anti-microbial activity. Hirapure and Pote, 2014 examined the antibacterial activity of *N. arbortristis* Linn. chloroform and ethanol extract of stem bark, roots bark and leaf according to inhibition zone of bacterial pathogens. Both chloroform and ethanol extracts exhibited various anti-bacterial potential against all the bacterial strains with the ranges of 3 to 13mm. The *A. precatorius* seeds contain steroids, flavonoids, alkaloids, lectins, anthocyanins, and fixed oils that is helpful to showing therapeutic potential especially antimicrobial property (Aswin *et al.,* 2022). A study conducted by Orozco-Nunnelly *et al.,* 2021 reported that methanol extract of *A. mexicana* outer root and leaf possessed the strongest antimicrobial activity, with greatest effects against pathogenic bacteria.Latex of Euphorbia species is known for its use in traditional medicines.Several studies confirmed biological activity of Euphorbia extracts and pure compounds. These compounds could be used for the treatment of different diseases caused by different micro-organisms (Mishra and Parida, 2020).

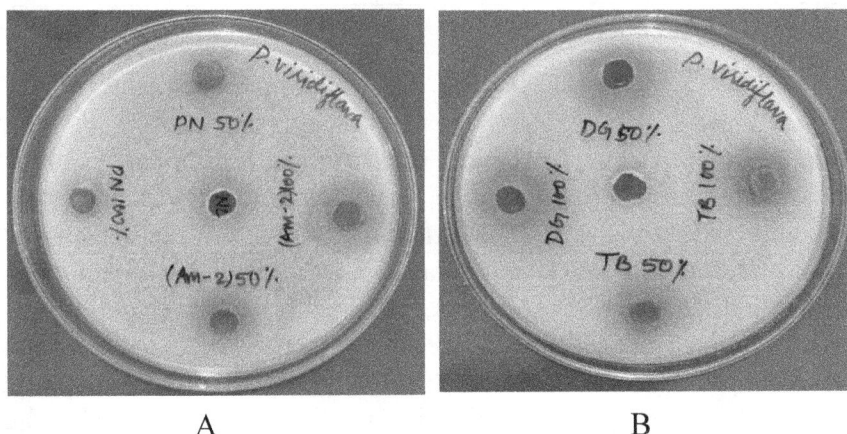

A   B

Figure 1: Maximum antibacterial activity of methanolic plant extract against *Pseudomonas virdiflava* A. *Argemone mexicana* leaf B. *Desmodium gangeticum*

Table 2: *In vitro* evaluation of methanolic plant extracts for inhibition of *Pseudomonas* virdiflava.

Methanol extract	Part used	*Pseudomonas viridiflava*	
		50% IA(mm^2)	100% IA(mm^2)
Desmodiumgangeticum	Resin	690.8	1406.72
Butea monosperma	Flower	794.42	904.32

Tribulus terrestris	Fruit	794.42	904.32
Pongamia pinnata	Leaf	904.32	1142.96
Eclipta prostrata	Leaf	741.82	794.42
Cassia fistula	Leaf	690.8	904.32
Argemone mexicana	Leaf	1476.58	2176.02
Bauhinia racemosa	Leaf	741.82	848.58
Terminalia bellerica	Fruit	904.32	1142.96
Catharanths roseus	Leaf	Nil	1271.1
Euphorbia caducifolia	Stem latex	Nil	690.8
Euphorbia nerrifolia	Stem latex	904.32	1020.5
Abrus precatorious	Seed	1142.96	1406.72
Gloriosa superba	Rhizome	690.8	1142.96

Conclusion

Pseudomonas virdiflava cause infection in cotton plants. The methanolic extracts of *Argemone mexicana* leaf showed maximum inhibition activity towards *Pseudomonas viridiflava* pathogens, at both 50% and 100% concentration. Other plant extracts also recognized as a good anti-bacterial agents. Overall, the results indicated that all 14 plants were prominent effective to inhibit bacterial pathogens. Hence, used Sariska plants extracts to inhibit harmful bacterial growth and their infection can be proved more effective in future due to being non-expensive, non-hazardous, and environmentally safe.

Acknowledgements

The authors are highly thankful to Principal Raj Rishi Govt. College, Alwar, Rajasthan for providing facilities and infrastructure and moreover his support to conduct the study. We also extend our thanks to the faculty members and staff of Department of Botany for their support in many ways.

References

Agrawal,K., Sharma, D.K., Jain, R., Jain, V.K. (2012). Seed borne bacterial diseases of tomato (*Lycopersicon esculentum* Mill) and their control measures: A review. J. Food Agri. Vat. Sci., 2, 173-182.

Agrawal, M., Bhagat, N., Agrawal, K. and Jain, R. (2010). Microbial quality of ready to eat products of groundnut. J. Phytological Res., 23(1), 105-107.

Aswin, R.K., Tridiganita, I.S., Arif, N.M.A., Gavrila, A.P., Dina, D.A., Gabrielle, A.V.P. (2022). *Abrus precatorius*: A comprehensive insight into the phytochemical, pharmacological, therapeutic activities and safety. Journal of Drug Delivery and Therapeutics, 12(1), 151-157.

Austin, D.J.,Kristinsson, K.G., Anderson, R.M. (1999).The relationship between the volume of antimicrobial consumption in human communities and the frequency of resistance. Proc Natl AcadSci USA; 96,11152-11156.

Dave, K., Darji, P. and Gandhi, F. (2019).Antimicrobial activity and phytochemical study of plant parts of *Butea monosperma.* Journal of Drug Delivery & Therapeutics, 9(4-A), 344-348.

Dular, A.K. (2015). Study of Some Fodder and Fuel Based Plants of Sariska Tiger Reserve in Aravallis. International Journal of Research and scientific innovation, 2(1), 129-133.

Iglewski, B.H. (1996). *Pseudomonas.* In: Baron S, editor. Medical Microbiology.4th edition. Galveston (TX): University of Texas Medical Branch at Galveston.

Jain, S.C., Jain, R., Singh, R. (2009). Ethnobotanical Survey of Sariska and Siliserh Regions from Alwar District of Rajasthan, India. Ethnobotanical Leaflets, 13, 171-88.

Karthikeyan, K., Selvam, S., Srinivasan, R., Chandran, C., Subramaniam, K. (2012). *In vitro* antibacterial activity of *Desmodium gangeticum* (L.) DG.Asian Pacific Journal of Tropical Disease.2, S421–S424.10.1016/S2222-1808(12)60195-9.

Khadi, B.M., Santhy, V., Yadav, M.S. (1970). Cotton: An Introduction. 10.1007/978-3-642-04796-1_1.

Lindeberg M, Cunnac, S., Collmer, A. (2009).The evolution of *Pseudomonas syringae* host specificity and type III effector repertoires. Mol. Plant Pathol, 10, 767-775.

Martín-Sanz A, Vega, M.P.D.L., Murillo, J. and Caminero, C. (2013). Strains of *Pseudomonas syringe* pv. syringae from pea are phylogenetically and pathogenically diverse. Phytopath, 103(7), 673-681.

Meena, R.C. (2018). Survey of Medicinal Plants in Sariska Tiger Reserve (Alwar). Shrinkhla Ek Shodh parak Vaicharik Patrika, 6 (1), 56-66.

Mishra, A. and Parida, S. (2020). Phytochemical and Antimicrobial Significance of Few Species Of Euphorbia. An international bilingual peer reviewed refereed research journal, 10(40), 82-89.

Nahak, G. and Sahu, R.K. (2017). Bio-controlling effect of leaf extract of *Tagetes patula* L. (Marigold) on growth parameters and diseases of tomato. Pak. J. Biol. Sci., 20, 12-19.

Orozco-Nunnelly, D.A., Pruet, J., Rios-Ibarra, C.P., Bocangel Gamarra, E.L., Lefeber, T., Najdeska, T. (2021). Characterizing the cytotoxic effects and several antimicrobial phytocompounds of *Argemone mexicana*. Plos one, 16(4), e0249704.

Perez, C., Paul, M. and Bazerque, P. (1990). An antibiotic assay by the agar-well diffusion method. Acta. Biol. Med. Exp., 15, 113-115.

Rolfs, F.M.(1914). Two Important Cotton Diseases and Their Control. 1-8.

Smale, M.J. and Keil, H.C. (1966). A biochemical study of the intervalrietal resistance of *Pyruscommunis* to fire blight. Phytochemistry, 5, 1113-1120.

Soltania, J. and Aliabadib, A.A. (2013). Antibacterial effects of several plant extracts and essential oils on *Xanthomonas arboricola* pv. Juglandis *in vitro*. J. of Essential Oil Bearing Plants, 16(4), 461-468.

Thornberry, H. (1959). A paper-disc plate method for the quantitative evaluation of fungicides and bactericides. Phytopathol., 40,950-954.

Dept. of Botany,
Raj Rishi Govt. College, Alwar (Raj.)
email : *pawan3223@gmail.com

17. Ethnobotany of Family Poaceae : Potential Medicinal Herbs for Tribes around The Globe

*Dr. Laxmikant Sharma and Ms. **Rinki Choudhary

Grasses, or more technically graminoids, are monocotyledonous, usually herbaceousplants with narrow leaves growing from the base. They include the "true grasses", of thePoaceae (or Gramineae) family, as well as the sedges (Cyperaceae) and the rushes (Juncaceae). The true grasses include cereals, bamboo and the grasses of lawns (turf) andgrassland. Sedges include many wild marsh and grassland plants, and some cultivated ones such as water chestnut (Eleocharis dulcis) and papyrus sedge (Cyperus papyrus). Uses for graminoids include food (as grain, sprouted grain, shoots or rhizomes), drink (beer, whisky, vodka), pasture for livestock, thatch, paper, fuel, clothing, insulation, construction, sports turf, basket weaving and many others.

Ecology

Graminoids are among the most versatile life forms. They became widespread toward the end of the Cretaceousperiod, and fossilized dinosaur dung (coprolites) have been found containing phytoliths of a variety of grasses that include grasses that are related to modern rice andbamboo. Grasses have adapted to conditions in lushrain forests, dry deserts, cold mountains and evenintertidal habitats, and are now the most widespread plant type; grass is a valuable source of food and energy for all sorts of wildlife and organics.

Graminoids are the dominant vegetation in many habitats, including grassland, salt-marsh, reedswamp and steppes. They also occur as a smaller part of the vegetation in almost every other terrestrial habitat. There are some 3,500 species of graminoids.

Many types of animals eat grass as their main source of food, and are called graminivores - these include cattle, sheep, horses,rabbits and many invertebrates, such as grasshoppers and the caterpillars of many brown butterflies. Grasses are also eaten byomnivorous or even occasionally by primarily carnivorous animals.

In the study of ecological communities, herbaceous plants are divided into graminoids and forbs, which are herbaceous dicotyledons, mostly with broad leaves.

Couch-Grass

Among these the Couch-grass (Agropyrum repens) is pre-eminent, though anything but a favourite with the farmer, for it has a slender, creeping rhizome, or underground stem, which extends for a considerable distance just beneath the surface of the ground, giving off lateral branches occasionally, and marked at intervals of about an inch by nodes, from which leaf-buds and slender branching roots are produced. These long, creeping, subterranean stems increase with great rapidity, and the smallest piece left in the ground will vegetate and quickly extend itself, so that it is almost impossible to extirpate it when once established in the soil, while its exhaustive powers render it very injurious to the crops. Its very name, Couch, is supposed to be derived from the Anglo-Saxon, civice (vivacious), on account of its tenacity of life. It is said that the only way to extirpate it, is to lay the ground down in pasture for some years, when the Couch will soon be destroyed by the close-growing Grasses, for it flourishes only in loose soil.

The name Agropyron is from the Greek agros (field), and puros (wheat).

On sandy seashores, the grass is often very abundant and assists in binding the sand and preventing the dunes from shifting, its long rhizome answering the purpose nearly as well as those of the Mat and Lyme Grasses.

Though commonly regarded in this country as a worthless and troublesome weed, its roots are, however, considered on the Continent to be wholesome food for cattle and horses. In Italy, especially, they are carefully gathered by the peasants and sold in the markets. The roots have a sweet taste, somewhat resembling liquorice, and Withering relates that, dried and ground into meal, bread has been made with them in time of scarcity.

Medicinal Action and Uses-Diuretic demulcent. Much used in cystitis and thetreatment of catarrhal diseases of the bladder. It palliates irritation of the urinary passages and gives relief in cases of gravel.

It is also recommended in gout and rheumatism. It is supposed to owe its diuretic effect to its sugar, and is best given in the form of an infusion, made from 1 OZ. to a pint of boiling water, which may be freely used taken in wineglassful doses. A decoction is also made by putting 2 to 4 oz. in a quart of water and reducing down to a pint by boiling. Of the liquid extract 1/2 to 2 teaspoonsful are given in water.

Darnel, Bearded

The Bearded Darnel, a common grass weed in English cornfields, is easily distinguished by its long glumes or awns and turgid, fruiting pales, containing the large grains, from the common Ray or Rye-grass (Lolium perenne), which is one of the best of the cultivated grasses, peculiarly adapted for both hay and pasture, especially in wet or uncertain climates. Both are often indiscriminately called Darnel or Ray-grass.

The seeds or grains of the Bearded Darnel were used medicinally by the ancient Greeks and Romans, but were never official in our Pharmacopoeia.

The admixture of the grain with those of the nutritious cereals amongst which it is often found growing should be guarded against, as its properties are generally regarded as deleterious. Gerard tells us: 'the new bread wherein Darnel is eaten hot causeth drunkenness. When Darnel has been given medicinally in a harmful quantity, it is recorded to have produced all the symptoms of drunkenness: a general trembling, followed by inability to walk, hindered speech and vomiting. For this reason the French call Darnel: 'Ivraie,' from Ivre (drunkenness); the word Darnel is itself of French origin and testifies to its intoxicating qualities, being derived from an old French word Darne, signifying stupefied. The ancients supposed it to cause blindness, hence with the Romans, lolio victitare, to live on Darnel, was a phrase applied to a dim-sighted person.

The alleged poisonous properties of Darnel are now generally believed to be due to a fungus.

Darnel is in some provincial districts known as Cheat, and there is reason to suspect that the old custom of using Darnel to adulterate malt and distilled liquors has not been entirely abandoned.

Culpepper terms it 'a pestilent enemy among the corn,' and in olden days its name was so commonly used as a synonym for a pernicious weed that it has been said that the expression in Matthew xiii. 25, would have been better translated Darnel than tares.

The Arabs still give the name zirwan to a noxious grass (which is only too common in the cornfields of Palestine) simulating the wheat when undeveloped, though easily distinguishable at 'harvest' time.

In connection with this similarity, it may be of interest to relate an experiment made by a friend of the writer. She procured some ears of Palestine wheat and also some of Palestine 'Darnel' ('tares'), for the purpose of illustrating the truth of the Parable of the Tares to her Bible class. After sowing both kinds in a patch of ground she asked her scholars to watch the appearance of the respective 'blades' as they appeared. They attached small strands of wool to distinguish each. In many cases wheat grew from the tare seeds, and tares from the wheat. It is said that the country people of Cheshire believed Darnel to be 'degenerated wheat.'

In the East it is a more serious enemy to the farmer, and in the low-lying districts of the Lebanon and other parts of Palestine it becomes alarmingly plentiful. If inadvertently eaten it produces sickness, dizziness, and diarrhoea. It would seem that the 'malice aforethought' of sowing this wild grass deliberately (as in our Lord's parable), was a not unusual practice. The following is a quotation from an old newspaper:

'The Country of Ill-Will is the by-name of a district hard by St. Arnaud, in the north of France. There tenants, when ejected by a landlord, or when they have ended their tenancy on uncomfortable terms, have been in the habit of spoiling the crop to come by vindictively sowing tares, and other coarse strangling weeds, among the wheat, whence has been derived the sinister name of the district. The practice has been made penal, and any man proved to have tampered with any other man's harvest will be dealt with as a criminal.'

Virgil speaks of 'unlucky darnel' (Georg., lib. i. 151-4) and groups it with thistles, thorns, and burs, among the enemies of the husbandman, and Shakespeare says: 'Darnel and all the idle weeds that grow in our sustaining corn.'

In the Middle Ages it was sometimes called Cokil, as well as Ray, and in the fourteenth century we hear of it being used against 'festour and morsowe,' and of Cokkilmeal being thought good for freckles and to make the face white and soft. Culpepper, after calling it 'a malicious part of sullen Saturn,' adds: 'as it is not without some vices, hath it also many virtues... the meal of darnel is very good to stay gangrenes; it also cleanseth the skin of all scurvy, morphews, ringworms, if it be used with salt and reddish (Radish) roots.' Also: 'a decoction thereof made with water and honey, and the places bathed therewith cures the sciatica,' and finally: 'Darnel meal applied in a poultice draweth forth splinters and broken bones in the flesh.'

Medicinal Action and Uses--Darnel is usually regarded as possessing sedative and anodyne properties. It was not only employed medicinally by the Greeks and Romans and in the Middle Ages, but in more modern practice in the form of a powder or pill in headache, rheumatic meningitis, sciatica and other cases. Cases are on record of serious effects having resulted from the use of bread, containing by accidental admixture the flour of Darnel seeds. Chemically the seeds contain an acrid fixed oil and a yellow glucoside, but as far as microscopical appearances indicate, the Darnel contains nothing that is not contained in wheat, and analysis has not yet revealed its poisonous elements.

Of late years, it has been questioned whether the ill-effects of Darnel are inherent in the grain themselves, or whether they may not be ascribed to their having been ergotized. Lindley in his Vegetable Kingdom takes the latter view, stating moreover, 'this is the only authentic instance of unwholesome qualities in the order of grasses," and Professor Henslow considers too that as the use of Darnel in the sixteenth century was similar to that of Ergot - a diseased condition of the grain of Rye-it is more probable that the injurious nature of Darnel has been due to an ergotized condition, especially as experiments have shown that perfectly healthy Darnel seeds have no injurious effects.

Vernal Grass, Sweet Scented

The Sweet-scented Vernal Grass - with yellow anthers, not purple, as so many other grasses gives its characteristic odour to newly mown meadow hay, and has a pleasant aroma of Woodruff. It is, however, specially provocative of hay fever and hay asthma. The flowers contain Coumarin, the same substance that is present in the Melilot flowers, and the volatile pollen impregnates the atmosphere in early summer, causing much distress to hay-fever subjects. The sweet perfume is due chiefly to benzoic acid.

A medicinal tincture is made from this grass with spirit of wine, and it said that if poured into the open hand and sniffed well into the nose, almost immediate relief is afforded during an attack of hay fever. It is recommended that 3 or 4 drops of the tincture be at the same time taken as a dose with water, repeated if required, at intervals of twenty to thirty minutes.

The name Anthoxanthum is from the Greek anthos (flower) and xanthos (yellow).

Scented Grasses

Among the Grasses may be included the SCENTED GRASSES, growing in tropical climates, largely cultivated in India, Ceylon and the Straits Settlements. They furnish very important essential oils for perfumery.

Lemongrass Oil is prepared from Cymbopogon citratus, formerly known as Andropogon Schoenanthus, a species growing abundantly in India and cultivated in Ceylon and Seychelles. It owes its scent almost entirely to its chief constituent, citral, and is one of the chief sources of the citral used in the manufacture of Tonone or artificial violet perfume. It is sometimes called Oil of Verbena from its similarity to the odour of the true Verbena Oil which is rarely found in commerce. It is frequently used to adulterate Lemon Oil. Samples of the oil produced experimentally in the West Indies, Uganda, and new districts of India were examined in the laboratories of the

Imperial Institute in 1911, and as a result of the recommendations made, the production of Lemongrass has been taken up on a considerable scale in Uganda.

Citronella Oil is derived from C. nardus, grown in Ceylon, Java and Burmah. The oil is distilled on an enormous scale and used for perfuming the cheapest household soaps and in the manufacture of coarse scents, and is also added as an adulterant to more expensive oils. Its scent is chiefly due to two substances, Geraniol and Citronellel.

Palmarosa, Rosha or Indian Geranium Oil, is derived from C. martine. It is grown in India and was formerly known as 'Turkish Geranium Oil, because it was imported into Europe via Turkey and Bulgaria as an adulterant to Otto of Roses. It has a strong geranium like odour and is used in the commercial preparation of pure Geraniol, its chief constituent. The distillation of this oil was started in the eighteenth century.

GINGERGRASS OIL is also the product of the last-named grass, an oil of poorer quality, which is only suitable for cheap perfumes.

Bibliography

- Chevalier, G., D. Mousain, Y. Couteaudier (1975). Associations ectomycorhiziennes entre Tubéracées et Cistacées. Annales de Phytopathologie 7(4), 355-356.
- Ferrandis, P., J. M. Herrantz, J. J. Martínez-Sánchez (1999). Effect of fire on hard-coated Cistaceae seed banks and its influence on techniques for quantifying seed banks. Plant Ecology 144 (1): 103-114. (Available online: DOI)
- Giovannetti, G, A. Fontana (1982). Mycorrhizal synthesis between Cistaceae and Tuberaceae. New Phytologist 92, 533-537.
- Hall, J. C.; Sytsma, K. J.; Iltis, H. H. (2002). "Phylogeny of Capparaceae and Brassicaceae based on chloroplast sequence data". American Journal of Botany 89 (11): 1826-42. doi:10.3732/ajb.89.11.1826. PMID 21665611.

- Heywood, V. H. (ed.) (1993), Flowering plants of the world, pp. 108-109. London: Batsford. ISBN 0-19-521037-9. Callaway, D.J. (1994). The World of Magnolias. Portland, Ongon, Timber Press. ISBN 0-88192-236-6
- Carlquist, S. 1971. Wood anatomy of Macaronesian and other Brassicaceae Aliso, 7/3: 365-384

- Laxmikant sharma(2022), Handbook of medicinal plants, pp. 30-36. ISBN 978-93-93857-22-4.

*Associate Professor,
**Research scholar,
Department of Botany,
Govt. R. R. College (Autonomous), Alwar,
Rajasthan

18. Role of Judiciary in Protecting Sustainable Development in India

Naveen

Abstract

Right to wholesome environment is a fundamental right protected under Article 21 of the Constitution of India. But the question is, can the environment be protected at present times when almost all the countries in South-East Asia are still at their developing stages? Development comes through industrialization, which in turn the main factor behind the degradation of environment. To resolve the issue, the experts worldwide have come up with a doctrine called 'Sustainable Development', i.e. there must be balance between development and ecology. Judiciary in India, more precisely, the Supreme Court and the High Courts has played an important role in preserving the doctrine of 'Sustainable Development'. Parliament has enacted various laws to deal with the problems of environmental degradation. In such a situation, the superior courts have played a pivotal role in interpreting those laws to suit the doctrine of 'Sustainable Development'. Sustainable development focuses on improving the quality standards of all human being in the earth without compromising the excessive use of natural resources beyond the capacity of the environment to supply them indefinitely; it requires and understanding that, this action has its consequences and we must find out innovative ways to change the institutional structures and individual behaviour, in other words it"s about taking action, changing policy and practice at all levels from the individualto international.

Keywords : Environment, Sustainable development, Judiciary, Constitution, Human being.

Introduction

The concept of 'Sustainable Development' is not a new concept. The doctrine had come to be known as early as in 1972 in the Stockholm declaration. It had been stated in the declaration that:

"Man has the fundamental right to freedom, equality and adequate conditions of life, in an environment of a quality that permits a life of dignity and well being and he bears a solemn responsibility to protect and improve the environment for present and future generation"

But the concept was given a definite shape in a report by world commission on environment, which was known as ' our common future'. The commission, which was chaired by the then Norway Prime Minister, Ms. G.H. Brundtland defined 'Sustainable Development' as:

"Development that meets the needs of the present without compromising the ability of the future generations to meet their own needs."

The report was popularly known as 'Brundtland report' the concept had been further discussed under agenda 21 of UN conference on environment and development held in June 1992 at Rio de Janeiro, Brazil.

Various Principles of 'Sustainable Development' :

Some of the basic principles of 'Sustainable Development' as described in'Brundtland report' are as follows:

a) **Inter-Generational Equity :** The principle talks about the right of every generation to get benefit from the natural resources. Principle 3 of the Rio declaration states that:

The right to development must be fulfilled so as to equitably meet developmental and environmental needs of present and future generations

The main object behind the principle is to ensure that the present generation should not abuse the non-renewable resources so as to deprive the future generation of its benefit.

b) **The Precautionary Principle :** This principle has widely been recognized as the most important principle of 'Sustainable Development'. Principle 15 the Rio declaration states that:

"In order to protect the environment, the precautionary approach shall be widely applied by States according to their capabilities. Where there are threats of serious or irreversible damage, lack of full scientific certainty shall not be used as a reason for postponing cost-effective measures to prevent environmental degradation."

1) Environmental measures by the state government and the local authority must anticipate, prevent and attack the causes of environmental degradation.
2) Where there are threats of serious and irreversible damage, lack of scientific certainty should not used as a reason for postponing measures to preventenvironmental degradation.
3) The 'onus of proof' is on the actor or the developer to proof that his action is environmentally benign.

c) **Polluter Pays Principle**
   Principle 16 of the Rio declaration states that:"
   National authorities should endeavor to promote the internalization of environmental costs and the use of economic instruments, taking into account the approach that the polluter should, in principle, bear the cost of pollution, with due regard to the public interest and without distorting international trade and investment."

From the beginning of the attendance in the Stockholm Conference in 1072, India has passed various major laws on environment, namely:

1. Water (Prevention and Control of Pollution) Act, 1974,
2. Air (Prevention and Control of Pollution) Act, 1981,
3. Environment (Protection) Act, 1986,
4. National Environment Tribunal Act, 1995,
5. National Green Tribunal Act, 2010.

The Supreme Court of India has also pointed out that the U.N. Conference on Human Environment created awareness for environment Protection.[1] The concept of Sustainable Development, was also introduced for the first time by the Stockholm Conference of 1972 and now a days this concept has been accepted as a part of the Customary International Law.[2]

In pursuance of United Nations Conference on Human Environment convened at Stockholm in 1972, the nations of the world decided to take appropriate steps to protect and improve human environment. The sequel to this, in India 42nd Amendment to the Indian constitution inserted articles 48-A directing the state to protect and improve the environment and to safeguard the forests and wildlife of the country and Article 51-A (g) mentioning fundamental duties of the citizens to protect and improve the natural environment including forests, lakes, rivers and wildlife and to have compassion for living creatures. The 42nd Amendment to the Indian Constitution also made certain changes in the seventh Schedule to the Constitution. Originally forest was a subject included in list II, entry 19.

since no uniform policy was being followed by the State in respect of protection of forests, now this subject has been transferred to List III and hence, now the parliament and state Legislature both may pass legislations. Protection of wild animals and birds has also been transferred from List II, Entry 20 to List III, Entry 17-B. 42nd Amendment Act for the first time inserted Entry 20-A in the List III which deals with population control and family planning because enormous increase in population is main cause for environmental problems. Under Article 253 of the Indian Constitution, the parliament is empowered to make any law for implementing any treaty, agreement or convention with any other country or countries or even any decision made at international conference, association or other body, this power is limited to implantation of decision and that too for a limited period.

The broad language of Article 253 suggests that in the wake of Stockholm Conference in 1972, Parliament has the power to legislate on all matters linked to the preservation of natural resources. This 42nd Amendment to Indian Constitution and insertion of Article 48-A and 51-A (g) marked the beginning of Environmental protection in India. Environmental Jurisprudence includes the laws, both statutory and judicial, concerning varied aspects of environmental protection and sustainable development. In India various laws have been enacted for the protection of environment. But the movement to protect environment got momentum with the judicial vigil in 1980s and 90s. Armed with the power of judicial review and constitutional scheme of independence of judiciary the Indian judiciary has performed a stellar role in protecting the environment and spreading environmental awareness among the Indian people.

The first case on which the apex court had applied the doctrine of ' Sustainable Development' was *Vellore Citizen Welfare Forum vs. Union of India*[3]. In the instant case, dispute arose over some tanneries in the state of Tamil Nadu. These tanneries were discharging effluents in the river Palar, which was the main source of drinking water in the state .The Hon'ble Supreme Court held that:

"We have no hesitation in holding that the precautionary principle and polluter pays principle are part of the environmental law of India."

The court also held that: Remediation of the damaged environment is part of the process of 'Sustainable Development' and as such polluter is liable to pay the cost to the individual sufferers as well as the cost of reversing the damaged ecology.

But before Vellore Citizen's case, the Supreme Court has in many cases tried to keep the balance between ecology and development. In *Rural Litigation and Entitlement Kendra Dehradun vs. State of Uttar Pradesh*[4], which was also known as Doon valley case, dispute arose over mining in the hilly areas. The Supreme Court after much investigation, ordered thestopping of mining work and held that:

"This would undoubtedly cause hardship to them, but it is a price that has to be paid for protecting and safeguarding the right of the people to live in healthy environment with minimal disturbance of ecological balance and without avoidable hazard to them and to their cattle, homes and agricultural land and undue affection of air, water and environment."

However in 1991, in the Rural Litigation and Entitlement Kendra vs. State of U.P.the Supreme Court allowed a mine to operate until the expiry of lease as exceptional case on condition that land taken on lease would be subjected to afforestation by the developer. But as soon as the notice was brought before the court that they have breached the condition and mining was done in most unscientific way, the Supreme Court directed the lessee to pay a compensation of three lacs to the fund of the monitoring committee. This has been directedon the principle of 'polluter pays'.

Likewise, various forests have also been protected. In a landmark case *Tarun Bhagat Singh vs. Union of India*[5], the petitioner through a PIL brought to the notice of the supreme court that the state government of Rajasthan though empowered to make rules to protect environment, failed to do so and in contrary allowed mining work to continue within the forest area. Consequently, the Supreme Court issued directions that no mining work or operation could be continued within the protected area.

Right to Water :

Various courts have upheld that the right to clean and safe water is an aspect of the right to life. For instance, in *Narmada Bachao Andolan v. Union of India*[6], the Supreme Court said that ¯water is the basic need for the survival of human beings and is part of right to life and human rights as enshrined in Article 21 of the Constitution of India . Pollution caused by tanning industry, existed in M. C. Mehta cases[7]. Though there is no reference to the right to life, the main judgment took for granted that the fundamental right is violated by the alleged pollution, and that this violation entails the court to interfere and issue directions for a remedy despite the mechanisms available in the Water Act.

In the supporting judgment, however, KN Singh J noted that the pollution of river Ganga is affecting the life, health and ecology of Indo-Gangetic plain and concluded that although the closure of tanneries might result in unemployment and loss of revenue; life, health and ecology had greater importance. The first time when the Supreme Court cameclose to declaring the right to environment in art 21 was in the early nineties. In *Chhetriya Pardushan Mukthi Sangarsh Samati v. State of Uttar Pradesh*[8], Sabyasachi Mukerjee CJ observed: Every citizen has a fundamental right to have the enjoyment of quality of life and living as contemplated in Art 21 of the Constitution of India.

In *MC Mehta v. Kamal Nath*,[9] it was made clear that any disturbance of the basic environmental elements, namely, air, water, and soil, which are necessary for life,,, would be hazardous to life,, within the meaning of art 21 of the Constitution,,. But judgments do not constitute law or policy; at best, they provide directions for the formulation of laws and policies. As yet, no laws or policies have been formulated asserting that water is a fundamental and inviolable right enjoyed by every citizen of the country. The right to water,, can therefore be obtained in India only on a case-by-case basis, by going to court.

Environment Protection and the Judiciary :

In *Virender Gaur v. State of Haryana*[10], the Apex Court confirmed that for every citizen, there exists a constitutional right to healthy environment and further conferred a mandatory duty on the state to protect and preserve this human right. Another landmark and revolutionary judgement is *Indian Council for Enviro-Legal Action vs. Union of India*, a case concerned serious damage by certain industries producing toxic chemicals to the environment of Bichchari District in Rajasthan. Directions for the closure of the industry were given and the decision in the Oleum Gas Leak case regarding absolute liability for pollution by hazardous industries was reaffirmed. Moreover, the polluter pays principle was explicitly applied for the first time in the Bichchari case.

Judicial Activism

Judicial awakening and activism for protection of the environment in India began formally after the 1972 Stockholm Conference on Human Environment. The term judicial activism denotes a process where at one end there are the logically principled rules in the hands of court and at other end there are demands, desires for expectations of society pressing it to accommodate with the framework of law. This process of accommodation by court is called the civilization of law and in term is known as activism. Environmental provisions are introduced in the Constitution of India by its 42nd amendment in 1974 under Article 48 (A) and 51-A (g) as a fundamental duty for every state and citizen of India to protect and improve the natural environment. Several laws pertaining to the protection of the environment were enacted in India prior to it. There were a number of public laws existed which had environmental overtones. The Indian Penal Code, 1860 and the Code of Criminal Procedure, 1973 dealing with public nuisance assume special significance in this regard.

The Environmental Protection Act, (EPA) of 1986 against industrial pollution and the Conservation of Forest and Natural Ecosystems Act of 1994 to stop deforestation and habitat destruction are, among others, good pieces of legislation for the protection of the environment in India. Public Interest Litigation (PIL) to prevent environmental degradation has been increasing in India and the judiciary has come to rescue the people on a number of occasions. There are several historic judicial decisions serving both man and environment in India. It can be seen that the Supreme Court of India has moulded a far-reaching and innovative environmental jurisprudence which no other constitutional court anywhere in the world has ever given shape to.

Public Interest Litigation :

Public Interest Litigation has had a profound effect on the development of environmental law in India. PIL allows any bona fide person to take a matter of public interest to the higher judiciary, even when the person who is supporting the cause is not personally or directly affected by the interest that is being brought to the courts.

The concept of public interest litigation (PIL) is well entrenched in India contrary to the past practices[11], today a person acting bonafide and having sufficient interest can move the courts for redressing public injury, enforcing public duty, protecting social and collective rights and interests, and vindicating public interest[12]. In the eighties and nineties, a wave of environmental litigation was witnessed. Most of such cases were in the form of class action and PIL, as environmental issues relate to diffusing of interests, rather than to ascertainable injury to individuals.

The concept of class action is embodied in the Code of Civil Procedure 1908, where if numerous persons have common interests, one or more of such persons can file a suit. A recent example of class action is the Bhopal Gas Leak disaster litigation. This community interest can also be agitated under the law of public nuisance incorporated in the CrPC. An individual, a group of individuals, or an executive magistrate, suo motu, can move the courts. This provision has proved to be a potent weapon for regulatory measures[13], as well as affirmative action516 by the government and local bodies for protection of the environment, provided that the executive magistrates exercise their discretion independently without undue influence from their bureaucratic or political superiors.

To summarize the environmental issues that have been brought to the courts underPILs in the past include,

- Riverine pollution by tanneries, industrial effluents, and untreated sewage;
- Soil and groundwater pollution;
- Indiscriminate mining;
- Protection of forests;
- Fencing of parks and sanctuaries;
- Preservation of monuments of archaeological and historical significance and their protection from vandalism and industrial pollutants; and
- Automobile pollution.

The judicial prescriptions have included

- Remedial measures offered by cleanup technologies;
- Liability measures based on application of the ¯polluter pays principle ; ?
- Revised environmental standards.

Tanneries and Discharge of Effluents :

Under the laws of the land the responsibility for treatment of the industrial effluents is that of the industry. However, it has been noticed that various tanneries operating in different parts of the country have not been complying with the laws of the land. They have been discharging effluents without any treatment and thus becoming one of the major sources of pollution. The courts in such cases have issued directions to such tanneries to either install primary treatment plant or stop working. The judiciary in India has followed the path of sustainable development in such case as well.

In *M.C. Mehta v. Union of India*[14], (popularly known as Ganga Water Pollution case or Kanpur tanneries case), a public interest litigation was filed for the issuance of directions restraining the tanneries from discharging trade effluent into the river Ganga till such time they put up necessary treatment plants for treating the trade effluents in order to arrest the pollution of water in the said river. The tanneries discharging effluents in the river Ganga did not set up primary treatment plant in spite of being asked to do so for several years. Nor did they care to put up an appearance in the Supreme Court expressing their willingness to set up pre-treatment plant. Consequently, the Supreme Court directed them to stop working.

Conclusion

The formulation and recognition of various doctrines and strategies signify a judicial awareness on the need for reconciliation of the developmental, socio-economic, and ecological conflicts in the present day Indian society. This awareness is reflected in the cases that came before the courts for review. Man must live and he must live well, in a healthy and safe atmosphere - this has been the judicial dictum and its entire efforts have been directed towards achieving that goal. It has, therefore, evolved diverse principles such as absolute liability, and public trust doctrine to preserve the human environment and to uphold man,,s right to live in a wholesome environment. It has ordered the closure of hazardous industries, the shifting of the place of industrial operation and the imposition of criminal responsibility on directors, for their failure in taking necessary anti-pollution measures.

The court has also directed the payment of compensation to victims of environmentalcalamities. It has clearly specified that there can be no compromise with environmental preservation; it has to be done to ensure the survival of the coming generations and to give them a life with human dignity. The Apex Court has also opined that the High Court has the proper authority to consider what should be the appropriate remedy for such type of cases. The decisions of the Apex Court, while strengthening the application of the principle of polluter pays, also adds new dimension regarding the qualification of punishment under this principle, though, the Apex Court has been silent about developing sound principles of quantification of pecuniary liability.

References

1. Rural Litigation and Entitlement Kendra Vs State of U.P. 1986 Supp SCC 517;Vellore Citizens' Welfare Forum Vs Union of India, (1996) 5 SCC 647; M.C. Mehta Vs Union of India, (1992) 1 SCC 358: M.C. Mehta

2. Vs Kamal Nath, (2000) 6 SCC 213.

3. Shastri. C. S, 2005. Environment Law. 2nd ed. New Delhi: Eastern Book Company.

4. AIR 1996 SC 2715

5. 1985 AIR 652

6. 1993 SCR (3) 21

7. AIR 2000 SC 3751, pp3825, 3830.

8. MC.Mehta v. Union of India AIR 1988 SC 1037. The tanning industries located on the banks of Ganga were alleged to be polluting the river. The court issued directions to them to set up effluent plants within six months from the date of the order. It was specified that failure to do so would entail closure of business.

9. AIR 1990 SC 2060.

10. AIR 2000 SC 1997, PP 2000,2003.

11. (1995) 2 SCC 577, (1997) 10 JT 600.1994 (

12. Locus standi was the biggest hurdle. JM Desai v. Roshan Kumar AIR 1976 SC 578

13. SP Gupta and others v. Union of India, AIR 1982 SC 149

14. State of Madhya Pradesh v. Kedia Leather and Liquor Ltd, (2003) 7 SCC389.

15. AIR 1988 SC 1037. See also MC Mehta v. Union of India, AIR 1988 SC 1115; MC Mehta v. Union of India,1991 Supp (1) SCC 181 and MC Mehta v. Union of India, 1992 Supp (2) SCC 637; MC Mehta v. Union of India, 1992 Supp (2) SCC 633; MC Mehta v. Union of India, 1993 Supp (1) SCC 434.

Registered as an Advocate on the Roll of Bar Council,
Punjab and Haryana
navhimshi@gmail.com

19. Green Chemistry and their Twelve Principles for Sustainable Development of Environment

D.T. Sakhare

Abstract

This paper provides an overview of applicability twelve principles and future trends of Green Chemistry. Green or Sustainable Chemistry is a term that refers to the creation of chemical products and processes that reduce or eliminate the use and production of harmful substances. They are used exclusively chemicals and chemical processes that do not have negative consequences for the environment. It is based on twelve principles that can be used to initially create or recreate molecules, materials, reactions and processes that are safer for human health and the environment. The processes of the Green Chemistry that have been developed to date include almost all areas of chemistry, including organic, inorganic, biochemistry, polymer, toxicology, environmental, physical, technological, etc. Through the several prevailing trends of the green program such as catalysis, biocatalysis and the use of alternative: renewable feedstock (biomass), reaction media (water, ionic liquids and supercritical fluids), reaction conditions (microwave irradiation) and new synthetic pathways (photocatalytic reaction), the dual goals – environmental protection and economic benefit can be achieved. This article shows examples of the prevailing trends in ways that Green Chemistry reduces the impact of chemical processes and technologies on the environment.

Keywords : Green Chemistry, Biocatalysis, Biomass, Ionic Liquids, Supercritical Fluids, Microwave Irradiation, Photocatalysis.

1. Introduction

Green Chemistry is defined as the "design of chemical products and processes to reduce or eliminate the use and generation of hazardous substances."[1,2]. This definition and the concept of Green Chemistry were first formulated at the beginning of the 1990s nearly 20 years ago [3]. In the years since, there has been international adoption that resulted in the creation of literally hundreds of programs and governmental initiatives on Green Chemistry around the world with initial leading programs located in the U.S., United Kingdom, and Italy [4]. These have played a significant role in informing sustainable design [5] Important early programs include the US Presidential Green Chemistry Challenge Awards established in 1995 [6]. the Green Chemistry Institute founded in 1997 [7] and the publication of the first volume of the now well-established Green Chemistry journal of the Royal Society of Chemistry in 1999 [8].

The most important aspect of Green Chemistry is the concept of design. Design is a statement of human intention and one cannot do design by accident. It includes novelty, planning and systematic conception. The Twelve Principles of Green Chemistry are "design rules" to help chemists achieve the intentional goal of sustainability. Green Chemistry is characterized by careful planning of chemical synthesis and molecular design to reduce adverse consequences. Through proper design one can achieve synergies—not merely trade-offs.

The Green Chemistry approach strives to achieve sustainability at the molecular level. Because of this goal, it is not surprising it has been applied to all industry sectors. From aerospace, automobile, cosmetic, electronics, energy, household products, pharmaceutical, to agriculture, there are hundreds of examples of successful applications of award winning, economically competitive technologies [9].

The concept of Green Chemistry has had this large impact due to the fact that it goes beyond the research laboratory in isolation and has touched industry, education, environment, and the general public. The field of Green Chemistry has demonstrated how chemists can design next generation products and processes so that they are profitable while being good for human health and the environment. Following the scientific enthusiasm of Green Chemistry, teaching initiatives, governmental funding, and the establishment of Green Chemistry Research Centers have multiplied in the past two decades. Many universities now offer classes on Green Chemistry and Green Engineering. Some institutions offer degrees in the field.

Governmental funding has also increased in several countries around the world [10].

1.1 Importance of Green Chemistry : Prevents pollution at the molecular level. Is a philosophy that applies to all areas of chemistry, not a single discipline of chemistry. Applies innovative scientific solutions to real-world environmental problems. Results in source reduction because it prevents the generation of pollution. Reduces the negative impacts of chemical products and processes on human health and the environment. Lessens and sometimes eliminates hazard from existing products and processes. Designs chemical products and processes to reduce their intrinsic hazards.

1.2 Chemistry & Society Pharmaceutical : Drugs (pain killers, antibiotics, heart and hypertensive drugs), disinfectants,vaccines, dental fillings, anesthetics, contraceptives. **Agriculture :** Fertilizers, pesticides. **Food:** Preservatives, packaging and food wraps, refrigerants. **Transportation:** Petrol and diesel, catalytic converters to reduce exhaust emissions. **Clothing:** Synthetic fibres, dyes, waterproofing materials. **Safety:**Polycarbonate materials for crash helmets. Sports:Composite materials for rackets, all weather surfaces Office inks, photocopying toners. **Homes:** Paints, vanishes and polish, detergents, pest killers.

1.3 History Of Green Chemistry :

1. In 1990 the Pollution Prevention Act was passed in the United States. This act helped create a modus operandi for dealing with pollution in an original and innovative way. This paved the way to the green chemistry concept.
2. Paul Anastas and John Warner coined the two letter word "green chemistry" and developed the twelve principles of green chemistry.
3. In 2005 Ryoji Noyori identified three key developments in green chemistry: use of supercritical carbon dioxide as green solvent, aqueous hydrogen peroxide for clean oxidations and the use of hydrogen in asymmetric synthesis.

1.4 Global Recognition of Green Chemistry : Australia: The Royal Australian Chemical Institute (RACI) presents Australia's Green Chemistry Challenge Awards. Canada: The Canadian Green

Chemistry Medal is an annual award given to any individual or group for promotion and development of green chemistry Italy: Green Chemistry activities in Italy centre on inter-university consortium known as INCA. In 1999, INCA has given three awards annually to industry for applications of green chemistry. Japan: In Japan, The Green & Sustainable Chemistry Network (GSCN), formed in 1999, is an organization consisting of representatives from chemical manufacturers and researcher. UK: In the United Kingdom, the Crystal Faraday Partnership, a non-profit group founded in 2001, awards businesses annually for incorporation of green chemistry. USA: United States Environmental Protection Agency (EPA).

1.5 Nobel Prize in Green chemistry :

.The Nobel Prize Committee recognized the importance of green chemistry in 2005 by awarding Yves Chauvin, Robert H. Grubbs, and Richard R. Schrock the Nobel Prize for Chemistry for "the development of the metathesis method in organic synthesis. 2. Frances Arnold won in 2018, it for the directed evolution of enzymes, a technique she has pioneered over the past 25 years and has used to pursue new avenues within green chemistry and to engineer reactions completely new to nature.

1.6 Green Chemistry and Sustainable Development : The UN defines sustainable development as 'meeting the needs of present without compromising the ability of future generation. Green chemistry focuses on how to achieve sustainability through science and technology. To better understand and solve the issue of environmental pollution, many approaches and models have been developed for environmental impact assessments. Some of these approaches and models have been successful in predicting impacts for selected chemicals in selected environmental settings. These models have joined air and water quality aspects to point and nonpoint sources and have been very useful for the development of emission control and compliance strategies. However, some of the approaches and models were aimed primarily at evaluating the quantity of pollutants that could be discharged into the environment with acceptable impact, but failed to focus on pollution prevention. However, some of the approaches and models were aimed primarily at evaluating the quantity of pollutants that could be discharged into the environment with acceptable impact, but failed to focus on pollution prevention. The concept of end-of-pipe approaches to waste management decreased, and strategies such as environmentally conscious manufacturing, eco-efficient production, or pollution prevention gained recognition.

2. Green Chemistry

(Green color is the color of chlorophyll and the color of the dollar. Being a green series of years is a battleground of environmental activists, and becoming a green becoming a trend in product marketing. And for chemists it becomes imperative to be green in applying the principles of green chemistry in all aspects of chemical sciences, in fundamental and applied research, production and education. [11].

2.1. Definition of Green Chemistry

According to the EPA definition, green chemistry is defined as a chemistry that designs chemical products and processes that are harmless to the environment, thus preventing the formation of pollution. Chemical products should be made so that they do not remain in the environment at the end of their application and that they are broken down into components that are harmless to the environment. Saving based on efficient synthesis without the use of "exotic" reagents, reducing the required energy, and replacing organic solvents with water are significant even at the laboratory level, while in industrial scale possible millions of savings [12].

Green chemistry is not a separate scientific discipline, but a responsible interdisciplinary approach to science, based on chemical, ecological and social responsibility, which enables creativity and the advancement of innovative research [13]. As a propulsive area of research, it tries to find and maintain a balance between the use of natural resources, economic growth and environmental conservation.

2.2. Trends in Green Chemistry

Green chemistry "program for the design, development and application of chemical products and processes that reduce or eliminate the use or production of substances that are hazardous to human health and the environment" and to achieving the main goals of the green program comes through several dominant trends [14] :

a. Research in the field of catalytic and biocatalytic reactions in order to obtain highly selective, pure compounds without the formation of toxic byproducts;
b. Seeking new raw materials, harmless and renewable, such as biomass;
c. Designing less toxic eco-compatible chemicals;
d. Finding and testing new alternative, non-toxic and renewable reaction media such as water, ionic liquids and supercritical fluids
e. Finding and testing new alternative reaction conditions, such as microwave, ultrasound and light reacting
f. Exploration of alternative routes for the purification of poisoned air and water to improve their quality, such as photocatalytic reactions [14].

Realizing the set goals, "green chemistry changes steady industrial practice - produces, pollutes, and then cleanses, and in the late twentieth century becomes the heart and soul of industrial ecology" [14].

Green chemistry is a Hippocratic oath for chemists, and in order to preserve natural resources and the environment, a new generation of scientists and technologists is being developed, which economically analyze the processes and materials used in production and development. Green chemistry or ecologically harmless, harmless and sustainable chemistry is the manufacture and application of chemical products and processes that reduce or eliminate the use and creation of hazardous substances. Instead of limiting the risk by controlling exposure to harmful chemicals, green chemistry seeks to reduce, and possibly eliminate, the danger, denying the need for exposure control. If no hazardous substances are used or produced, then the risk is zero and there is no need to worry about removing hazardous substances from the environment or limiting exposure to them or "Green chemistry is about reducing waste, raw materials, risks, energy, environmental impact and cost" [14].

3. Twelve Principles of Green Chemistry

Twelve principles of green chemistry have been developed by Paul Anastas and John Warner of EPA, and in their Green Chemistry Theory and Practice book, 1998, they explained their meaning in practice. The principles of green chemistry speak about the reduction or removal of dangerous or harmful substances from the synthesis, production and application of chemical products and thus the use of substances dangerous to human health and the environment is reduced or eliminated. When designing a green chemistry process, it is impossible to meet the requirements of all twelve principles of the process at the same time, but it attempts to apply as many principles as possible during certain stages of synthesis.

Twelve Principles of Green Chemistry :
1. Prevent Waste.
2. Atom Economy.
3. Less hazardous synthesis.
4. Design Benign Chemicals.
5. Benign Solvents and auxiliaries.
6. Design for energy efficiency.
7. Use of renewable feedstock's.
8. Reduce derivatives.
9. Catalysis
10. Design for degradation.
11. Real time analysis for pollution prevention.
12. Inherently benign chemistry for accident prevention
The twelve principles as shown in below Fig.1

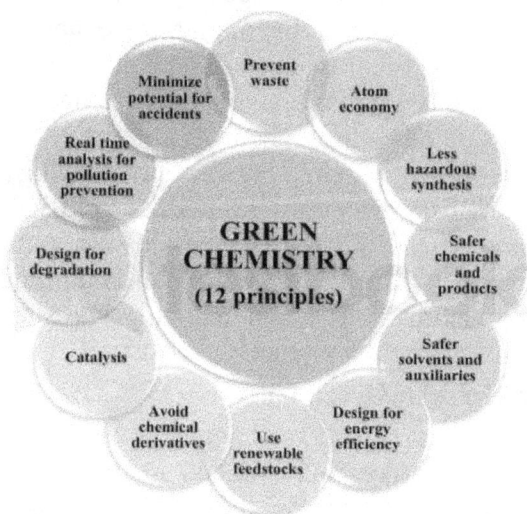

Fig. 1 Twelve Principles Of Green Chemistry

3.1. Prevention :

It is better to check or avoid the synthesis of hazardous, toxic, explosive, bio-accumulative and waste chemical product rather than to treat or clean up [15].

For example :

(a) Check or avoid over manufacturing/synthesis of nuclear and non-nuclear weapons, explosive and harmful bio-chemical substances from various developed and developing countries because it create various type of environmental pollution and human diseases [16].

(b) Check or avoid over exploitation of natural resources like coal and petroleum because its burning produces various harmful gases like oxides of carbon and oxides of nitrogen and sulphur which result into global warming and acid rain respectively [17].

(c) Check or avoid the over production of bio-accumulative, bio-transforming, non-biodegradable substances like polythene, Aldrin, Chlordane, DDT, and methyl mercury compounds[18].

Pollution Prevention : Drive smaller, more efficient cars, Take the commuter train, Riding a bike, Fix a leaky faucet, Recycle paper or compost leaves.

3.2. Atom Economy :

Synthetic methods should be designed to maximize the incorporation of all materials used in the process into the final product. The principle of Atom Economy is logically linked to the principle of waste prevention, since it requires all raw materials used in production to maximize utilization or inclusion in the final product to ultimately reduce the amount of waste. This means that the chemical synthesis should be designed in such a way that the final product maximizes the input of raw materials or design such synthetic products that will use the entire material used for synthesis in the final product.

The principle of increasing atomic usability was defined in 1991 by Barry Trost of Stanford University. Trost believes that introducing the concept of usability atoms is essentially the prevention of waste at the molecular level. Barry Trost's concept initiated the redesign of existing synthetic reactions until then established on the principle of "making a product regardless of price". These modifications are useful and because they generally lead to increased yields.

155

There is a known progress in the synthesis of ibuprofen [19]. The main problem of old synthesis (boots process) is low economic cost, because the utilization of input raw materials is only about 40%. In the 1990s a new "green" method of ibuprofen synthesis was developed, involving only three steps, and almost all transitional materials were converted to the product (up to 99%) or regenerated and returned in the process and almost almost eliminated the generation of waste materials And this process is one of the processes of "green synthesis" [20, 21].

Design the chemical processes in such a way that the final product contains maximum proportion of the reactant or the starting raw materials and leaving a few numbers of atoms of raw materials[22].

Example :

Calculation of atom economy When one mole of Benzene react with 4 ½ mole of oxygen molecule then it produced one mole of maleic anhydride and 2 mole of carbon dioxide and 2mole of Water [23].

Atom economy= (mass of atom in desired product/mass of atomic reactant)*100

$$= (98/222)*100$$
$$= 44.1\%$$

3.3 Less Hazardous Chemical Synthesis :

The Less Hazardous Chemical Synthesis advocates, wherever possible, the creation of synthetic methods for the use and creation of substances that are little or no toxic to human health and the environment. Replacing harmful chemicals with biological enzymes makes many industrial processes cleaner and cheaper [24].

Design the chemical processes/product in such a way that use and generation of chemical substances should not exceed the critical limit of toxicity to avoid environmental deterioration and harmful for human being.

Example :

(a) Avoid the synthesis of chemicals like organ mercurial's compounds; which caused minamata disaster [25].

(b) Avoid the synthesis of methyl isocynate (MIC); which caused Bhopal gas tragedy [26].

3.4. Design Benign Chemicals :

An example is the production of polymers of polyphenylene sulfone (PPSU), which is now widely used for indoor airplanes and is also introduced in underground trains where it is also important to use non-flammable materials. It is a new engineering plastic characterized by a unique combination of useful environmental, mechanical, and flame resistant properties [27]

Chemical processes and products should be designed in such a way that, it is highly selective in nature and affect their desired functions and minimizing their toxicity, bio-accumulation and bio-transformation.

Example :

2, 4-D: It is a selective pesticide which selectively kills only broad leaf weeds[28].

3.5 Benign Solvents and Auxiliaries :

The use of auxiliary substances (e.g., solvents, separation agents, etc.) should be made unnecessary wherever possible and innocuous when used.

Chromatographic separations, where large quantities of solvents are used, are problematic due to environmental pollution. Most conventional organic solvents are toxic, flammable and corrosive. Their recycling is linked to energyefficientdistillation with considerable losses and therefore the development of environmentally-friendly solvents is necessary. For now, it is promising to replace the known organic solvents with recyclable solvents, which are ionic liquids - salts at room temperature in the liquid state. Unlike volatile organic compounds, ionic liquids have low vapor pressure, do not vaporise and do so easily, resulting in safer chemical processes [29].

The use of auxiliaries substances in the form of solvents, separating agent, extractive agent should be nontoxic, non- explosive, non-hazardous, non- cancer causing, non-bio accumulated and non-mutation inducing.

Example :

Super critical Carbon dioxide is a better solvent because it is a non-toxic and non- explosive fluid [30].

3.6 Design for Energy Efficiency :

Energy requirements of chemical processes should be recognized for their environmental and economic impacts and should be minimized. If possible, synthetic methods should be conducted at ambient temperature and pressure.

The oil crisis in 1973 has initiated the development of a number of processes in which energy savings are taken into account, with the aim of exploiting every kJ of energy in the production process. Following the above-mentioned Principle of Energy Efficiency, whose other name is Design for Energy Efficiency, as a fundamental requirement, minimizes the use of energy. The possible ways to improve energy efficiency in the chemical industry [31].

It is necessary to design the chemical processes /products in such a way that it utilizes less energy to form desired product, this can accompanied by keeping the chemical processes at ambient temperature and pressure in the presence of suitable catalyst.

Example:

Formation of ammonia from Haber's process [32].

$$N_2 + 3H_2 \rightarrow 2NH_3$$

Temperature = 673-723 Kelvin, pressure = 200 atm, catalyst = Iron

3.7 Use Of Renewable Feedstock'S :

The seventh principle of green chemistry advocates Use of Renewable Feedstocks wherever it is technically and economically acceptable. For example, it is more convenient to use renewable raw materials than a variety of plastic materials, and then to waste away the waste materials. Because of this, the making of biodegradable plastic materials is a current trend. Biodegradable packaging has a future in the food industry. Numerous factors, including politics and changes in legislation, as well as global demand for food and energy resources, certainly affect the development of biodegradable packaging [33].

In the case of bioplastics, the use of renewable raw materials in production positively affects energy consumption and CO_2 emissions. Coca-Cola, a world-widescale company for the time being, manufactures bottles made of 30% polyethylene (PE) blends, while American company NatureWorks uses bottles made from lactic acid polymers (PLA) made from lactic acid, obtained by fermentation of dextrose obtained from starch, Most commonly corn. About 1 kg of PLA requires about 2.5 kg of corn [34].

For sustainable development, it is better to avoid exploitation of non-renewable natural resources like petroleum, coal and natural gas etc.

But use of renewable resources for its sustainable development did not create much problem because it is restored by natural processes and biogeochemical cycle.

Example :

Formation of furfural from bagasse and waste biomass of wheat and rice plant etc [35]

3.8 Reduce Chemical Derivatives :

During a chemical processes, waste product are formed or generated if additional chemical reagent are used to block or protect any groups, so avoid such type of blocking, protecting groups or even any modifications, if possible.

Reduced usage of derivatives and protecting groups in the synthesis of target molecules is one of the main concepts of green chemistry. Derivatization demands the consumption of additional energy and reagents, as well as the formation of additional waste during the synthesis. It also involves the application of protective or deprotecting substances, as well as any short-term changes to the physical and chemical process. The selection of the protective group is a critical aspect in the effective implementation of a synthetic process. The choice of the protective group has a significant impact on the overall efficiency and length of the synthetic process. Selectivity in the reaction will be induced by derivatizing the desired reactive site to make it more receptive to the reacting species. Using derivatives as little as possible in chemical synthesis can be achieved by avoiding the use of protecting groups which will result in an increase of atom economy on the reaction.

A prominent example is the manufacturing of penicillin-based antibiotics (Fig.2) or the substitution of traditional chemical enzymatic techniques in which 6-aminopenicillic acid is produced by interacting with the catalyzed immobilized enzyme penicillin amide. This resulted in the substitution of many chemical processes by an enzymatic reaction, which no longer required a low temperature (-60°C), organic solvents, and completely improper conditions, which increased and complicated production in the case of chemical synthesis [36].

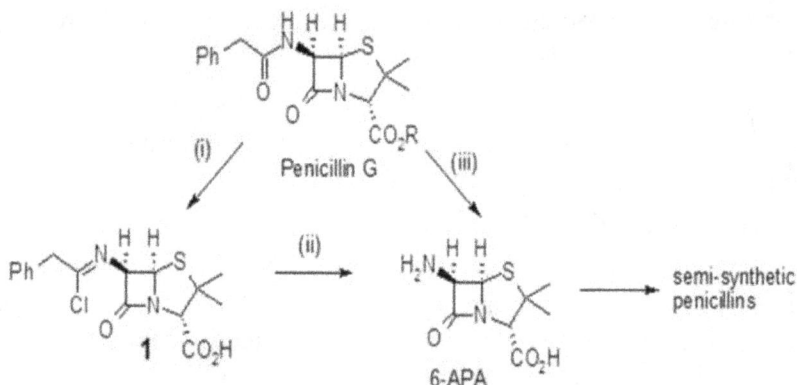

Fig.2: Synthesis of 6-aminopenicilic acid catalyzed by immobilized penicillin G amide.

In this manner another newer technique involving greener route to produce ethanal commercially can be prepared by oxidation of ethene, in the presence of an ionic catalyst in an aqueous medium. This is also greener method and gives 90% of yield.

Likewise, Tetrachloroethene was used as a solvent for dry cleaning purposes. It is a suspected carcinogen and groundwater contaminant. It is replaced by greener solvent like supercritical CO_2.

The synthetic methods should avoid using or generating substances toxic to humans and/or the environment. Hence less hazardous chemical synthesis is an important principle.

Photochemical reaction occurs when light energy gets absorbed by a substances' molecule. It is a green route as no by product will be formed. Vitamin D3 synthesis is assisted by a photochemical reaction.

We were bleach the paper, by using chlorine gas because it have excellent oxidising characteristics. Now H_2O_2 with a proper catalyst is being utilised for bleaching since it does not pollute groundwater. Halogenated solvents contaminate groundwater. Whereas liquified CO_2 leaves a lower amount of residue. It is also a non-toxic and attractive solvent for temperature-sensitive materials.

Hydrogen peroxide can easily breakdown into water and oxygen. It is a good oxidizing agent and a strong bleaching agent. Use of H_2O_2 gives better results and makes use of a lesser amount of water.

When compared to conventional solvents, liquified CO_2 leaves a lower amount of residue. It is also a non-toxic and attractive solvent for temperature-sensitive materials

thus these all are excellent example of Green Chemistry making a genuine difference.

Example:

Use of enzymes to avoid protecting groups and cleanup process is the industrial synthesis of semi synthetic antibiotics such as ampicillin and amoxicillin [37].

3.9 Catalyst:

In order to protect the environment, the catalysis principle promotes the use of biodegradable catalysts, which imply less energy use, avoiding the use of organochlorine compounds and reducing the use of water or less waste water.

Like all catalysts, enzymes function in a way that lowers the activation energy of an individual reaction, and thus accelerates, up to several million times. In doing so, the enzyme remains unchanged throughout the duration of the reaction to which it affects, and this allows it to become completely unchanged when the reaction comes to an end. Also, enzymes do not affect the relative energy between the reactants and the products, nor to the related reactions.

Catalyst is the chemical substance which is used in small quantities, enhance the rate of reaction by decreasing activation energy and regenerate itself at the end of reaction [38]. But the stoichiometric reagent are used in large quantities and do not generate at the end of reaction [39].

Example:

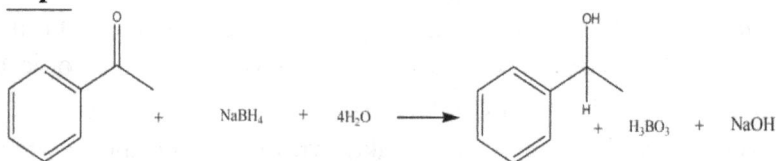

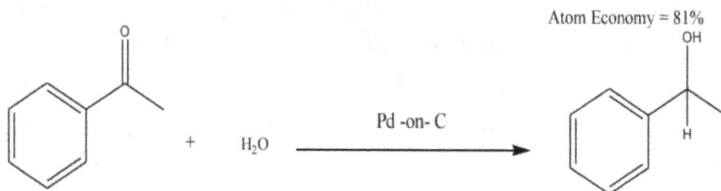

3.10. Design for Degradation :

The principle of creating degradable chemicals and products or design for degradation demands the creation of enzymatic processes whereby the 6-aminopenicillic acid is obtained by reacting with the catalyzed immobilized enzyme penicillin amide. This resulted in several chemical steps being replaced by an enzymatic reaction, and no longer required a low temperature (-60°C), organic solvents, and completely unsuitable conditions that increased and complicated production in the case of chemical synthesis [36].

The chemical processes and products should be design in a way that the desired products and waste product formed by the process are biodegradable in natural environment. The desired products are break down into harmless small substances by physical, chemical and biological means and do not persist in the natural environment.

The product should not be bio accumulative in nature and do not show biomagnifications

Example :

Biodegradable and bioactive thermoplastic aliphatic polyester polylactic acid (PLA) [40]

3.11. Real Time Analysis for Pollution Prevention :

Traditional analytical chemistry implies large amounts of sample for analysis, abundant use of solvents and energy. With the development of new methods and precision mobile instruments, it is possible that the analyzes work with a small sample size at the sampling site and with much less solvent.

The principle of Real-Time Analysis for Pollution Prevention requires further development of analytical methodology to enable real-time monitoring of the chemical production process with the aim of preventing the formation of dangerous substances, ie it is necessary to constantly monitor the production process at each stage Would prevent the occurrence of errors that could lead to the emergence of dangerous substances, harmful to the environment and human health.

It is important to know the event's or the products formation during a chemical processes at different temperature, pressure, and time to control the formation of desired products and to avoid formation of any hazardous substances or waste substances as byproduct. [41]

Example:

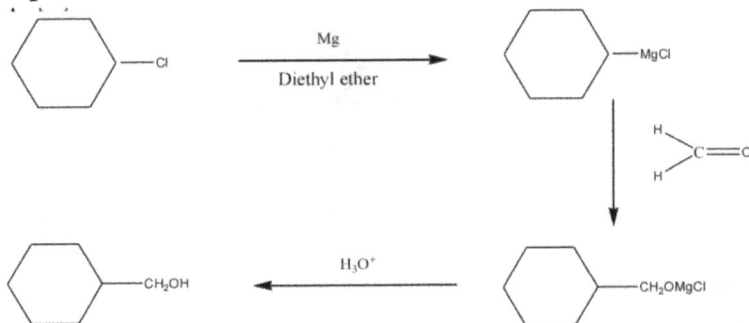

3.12. Inherently benign Chemistry for Accident Prevention:

The Twelfth Principle of Green Chemistry is the principle of Inherently Safer Chemistry for Accident Prevention. The basic requirement is to reduce the use of substances in chemical processes that can cause adverse effects (explosion, fire and harmful vapor). An example is today the increasing use of supercritical CO_2 that replaces organic solvents and which, unlike organic solvents, is not toxic or explosive and is environmentally acceptable.

Safety can be defined as a control of known hazards by achieving an acceptable level of risk and is achieved at several levels of the lowest use of Personal Protective Equipment. Then it follows the level of Administrative and Work Practice Controls) and implies establishing effective procedures, rotating work tasks, adjusting work schedules so that workers are not over-exposed to the impact of dangerous chemicals, etc. The next higher level of security control is the expert Engineering Controls, which implies the implementation of physical process change To reduce contact with hazardous chemicals, isolate the process, use wet methods to reduce dust formation, ventilation, digestion, etc. The highest level of safety control is achieved by eliminating or replacing the procedure with safer alternatives (Fig. 3).

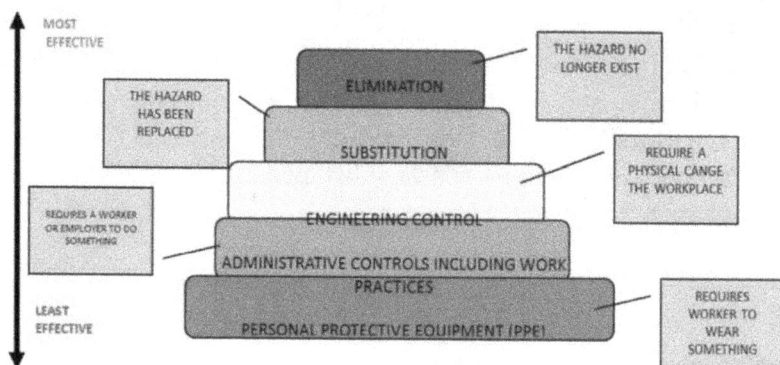

Fig. 3. Hierarchy of security control.

Design chemical processes and products and their physical states like solid, liquid and gaseous form to minimize or eliminate the potential of chemical accident's including explosion, fire, and smoke produce due to chemical and release into the natural environment. Hazardous Substances are Corrosive, Flammable, Explosive, Reactive, Toxic etc.

To prevent accidents and injuries the following right steps should be taken before handling any hazardous substances, Read labels and SDSs to learn about hazardous and required safety precautions. Check for adequate ventilation. Remove items from the work area that could ignite or react with the hazardous materials. Know the location of fire extinguisher, emergency alarms, eyewash stations and first-aid kits [42].

Disadvantages of Green Chemistry :

This goal is also the biggest handicap-lack of green chemistry that is reflected in time, costs and lack of information. More specifically, switching from an old, conventional product or process to a new "green" product or process requires a lot of time, designor redesign of a new product and process is often difficult and quite expensive, and there is also a lack of unity on what is considered safe. With the high cost of implementation and the lack of information, the lack of green chemistry is also the fact that there is no known alternative to used chemical raw materials or alternative technologies for green processes. In addition, there is also a lack of human resources and skills.

The risks of switching to green products and processes are not divided within the supply chain, and there is a lack of resources for further research. Ionic liquids are considered to be the future of green chemistry. Although there is no doubt that those are useful in chemical synthesis, the question is increasingly raised whether they meet expectations. When applying twelve principles that describe green chemicals, ionic liquids do not look particularly green. There is an opinion that at the presentstage of science progress it is unrealistic to expect that in the next ten years a wide application of ionic liquids will be seen.

Although, as is well known, ionic liquids are slightly volatile due to the low vapor pressure, yet it is only one of the many things that make a substance really green. For example, ionbased, imidazole-based and fluoro-anion-based liquids are likely to be poisonous but can not reach the environment by evaporation. The problem is that most ionic liquids are watersoluble and can easily reach the biosphere through that pathway [43].

5. Conclusions

Establishing a balance in the use of natural resources, economic growth and environmental conservation is possible through the introduction of a green chemistry process whose task is to design such chemical processes and products that are harmless to human health and the environment. The application of the concept of green chemistry that introduces chemical safety implies adequate legal support through the legal regulation of certain procedures and activities that are unavoidable for the implementation of such a concept.

The concept of green chemistry is based on twelve principles that speak of reducing or eliminating hazardous or harmful substances from the synthesis, production and application of chemical products and thus the use of substances that are hazardous to human health and the environment is reduced or eliminated. When designing a green chemistry process, it is impossible to meet the requirements of all twelve principles of the process at the same time, but it attempts to apply as many principles as possible during certain stages of synthesis. The goals of green chemistry in environmental protection and economic gain are achieved through several dominant directions. Some of them are: biocatalysis, catalysis, use of alternative renewable raw materials (biomass), alternative reaction media (water, ionic liquids, supercritical fluids), alternative reaction conditions (microwave activation) as well as new photocatalytic reactions.

Catalysis as the foundation of green chemistry with new catalytic reactions and types of new catalysts offers a number of benefits in terms of process utilization, selectivity, energy reduction and the use of alternative reaction media. The huge potential of microorganisms and enzymes in the transformation of synthetic substances with selectivity gives biocatalyst a dominant position in the "green" program. Photocatalytic reactions that represent new methods of cleaning contaminated air and water also contribute to green chemistry creating conditions for achieving sustainability.

References:
[1].P. T. Anastas and J. C. Warner, in Green Chemistry: Theory and Practice, Oxford University Press, New York, 1998 Search PubMed; I. Horvath and P. T. Anastas, Chem. Rev., 2007, 107, 2167 Search PubMed.
[2].P. T. Anastas and T. C. Williamson, in Green Chemistry: Designing Chemistry for the Environment, American Chemical Series Books, Washington, DC, 1996, pp. 1–20 Search PubMed.

[3].T. J. Collins, in Green Chemistry, Macmillan Encyclopedia of Chemistry, Simon and SchusterMacmillan, New York, 1997, vol. 2, pp. 691–697 Search PubMed.

[4]. P. T. Anastas, Green Chem., 2003, 5, 29 Search PubMed.

[5].W. McDonough, M. Braungart, P. T. Anastas and J. B. Zimmerman, Environ. Sci. Technol., 2003, 37, 434A CAS.

[6].Office of Pollution Prevention and Toxics, The Presidential Green Chemistry Challenge Awards Program, Summary of 1996 Award Entries and Recipients, US Environmental Protection Agency, Washington, DC, EPA744K96001, 1996 Search PubMed.

[7]. Forum, Green Chem., 1999, 1, G11 Search PubMed.

[8]. J. Clark, Green Chem., 1999, 1, G1 RSC.

[9].Office of Pollution Prevention and Toxics, The Presidential Green Chemistry Challenge, Award Recipients, 1996–2009, US Environmental Protection Agency, Washington, DC, EPA 744K09002, 2009 Search PubMed.

[10]. S2669, Green Chemistry Research and Development Act of 2008, 2008.

[11] Ritter, S. K. (2001): Green Chemistry. Chem. Eng. News, 79 (29), 27-34.

[12] Vojvodić, V. (2009): Environmental Protection: Green Manufacturing in the Pharmaceutical Industry and Cost Reduction, Kem Ind 58 (1): 32-33, In Croatian.

[13] Riđanović, L., Ćatović, F., Riđanović, S. (2013): The Green Chemistry-Ecological Revolution in the Classroom. 8thResearch/Expert Conference with International Participations "QUALITY 2013", Neum, B&H, June 06 – 08, 447-452., In Bosnian.

[14] Jukić, M., Djaković, S., Filipović-Kovačević, Ž., Kovač, V. and Vorkapić-Furač, J. (2005): Dominant trends of green chemistry. Kem Ind 54 (5): 255-272, In Croatian.

[315]

[16] Environmental effect of war-Lenntech, www.lenntech.com

[17] Fundamental concept of Environmental chemistry, G.S. Sodhi

[18] Pesticide chemistry and toxicology-Bentham e books

[19] Mijin, D., Stanković, M. I., Petrović, S. (2003): Ibuprofen: Gain and Properties, Hem. Ind. 57 (5) 199-214, In Serbian.

[20] Anastas, P. T., Warner, J. C. (1998): Green Chemistry Theory and Practice. New York: Oxford University Press, 10-55.

[21] Anastas, P. T., Kirchhoff, M. M., Williamson, T. C. (2001): Catalysis as a foundational pillar of green chemistry. Appl Catal A: General, 221: 3-13.

[22] Fisher science education, www.fisheredu.com

[23] Atom economy –yield Green industry www.greens-industry.org.uk

[24] Riđanović, L., Ćatović, F., Riđanović, S. (2013): The Green Chemistry-Ecological Revolution in the Classroom. 8thResearch/Expert Conference with International Participations "QUALITY 2013", Neum, B&H, June 06 – 08, 447-452., In Bosnian.

[25] Environmental Chemistry by A.K.DE

[26] Fisher science education, www.fisheredu.com

[27] Wayne Hill, H. and Brady, D. G. (1976): Properties, environmental stability, and molding characteristics of polyphenylene sulfide, Polymer Engineering & Science, Vol 16, Iss 12,pp 831–835

[28] 2, 4-D-Beyond pesticide, www.beyondpesticides.org

[29] Kärkkäinen, J. (2007): Preparation and characterization of some ionic liquids and their use in the dimerization reaction of 2-methylpropene. Dissertation, University of Oulu.

[30] Handbook of green chemistry Volume.IV, green solvents, supercritical solvents, By Paul T. Anastas.

[31] Hoffert, M. I., Caldeira, K., Benford, G., David R. Criswell, D. R., Christopher Green, C., Herzog, H., Jain, A. K., Kheshgi, H. S., Lackner, K. S., Lewis, J. S., Lightfoot, H. D., Manheimer, W., Mankins, J. C., Mauel, M. E., Perkins, L. J., Schlesinger M. E., Volk, T., Wigley, T. (2002): Advanced Technology Paths to Global Climate Stability: Energy for a Greenhouse Planet, Science, Vol. 298, Issue 5595, pp. 981-987, DOI: 10.1126/science.1072357

[32] The Haber process for manufacture of Ammonia, www.chemguide.co.uk

[33] Ivanković, A., Zeljko, K., Talić, S., Martinović Bevanda, A. and Lasić, M.(2017): Biodegradable packaging in the food industry, Archiv für Lebensmittelhygiene 68, Heft 1.
[34] Rujnić-Sokele, M. (2007): Truths and mistakes about bioplastics. Polymers: Journal of Rubber and Plastics, Rubber and Plastics Corporation, Zagreb, 28_3: pp178-181. In Croatian.
[35] Green synthesis from biomass by, Paulo M. Donated/Springer Open
[36] Findrik Blažević, Z. (2013): Bioreactivity Technique I, Internal Script. Zagreb: University of Zagreb, Faculty of Chemical Engineering and Technology, In Croatian
[37] American chemical society/Green chemistry principle #8
[38] Handbook of green chemistry Volume-I, Green catalysis, Homogeneous catalysis by, Paul T. Anastas
[39] Introduction: Green Chemistry and catalysis by Wiley –VC
[40] Production process for polylactic acid (PLA) Industrial Plant: Hitachi, www.hitachi.com
[41] March Advanced organic chemistry
[42] Green chemistry principle # 12 (ACS), minimize the potential for accident, ehsdailyadvisor.blr.com
[43] Bharadwaj, M. and Neelam (2015): The Advantages and Disadvantages of Green Technology, Journal of Basic and Applied Engineering Research, p-ISSN: 2350-0077; e-ISSN: 2350-0255; Volume 2, Issue 22; October-December, 2015, pp. 1957-1960.

U.G, P.G. & Research Centre,
Department of Chemistry,
Shivaji, Art's, Comm. & Science College Kannad.
Aurangabad.Maharashtra
email : <u>sakharedhondiram@yahoo.com</u>

20. Phytochemical Activity of Date Fruit (Barari)

S. Mohamed Musthafa

1. Introduction

Phoenix dactylifera, commonly known as date or date palm, is a flowering plant species in the palm family, Arecaceae, cultivated for its edible sweet fruit called dates. It's relief from constipation, it cures anemia, it help to cure diarrhea and abdominal cancer. Dates will boost energy, relieve intoxication, promote heart health reduce inflammation encourage weight gain. The species is widely cultivated across northern Africa the middle east and south Asia and is naturalized in many tropical and subtropical region worldwide *phoenix dactylifera* is the type of genus phoenix, which contains 12-19 species of wild date palm Dates have been cultivated in the Middle East and Indus valley for thousands of years. There is archaeological evidence of date cultivation in Arabia from the 6th millennium BCE. The total world production dates amount of 8.5millions metric tons, countries of the Middle East, North Africa being the largest producers and consumers

Scientific classification

> Kingdom : Plantae
> Clade : Tracheophytes
> Clade : Angiosperms
> Clade : Monocots
> Clade : Commelinids
> Order : Arecales
> Family : Arecaceae
> Genus : Phoenix
> Species : *P. dactylifera.*

The date provides various kinds of antioxidants to treat different diseases. Antioxidant protects your cells from free radicals that may cause harmful reaction in your body lead to disease. Dates are rich in antioxidants including

1. Carotenoids : it is very beneficial for your heart health. It also reduces the risk of eye related disorder

2. Flavonoids : It is powerful antioxidant with multiple benefits. It is known for its anti- inflammatory properties. Studies have been shown that it is used to reduce the risk of diabetes, Alzheimer's disease and certain types of cancers.

3. Phenolic Acid : it has anti-inflammatory properties and helps to reduce the risk of some cancers and heart issues.

People all over the world dates are of very importance and are growing in many places in the world. They are customarily used to break the day long fast during the holy month of Ramadan (**Al Farsi and Lee, 2008; Al-Sahib and Marshall, 2003).** Date palms are monocotyledon, dioeciously and can grow up to an altitude of 1500 m in well-drained soils. Currently they are cultivated in the Middle East, North Africa, parts of Central and South Amen.

Varieties of Dates :

Estimates are that based on the shape and organoleptic properties of the fruits, there are more than 600 varieties of dates (**Ahmed et al., 1995; Zaid, 1999).** Some of the important date varieties grown around the world are Aabel, Ajwah, Al-Baraka, Amir Hajj, Abide Rahim, Barari, Baht, Bekreri, Bomaan, Bouhattam, Barakawi, Bireir, Deglet Noor, Dabbas, Dayri, Empress, Fard, Ftimi, Garn ghzal, Halawi, Haleema, Hayany, Iteema, Jabri, Kenta, Khadrawy, Khlas, Kenta, Kodary, Korkobbi, Khusatawi, Lulu, Maktoomi, Maghool, Manakbir, Mermilla, Medjool, Mejraf, Mishriq, Nabtat-seyf, Naptit Saif, Nefzaoui, Raziz, Rotab, Rotbi, Sagai, Smiti, Shikat alkahlas, Sagay, Shishi, Shikat alkahlas, Sokkery, Saidi, Sayir, Sekkeri, Shabebe, Sellaj, Sultana, Tagyat, Tamej, Thoory, Umeljwary, Umelkhashab, Zahidi and Bericcha Paz- ham (**Al Noimi and Al Amir, 1980; Al-Shahib and Marshall, 2003; Chaira et al., 2009; Chandra et al., 1992-; Habib and Ibrahim, 2009).** Dates are influenced by environmental conditions and this has at times led to 'cultivars' with similar morphological characters being given the same varietal name e.g. Khalas Oman and Khalas Bahraini (**Al Noimi and Al-Amir, 1980; Fadel et al., 2006).**

Benefits of Dates with Milk at Night :

171

> Reinforces and refreshes the skin.
> Thickens and strengthens hair texture.
> It helps prevent anemia and better blood circulation.
> Improve eyesight and eye health.

Benefits of Dates Soaked Overnight in Water :

Soak them overnight and consume them the next morning. The results have been great for weak hearts. Overnight soaked dates reduce heart strokes and other heart-related diseases. The same overnight soaked dates are helpful in reducing alcoholic intoxication and hangovers. Dates exude natural cooling effect and pacify the body besides boosting immunity. Traditional medical practitioners recommend soaking 4 to 6 dry dates overnight and consuming it daily in the morning, along with water for boosting immunity. Ayurveda describes that the phytohormones present in these tasty fruits mimic the functioning of oxytocin often touted as a cuddle or love hormone. If you are on a weight-gain regimen, bring home dry dates to expedite the process.

Researchers believe that the sugars in this fruit are complex carbohydrates, heavy to digest and aid in slow release of energy into the bloodstream by keeping you satiated for a long time and that's why Ayurveda strongly recommends eating soaked dry dates before eating lunch or dinner to feel food and cut down on food. Dry Dates For Children:

Properties and Nutritional of Sate Syrup :

Acidity	Date syrup should have an acidity of 0.5-1.3% of acetic acid.
Color	Date syrup is transparent if produced in natural and healthy conditions.
Ph	The syrup should have a pH of 3.5-4.3.
Soluble Solids:	The allowed amount of soluble solids in the date syrup is 67-73.
Ash	The syrup should have a maximum of 1.5% ash.

Reducing Sugars	The amount of reducing sugars in date syrup is 58%.

2. Review of Literature

Phoenix dactylifera commonly known as the date palm is a primeval plant and has been cultivated for its edible fruit in the desert oasis of the Arab world for centuries. The fruits are a rich source of carbohydrates, dietary fibers, certain essential vitamins and minerals. The date pits are also an excellent source of dietary fiber and contain considerable amounts of minerals, lipids and protein. In addition to its dietary use the dates are of medicinal use and are used to treat a variety of ailments in the various traditional systems of medicine. Fruit quality is strongly affected by genotype and harvest date. In this study, parameters regarding fruit quality, bioactive compounds, and antioxidant capacity of different dates cultivars at three harvesting dates were quantified to elucidate the influence of genotype and harvest date on strawberry quality(**Min yong 2022**). Phytochemical investigations have revealed that the fruits contain anthocyanins, phenolics, sterols, carotenoids, procyanidins and flavonoids, compounds known to possess multiple beneficial effects. Preclinical studies have shown that the date fruits possess free radical scavenging, antioxidant, antimutagenic, antimicrobial, anti-inflammatory, gastroprotective, hepatoprotective, nephroprotective, anticancer and immunostimulant activities. Date fruit is an excellent source of nutritional and health benefits. The chemical composition of dates includes carbohydrates, dietary fibre, proteins, fats, minerals and vitamins, enzymes, phenolic acid and carotenoids, all of which are directly linked to nutritional and health benefits for consumers(**Salam A Ibrahim 2020**) This review presents a comprehensive analysis of the phytochemistry and validated pharmacological properties of date fruits and the seeds.(**Yen2010**).

Adventitious plantlets were obtained from lateral buds, shoot tips, embryos, and pieces of stem and rachilla tissue of Phoenix dactyl"fera L. cultured on a modified Murashige and Skoog medium containing 3 mg 1 ' N-(d 2-isopentyl)adenine, 0- 1— I €D mg l ' e-naphthaleneacetic acid or 2,4- dichlorophenoxyacetic acid, and 3 g 1

' activated charcoal. Additions of auxins were necessary to induce esplants to produce callus, adventitious plantlets, and roots. Plantlets were obtained from explants cultured months in vitro. No difference in growth responses between mate and female explants was observed during culture. Complex addenda of activated charcoal and polyvinyl- pyrrolidone were tested in the nutrient media at various concentrations to prevent explant browning. Activated charcoal fostered satisfactory growth by reducing the browning and inhibition of growth of explants(**Brent tissert, 1979**).

Date palm is one of the oldest trees cultivated by man. In the folk-lore, date fruits have been ascribed to have many medicinal properties when consumed either alone or in combination with other herbs. Although, fruit of the date palm served as the staple food for millions of people around the world for several centuries, studies on the health benefits are inadequate and hardly recognized as a healthy food by the health professionals and the public. In recent years, an explosion of interest in the numerous health benefits of dates had led to many in vitro and animal studies as well as the identification and quantification of various classes of phytochemicals. On the basis of available documentation in the literature on the nutritional and phytochemical composition, it is apparent that the date fruits are highly nutritious and may have several potential health benefits. Although dates are sugar-packed, many date varieties are low GI diet and refutes the dogma that dates are similar to candies and regular consumption would develop chronic diseases. More investigations in these areas would validate its beneficial effects, mechanisms of actions, and fully appreciate as a potential medicinal food for humans all around the world. Therefore, in this review we summarize the phytochemical composition, nutritional significance, and potential health benefits of date fruit consumption and discuss its great potential as a medicinal food for a number of diseases inflicting human beings. (**Praveen K.** and **Vayalil, 1998**).

3. Scope and Plan of Work

This article describes the purpose of antimicrobial activity, phytochemical activities, and total antioxidant test, health and medicinal studies of dates

Plan of Work

3.1 Collection of the sample –date fruit(*Phoenix dactylifera) barari*

3.2 Extraction of phytochemical by solvent extraction method

3.3 Screening for phytochemicals

3.4 Antimicrobial activity of extract

3.5 DPPH assay

3.6 Screening by paper chromatography

3.7 UV analysis

3.8 GC/MS analysis

4. Materials and Methods

4.1 Sample Collection

Dates fruit of Barari variety was purchased from the local grocery shop situated in Tenkasi.

4.2 Extraction of Metabolites

The different extracts from date fruits were obtained by:

4.2.1 Acid Hydrolysis

First order, an acid hydrolysis was performed on 5 g dry plant material blinded with 40 mL of hydrochloric acid (2N HCl). The mixture prepared was transferred into Erlenmeyer flasks and was boiled in water bath at 100 °C for 40 minutes. (Lebreton and co-workers -1967)

4.2.2 Extraction of Bioactive Compounds

At the end, the acid mixture was separated twice into two fractions with diethyl ether (60-60 mL). The organic fraction containing the metabolites was collected and used for further analysis.

4.3 Phytochemical Screening of Extract

Phytochemicals (from Greek Phyto, meaning "plant") are chemical produced by plants through primary or secondary metabolism. The screening was performed for triterpenes/ steroids, alkaloids, anthraquinones, coumarins, flavonoids, saponins, tannins and phenolic acids. The colour intensity or the precipitate formation was used as analytical responses to these tests.

4.3.1. Flavonoids Test

Flavonoids (from the Latin word flavus meaning yellow, their color in nature) are a class of plant and fungal secondary metabolites.

Flavonoids are reduced risk of cancer, heart disease, asthma and stoke. They play a vital role in protecting the brain.

Procedure

1. 0.1g of each sample were taken in test tubes and 2ml of ethyl acetate was added The mixture was boiled at 60•c for 3 minutes using water bath.
2. After that filtrate was separated from the mixture of solution. 1% of diluted Ammonia was added in each tube.
3. The color change was observed and OD was taken using colorimeter. A positive observation is indicated by the development of yellow color.

4.3.2. Tannin Test :

The term tannin originated from the word tanna, which is an Old High German word meaning of oak or fir tree. The words 'tan' and 'tanning' are also named for the treatment of leather. Tannins were water-soluble polyphenols that were present in many plant foods.

Procedure

1. 0.25g of each sample were taken in sterile test tubes and 10 ml of boiled distilled water was added in each tube.
2. The tubes were mixed well.
3. Finally, 1% of ferric chloride was added in each tube.
4. The color change was observed and read out OD value was observed in colorimeter. The positive observation is indicated by the development of blue-black and blue green precipitate.

4.3.3. Phenolic Compound (Ferric Choloride Test)

Phenolic compounds are mostly found in vascular plants. It is one of the secondary metabolites of plants. Natural phenolic compounds play an important role in cancer treatment and prevention.

Procedure

1. 1g of each sample were taken in sterile test tubes and 5ml of ethanol was added in each tube. The tubes were mixed well.
2. The filtrate from the mixture of solution was separated out. 5% of ferric chloride was added drop by drop in each tube.
3. The color change was observed and OD value was observed in a colorimeter (650nm) Positive result in indicated by the development of brown and green color change.

5. Result and Discussion

5.1. Extraction of the Samples :

Acid hydrolysis First order, an acid hydrolysis was performed on 5 g dry plant material blinded with 40 mL of hydrochloric acid (2N HCl). The mixture prepared was transferred into Erlenmeyer flasks and was boiled in water bath at 100 °C for 40 minutes. (Lebreton and co-workers -1967)

5.2. Phytochemical screening the samples result was tabulated in the **table 1**

5.2.1. Flavonoid Test :

The color change was observed and OD was taken using colorimeter. A positive observation is indicated by the development of yellow color. Table 1 shows that flavonoid test is negative

5.2.2. Tanin Test :

The color change was observed and read out OD value was observed in colorimeter. The positive observation is indicated by the development of blue-black and blue green precipitate Table 1 shows that tannin test is positive

5.2.3. Phenolic Compound (Ferric Chloride Test) :

The color change was observed and OD value was observed in a colorimeter (650nm) Positive result in indicated by the development of brown and green color change. Table 1 shows that phenolic compound is positive

5.2.4. Terpenoids Test :

Positive result is indicated by the formation of a reddish-brown layer at the interface. Table 1 shows that terpenoid test is positive

5.2.5. Saponins Test :

Positive result is indicated by froth appearance while shaking the tube. Table 1 shows that saponins test is positive

5.2.6. Cardiac Glycoside Test :

Positive results in indicated by a violet ring. In some case the violet ring can be accompanied by a brown ring which in appear in the bottom layer of the tubes. (The appearance of a green ring indicated the presence of acetic acid) Table 1 shows that cardiac glycoside test is positive

5.2.7. Protein Test / Biuere Test :

positive results is indicated by the appearance of dark brown color change and a blue colored ring formation in the upper layer with precipitation. Table 1 shows that protein test is positive

5.2.8. Salkowski's Test :

Positive result in indicated by the appearance of dark reddish-brown color change. Table 1 shows that salkowski's test is positive

5.2.9. Steroid Test :

Positive result in indicated by the development of red ring in the lower part of the tube and if golden yellow color is formed it denote the presence of triterpenes. Table 1 shows that steroid test is positive

5.2.10.Anthroquinone Test :

Positive result in indicated by the pink, violet or red color. Table 1 shows that Anthroquinone is positive

5.3. Antimicrobial Testing of the Extract of Date Palm (Barari)

5.3.1. E.coli sp. Cultivated in the Muller Hinton Agar :

Antimicrobial activity of *E.coli sp.* in date extract (barari) plate 1 having four zones in the muller hinton media by, using well cut method 4th zone is greater than other zones(0.6mm) and plate 2 consist of four wells 4th zone is larger than other 3 zones (1.5mm)and plate 3 consist of 2 zones and 2nd zone forms maximum in size(1mm)

5.3.2. Pneumonia sp. Cultivated in Muller Hinton Agar :

Antimicrobial activity of *pneumonia sp.* in date extract (barari) plates have four zones in the muller hinton media by using well cut method plate 4 having 4 zones 4 th zone is greater than other 3zones (2.0mm) and plate 5 consist of 5 wells and 4th zone is larger (3.0mm) and plate 6 consist of 2 zones 2nd zone in maximum in size(3.4mm)

6.Photos

Date Fruit (Barari)

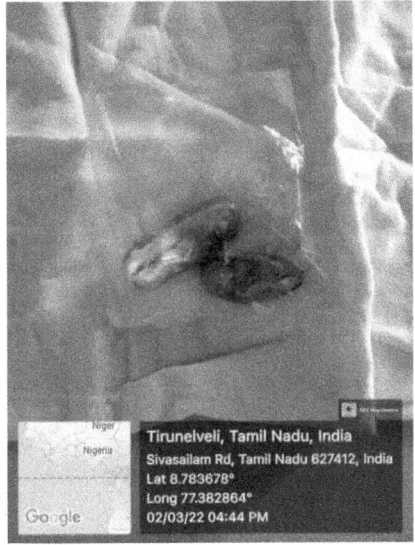

Extraction Of Date Fruit (Barari) using Hcl (Hydrochloric Acid)

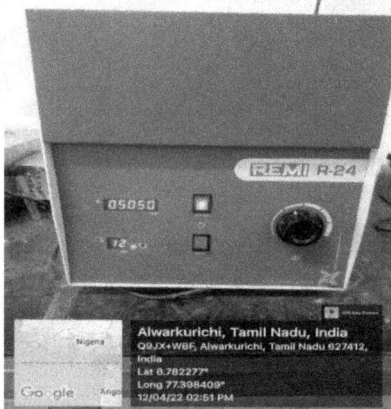

7. Tables

Phytochemical Analysis For Extraction Of Date Sample (Barari)
TABLE-1

S.NO	PHYTOCHEMICAL TEST	RESULTS
1	Flavonoid test	-
2	Tanin test	+
3	Phenolic compound test	-
4	Terpenoid test	+
5	Saponin test	+
6	Cardiac Glycoside test	+
7	Protein test	+
8	Salkowski's test	+
9	Steroid test	+
10	Anthroquinone test	+

TABLE-2 Antimicrobial Testing of the Extract Against *Escherchia Coli* SP.

Test Organism	Concentration of Samples	Zone of Inhibition in Diameter(mm)
E.coli SP.	10	0.3
	20	0.4
	30	0.5
	40	0.6
	50	0.7
	60	0.8
	70	0.9
	80	1.5
	90	1
	100	1

TABLE-3 Antimicrobial Testing of the Extract Against *Streptococcus SP.*

Test Organism	Concentration of Samples	Zone of Inhibition in Diameter(Mm)
Streptococcus sp.	10	0.1
	20	1.3
	30	1.6
	40	2.0
	50	2.5
	60	2.8
	70	3.0
	80	3.2
	90	3.3
	100	3.4

Analysis of different antibiogram of phtochemical compounds from date palm (barari)

Z

1. Flavonoid test   2. Tanin test   3. Phenolic compound test

Sustainable Development and Climate Change

4.Terpenoid test   5.Saponin test   6.Cardiac glycoside test

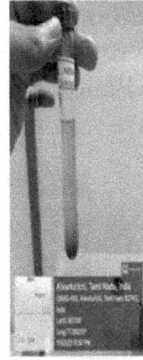

7.Protein test

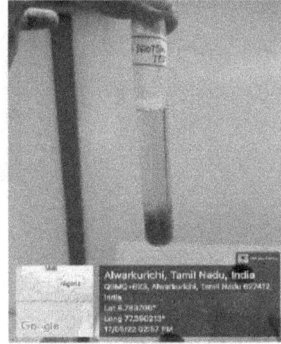

8.Salkowski's test

9.Steroid test

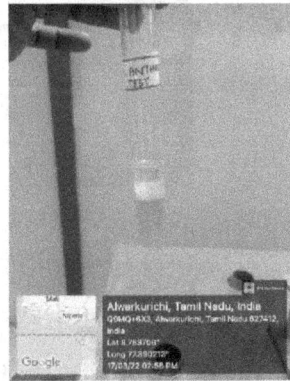

10.Anthroquinone test

8. Plates
Plate number: (1,2,3)
This Plates shows the antimicrobial activity of Date palm extract against various concentration of the ***E.coli sp*** .in **MH media**

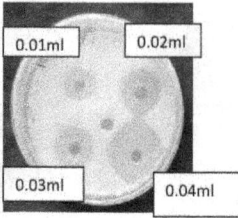

Plate-1

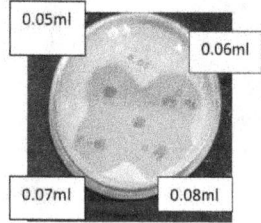

plate-2

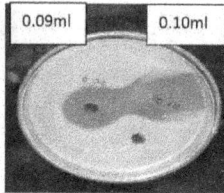

Plate-3

Plate: (4,5,6)
This plates shows the antimicrobial activity of Date palm extract against various concentration ***Pnuemoniae sp.*** in **MH media**

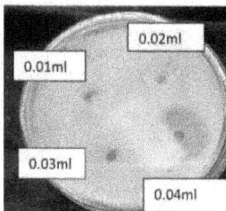

Plate-4

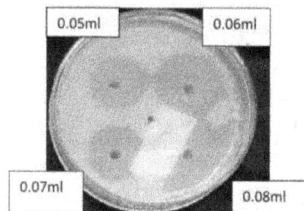

plate-5

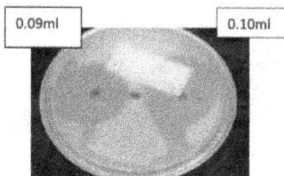

Plate-6

GRAPH-1(UV Analysis Date Palm Fruit Barari, with Water)

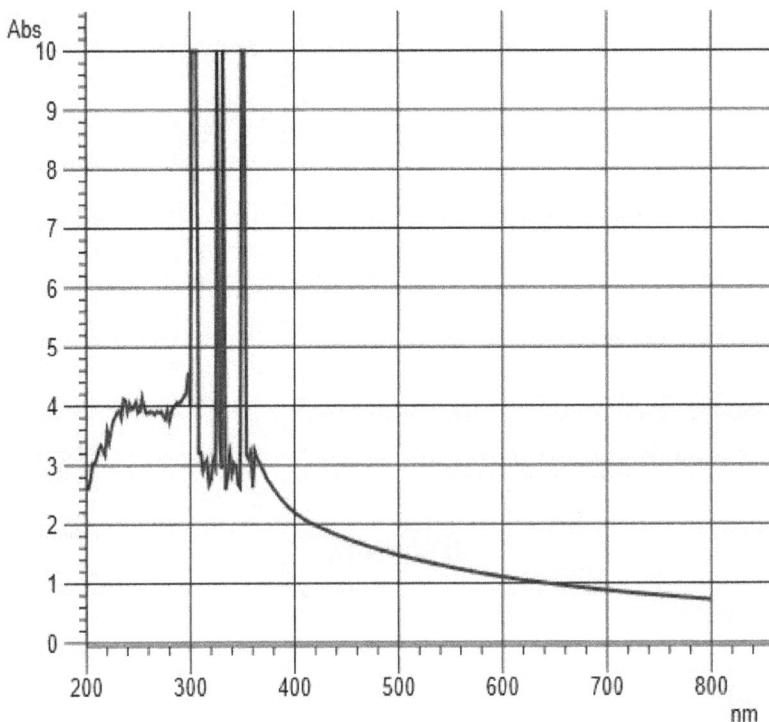

Sample Name :   PCMUV
File Name :   PCMUV1
Run Date :   2022/03/16 16:14
Operator :
Spectrophotometer
Model :   UH5300 Spectrophotoeter
SERIAL No. :   3048-007
(CPU1)Program No. : 3J15300-04
(CPU2)Program No. : 3J15310-10
Option :   6 Cell

GRAPH-2 (UV ANALYSIS IN nm)

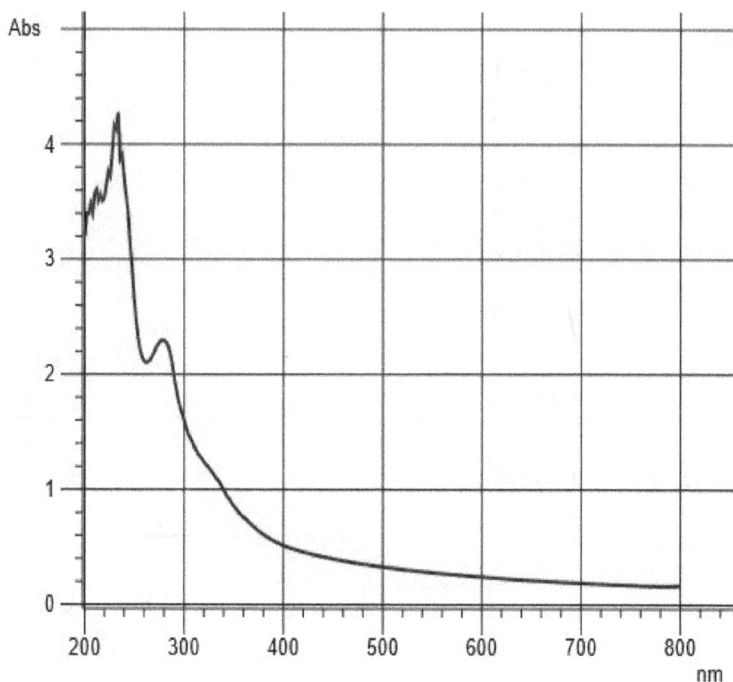

Sample Name :	PCMUV
File Name	: PCMUV2
Run Date	: 2022/03/16 16:25
Operator:	
Spectrophotometer	
Model :	UH5300 Spectrophotometer
SERIAL No. :	3048-007
(CPU1)Program No :	3J15300-04
(CPU2)Program No.:	3J15310-10
Option :	6 Cell

GRAPH-3 GC/MS Analysis For

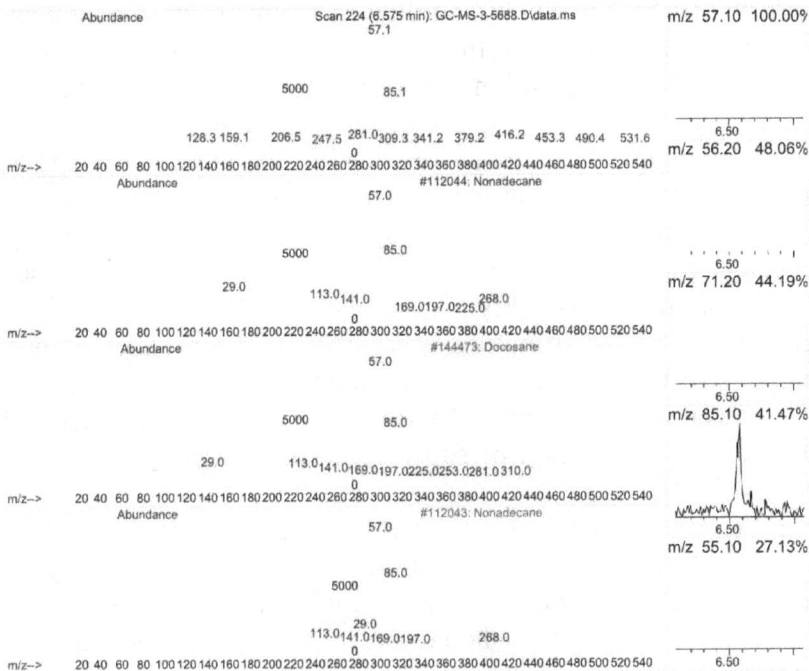

Abundance   Scan 224 (6.575 min): GC-MS-3-5688.D\data.ms   m/z 57.10 100.00%
57.1

5000   85.1

128.3 159.1   206.5   247.5   281.0 309.3 341.2   379.2   416.2   453.3   490.4   531.6   6.50
0   m/z 56.20 48.06%
m/z-->   20 40 60 80 100 120 140 160 180 200 220 240 260 280 300 320 340 360 380 400 420 440 460 480 500 520 540
Abundance   #112044: Nonadecane
57.0

5000   85.0   6.50
                       m/z 71.20 44.19%
29.0   113.0 141.0
           169.0 197.0 225.0   268.0
0
m/z-->   20 40 60 80 100 120 140 160 180 200 220 240 260 280 300 320 340 360 380 400 420 440 460 480 500 520 540
Abundance   #144473: Docosane
57.0

5000   85.0   6.50
                       m/z 85.10 41.47%
29.0   113.0 141.0 169.0 197.0 225.0 253.0 281.0 310.0
0
m/z-->   20 40 60 80 100 120 140 160 180 200 220 240 260 280 300 320 340 360 380 400 420 440 460 480 500 520 540
Abundance   #112043: Nonadecane
57.0   6.50
                       m/z 55.10 27.13%
85.0
5000

29.0
113.0 141.0 169.0 197.0   268.0
0
m/z-->   20 40 60 80 100 120 140 160 180 200 220 240 260 280 300 320 340 360 380 400 420 440 460 480 500 520 540   6.50

Sample : T-17590-1-PURITY
Peak Number: 1   at   6.575 min Area: 1684   Area % 2.23 The
3 best hits from each library. Ref\#   CAS\# Qual
C:\Database\NIST08.L
1 Nonadecane   112044 000629-92-5 60
2 Docosane   144473 000629-97-0 53
3 Nonadecane   112043 000629-92-5 49

10. Summary

In the current work, to evaluate the antimicrobial activity of dates (barari) dates companies was checked by subjecting the selected products to diverse physical, chemical preservative, adulteration and biological test generally employed in dates industries as per FSSAI in addition to their antioxidant role.

Natural resources have been the crucial origin of chemical elements. They have been used in many tradition as alternative medicenes.

The chemical profiling of small plants extracts and essential oils related to different plants were followed to unveil their most active components. Phoenix dactylifera was selected as a host plant to investigate the composition of different organs with different cultivars.

The microbiological parameter recorded in the current work raises efficiency of antimicrobial activity employed during the production due to the growth of *E.coli sp.,streptococcus sp., Enterococcus sp.,pneumonia sp., pseudomonas sp.,*. There may be several reasons for the poor microbial quality.

Pseudomonas sp., distribution was noted in the product as good design. Screening effect of antibacterial role in MH media at different concentration showed the increased antibacterial effect in response to concentration of supernatant against *streptococcus sp., and pseudomonas sp.,*

From the current works, it was found the dates gurantees the fibre, nutrients, sugar content but with some threat from biological agents. It could be avoided only throughstorage, handling transport and distribution. Government should be more vigilant regarding the quality of eatables.

More care should be given to justify the reliability of the consumers on the product. Making the manufacture to produce quality products and their supply and better future.Which could be possible only through these kind of applied research.

Accordingly to our studies, date fruits are used for prophylaxis and treatment of many huma diseases. According to an ethnobotanical study, parts of date palm are traditionally used to treat anemia, and dimmenrilization, infusion for cold, as a gargle for sore throat crushed in water to treat hemmorhoids, constipation and jaundice

Bibilography

Abbasi S, Mahjobipoor H, Kashefi P, Massumi G, Aghadavoudi O, Fara- jzadegan 2013.. The effect of lidocaine on reducing the tracheal mu- cosal damage following tracheal intubation. *J Rese Med Sci: The Official J Isfahan Unive Med Sci.* ;18(9):733.

Abedi A,aliga, Mufeed, Baliga and aAl kadir. 2011. Compositional and functional characteristics of dates, syrups, and their by-products. *Food Chemistry.* 104(3): 943–947.

Al Farsi, Lee, 2008, Al-Sahib and Marshall. 2003. Antioxidant activity Scavenges free radical, inhibit iron-induced lipoperoxidation and protein oxidation *Academia journals of biotechnology.* 3: 251-280.

Al Noimi and Al Amir. 1980. Antimutagenic Inhibits benzo (a) pyrene-induced mutagenecity in the activity Ames test. *International journal of current microbiology* 4: 112-158.

Al Noimi and Al-Amir, Fadel 2006. Antifungal activity against Candida albicans and C. krusei *Springer* 9(1): 44-66.

Almana S.1994. . Biological activities of the essential oil and methanolic extract of Micromeria fruticosa (L) Druce ssp serpyllifolia (Bieb) PH Davis plants from the eastern Anatolia region of Turkey. *J. Sci. Food Agric.* 2004, 84: 735–741

Al-Shahib and Marshall. 2003. Antiheamolytic Inhibits haemolytic activity Al Noimi and of streptolysin O *Electronic journal of biology* 5: 234-256.

Andreou Ho and Wan 2002. According to Duke's Phytochemical and Ethnobotanical Databases, DF con- tains 30,000 ppm (3.0 g/100 g) of polyphenols. *Bulletin of plant health production in Africa* 54: 2334-2390.

Aninane W. 2018. Recently, the neuro-protective effect of aqueous extract of DF in rats has been investigated. Pretreatment of the animals with DF at a dose of 250 mg/kg significantly decreased neural death of CA1 hippocampal neurons induced by focal cerebral ischemia compared to the control group . *Springer* 80: 178-220.

Bai and Perron y. 2003. The same group has also reported that DF extracts ameliorate CCl_4 –induced hepatotoxicity *Academia journal of science* 3: 2787-2890.

Baillard C. Fosse JP, Sebbane M, Chanques G, Vincent F, Courouble P, 2006. Noninvasive ventilation improves preoxygenation before intubation of hypoxic patients. *Am J Respir Crit Care Med.* 174(2):171–7. doi: 10.1164/rccm.200509-1507OC. [PubMed: 16627862].

Beebe DS. 2001. Complications of tracheal intubation. 20. Seminars in Anes- thesia, Perioperative Medicine and Pain: *Elsevier*

Beltsville Human, H. 2006. Coronary heart disease is strongly related to decrease in the concentrations of high density lipoprotein cholesterol and increase in the low density lipoprotein cholesterol. *Science today* (India) 378-429.

Bernanke 2011. Studies have shown that feeding rats with the aqueous extract of date flesh or pits significantly reduced CCl₄-induced elevation in plasma enzyme and bilirubin concentration *Annals of Biological Research* 5: 317-385.

Bessec and Bouabdallah 2005. studies pertaining to the detailed identification, characterization, and quantification of phytochemicals in differ- ent DF varieties at different stages of fruit ripening are still in- sufficient. *Journals of Applied biotechnology* 35: 888-899

Boulenouar and Aslam and Qasi . 2009.). Analysis of carotenoids with emphasis on 9-cis [beta]-carotene in vegetables and fruits commonly consumed in Israel. *Food Chemistry.* 62(4): 515.

Boulenouar and rahuman , Cragg, Mulles B. 2009. They have shown that in human subjects a con- sumption of 100 g/day of DF, *Hallawi* or *Medjool*, for 4-weeks did not alter their body mass index, glucose or total cholesterol, VLDL, LDL, or HDL levels in the serum. However, serum triacylglycerol and VLDL was significantly reduced after con- sumption of DFs. *Springer* 55: 109-139.

BRENT TISSERAT 1979. Angiotensin-converting enzyme inhibition by Brazilian plants. *Fitoterapia.* 78(5): 353–358.

Chandra , Habib and Ibrahim. 2009. Antiviral activity Prevent lytic activity of Pseudomonas phage ATCC 14209-B1 on *Pseudomonas aeroginosa African journals of biotechnology* 6: 867-910.

Cooper JD, Grillo HC. 1969. Experimental production and preven- tion of injury due to cuffed tracheal tubes. *Surg Gynecol Obstet.*;129(6):1235–41. [PubMed: 5353420].

Cooper JD, Grillo HC.1969. The evolution of tracheal injury due to venti- latory assistance through cuffed tubes: a pathologic study. *Ann Surg.* ;169(3):334–48. [PubMed: 5266019].

Crawford and Fratantoni E 2003. The protective effects of fruits against chronic diseases are at- tributed to bioactive non-nutrients called phytochemicals. Phy- tochemicals are secondary plant metabolites. *Journals of experimental botany* 30: 2290-2298.

Dacco and Satchell 1999 . Phytoestrogens are a group of biologically active plant com- pounds with a chemical structure similar to that of estradiol. These compounds have the ability to bind to estrogen receptors and exert various estrogenic or antiestrogenic effects. There are three major classes of phytoestrogens—isoflavones, coumes- tans, and lignans that occur in plants, their fruits, or seeds.. *Electronic journal of Biology 12:* 4778-4980.

M.Sc.,Microbiology,
Spk, College, Alwarkurichi, Tenkasi District
Manonmaniam Sundaranarbuniversity,Tirunelveli.